GOTTFRIED
HELNWEIN

KÖNEMANN

CONTENTS
INHALT
TABLE DES MATIÈRES

Head of a Child/Kindskopf/Tête d'enfant, 1991
Mixed media on canvas, 236 × 157 inches, 600 × 400 cm
Ludwig Museum in the Russian Museum, St. Petersburg

Helnwein:
The Artist as Provocateur
Der Künstler als Provokateur
L'Artiste, le Provocateur

Peter Selz

It is no longer the myths which need to be restructured… it is the sign itself which must be shaken; the problem is not to reveal the (latent) meaning of an utterance, of a trait, of a narrative, but to fissure the very representation of meaning, it is not to change or purify the symbols, but to challenge the symbolic itself.

Roland Barthes

In 1979 Gottfried Helnwein painted a watercolor of a pretty little girl asleep on the table, her head on her plate and a spoon next to her hand. Its title is *Life not Worth Living,* and its text, an integral part of the work, reads:

"Dear Dr. Gross! When I was watching 'Holocaust' (the TV program), I thought again about your attitude as reported in the *Kurier*. And since this is the Year of the Child, I want to take this opportunity to thank you on behalf of the children who were taken to heaven under your care. I want to thank you that they were not 'injected to death' as you have called it, but simply died by having poison mixed into their meals. With German Greetings, Yours, Gottfried Helnwein."

The watercolor was prompted by an interview in which Dr. Heinrich Gross was asked by a reporter about the Nazi's euthanasia program in which he and other physicians had killed children considered "not worth living". He tried to vindicate his murders by claiming that he simply poisoned their food, so that they could die quietly and without pain.

Im Jahr 1979 malte Gottfried Helnwein ein Aquarell eines hübschen kleinen Mädchens, das am Mittagstisch eingeschlafen ist. Ihr Kopf ruht auf dem Suppenteller, den Löffel noch in der Hand haltend. Der Titel des Bildes lautet *Lebensunwertes Leben* und illustriert den folgenden Brief:

»Sehr geehrter Dr. Gross! Wie ich ›Holocaust‹ (die Fernsehserie) angeschaut habe, ist mir Ihre Stellungnahme im *Kurier* wieder eingefallen. Und da wir gerade das Jahr des Kindes haben, will ich die Gelegenheit ergreifen und Ihnen im Namen der Kinder, denen unter Ihrer Obhut in den Himmel geholfen wurde, herzlich dafür danken. Danken dafür, daß sie nicht ›totgespritzt‹ wurden, wie Sie sich ausdrücken, sondern daß ihnen das Gift lediglich ins Essen gemischt wurde. Mit deutschem Gruß, Ihr Gottfried Helnwein.«

Das Aquarell entstand nach einem Interview, in dem Dr. Heinrich Gross von einem Reporter über das Nazi-Euthanasie-Programm befragt wurde. Im Zuge dieser Maßnahme hatten Gross und andere Ärzte Kinder umgebracht, die als »lebensunwertes Leben« eingestuft worden waren. Gross

En 1979, Gottfried Helnwein peint à l'aquarelle une jolie petite fille endormie sur une table ; sa tête repose sur son assiette, une cuiller est à côté de sa main. Son titre, *Indigne de vivre* ainsi que le texte adjoint, sont partie intégrante de l'œuvre :

« Cher docteur Gross ! Alors que je regardais ‹ Holocauste › (le film télévisé), je me suis souvenu d'un article du *Kurier* à propos de votre attitude. Or, comme nous sommes dans l'année de l'enfance, je profite de l'occasion pour vous remercier au nom des enfants qui ont été envoyés au paradis sous votre protection. Je tiens à vous remercier – et je parle en vos propres termes – de ne pas les avoir ‹ éliminés par injection › mais de les avoir fait mourir simplement en mélangeant du poison à leurs repas. Recevez, Monsieur, mes salutations d'Allemagne, Gottfried Helnwein. »

Cette aquarelle lui avait été suggérée par une interview au cours de laquelle un journaliste interrogeait le Dr Heinrich Gross sur le programme nazi d'euthanasie, sur son rôle et celui d'autres médecins qui tuaient des enfants considérés comme « indignes de vivre ». Gross tentait de se disculper en

When, in 1979, this same man became Austrian head of state psychiatry, no one so much as wrote a letter of protest. Helnwein, incensed over this profound political apathy, painted the watercolor, appended the sarcastic letter, and published it in a Viennese journal. His painting-cum-letter aroused discussion and was probably the cause for Gross' subsequent resignation in disgrace.[1] By this time Helnwein was well aware that art can have a bearing on life.

Although the watercolor at first glance resembles the paintings of American photorealists of the period, it also differs from them significantly. Like their work, it is based on precise and detailed observation and is done with a meticulous manner and pristine finish. But Helnwein diverges sharply from the photorealists in the meaningful content that is the essence of his work. For him, art, like philosophy, raises moral issues and becomes a denotative method of instruction, often by subverting accepted norms and by provoking social change, it does not simply reflect on itself. The British-American painter Malcolm Morley, considered the first of the photorealist painters, asserted: "I have no interest in subject matter as such or satire or social comment or anything lumped together with subject matter … I accept the subject matter as a by-product of the surface."[2] For Helnwein, by contrast, the What of a picture is more important than the How. He is a master of paradox, and much of his work is characterized by its ambiguity.

Helnwein frequently turned to children for his subjects – children as innocent, weak, defenseless, and abused objects victimized by adults. Typical also is a work such as *Embarrassing* (1971), a watercolor depicting a small girl in her Sunday dress, sitting on the floor against a white wall. Her bandaged left hand is placed on a comic book, while her other emaciated arm and bandaged hand dangle on her right. A horrible wound cuts across her face from

versuchte, seine Morde zu beschönigen, indem er behauptete, er habe einfach das Essen der Kinder vergiftet, so daß sie still und schmerzlos hätten sterben können.

Als derselbe Mann 1979 zum Leiter der Staatlichen Österreichischen Psychiatrie ernannt wurde, gab es keinerlei Proteste. Helnwein, der über diese grundlegende politische Apathie entsetzt war, malte das Aquarell, fügte den sarkastischen Brief hinzu und veröffentlichte sein Werk in einer Wiener Zeitschrift. Die darauf folgende Diskussion bewirkte wahrscheinlich Gross' unehrenhafte Amtsniederlegung[1]. Damals war Helnwein bereits bewußt, daß Kunst in das Leben eingreifen kann.

Zunächst ähnelt das Aquarell den Gemälden zeitgenössischer amerikanischer Fotorealisten, denn es basiert auf einer präzisen Wiedergabe und ist bis ins kleinste Detail ausgeführt. Der bedeutungsvolle Bildinhalt jedoch distanziert Helnweins Arbeit von denen der Fotorealisten. Für ihn soll die Kunst, ebenso wie die Philosophie, moralische Debatten initiieren und durch das Unterminieren anerkannter Normen und das Provozieren sozialer Veränderungen zur denotativen Unterrichtsmethode werden. Kunst beziehe sich nicht einfach auf sich selbst. Der Angloamerikaner Malcolm Morley, der als erster fotorealistischer Maler gilt, erklärte: »Mich interessiert weder der Inhalt als solcher noch die Satire oder der gesellschaftliche Kommentar oder irgendetwas, das mit dem Inhalt zusammenhängt … Ich akzeptiere den Inhalt als ein Nebenprodukt der Oberfläche.«[2] Für Helnwein hingegen ist das Was eines Bildes wichtiger als das Wie. Er ist ein Meister des Paradoxons, und ein Großteil seines Werkes zeichnet sich durch diese Doppeldeutigkeit aus.

Eines der Hauptmotive Helnweins sind Kinder – unschuldige, schwache, wehrlose und mißbrauchte Wesen, von Erwachsenen zu Opfern gemacht. Zu dieser Werkgruppe gehört auch das Aquarell *Peinlich* (1971): Ein kleines Mädchen im Sonntagskleid sitzt auf dem Boden und lehnt gegen eine weiße

soutenant qu'il s'était contenté d'empoisonner leur nourriture de façon à ce que leur mort fût douce et sans douleur.

Quand en 1979, ce même homme devient le chef de la psychiatrie autrichienne, personne ne proteste. Exaspéré par cette profonde apathie politique, Helnwein peint alors cette aquarelle qu'il joint à cette lettre sarcastique, publiées dans une revue viennoise. Ce message qui enflamme les débats est sans doute à l'origine de la disgrâce de Gross qui suivit[1]. A l'époque, Helnwein a déjà parfaitement conscience que l'art peut avoir un rapport avec la vie.

A première vue, cette aquarelle ressemble aux œuvres des photoréalistes américains de l'époque. Comme leurs travaux, elle se fonde sur une observation précise et détaillée, c'est une peinture exécutée de manière méticuleuse. Mais Helnwein s'oppose radicalement aux photoréalistes par le contenu expressif. Pour lui, l'art comme la philosophie soulèvent des questions morales ; l'art est une méthode pédagogique efficace opérant souvent par la subversion des normes établies et en provoquant des changements dans la société : il ne se contente pas de méditer sur lui-même. Le peintre angloaméricain Malcolm Morley, considéré comme le premier photoréaliste, déclarait : « Je ne m'intéresse ni au sujet en tant que tel, ni à la satire ou au commentaire sur la société, ou à tout ce qui peut avoir un rapport avec le sujet … J'accepte le thème en tant que dérivé de la surface. »[2] A l'inverse, pour Helnwein, le Quoi du tableau est plus important que le Comment. Il est le maître du paradoxe, et la plupart de ses œuvres sont caractérisées par cette ambiguïté.

Il se tourne souvent vers les enfants qu'il prend comme sujets – enfants innocents, faibles, sans défense, des êtres maltraités et transformés en victimes par les adultes. Une aquarelle telle que *Gênant* (1971), montrant une petite fille dans sa robe du dimanche, assise par terre devant un mur blanc, est caractéristique. Sa main gauche bandée repose sur un album de bandes dessinées,

nose to chin and neck, while her eyes bulge. No expression or affect appears in this doll-like child's face.

What, we must ask, prompted this artist to turn to images of suffering, torture, and death? We must remember that during the postwar years, when Helnwein was growing up in Vienna, nobody spoke of the brutality of the Nazi period. Memories were suppressed, and Austria's unrestrained embrace of Nazi savagery was denied as the country attempted to pose as the "first victim of Fascism". This depressing silence on the part of the Austrian petite-bourgeoisie was very difficult for Gottfried to accept – he was a rebellious child, interested in social and political questions, and curious and inquisitive about the recent past.

Two further experiences left an indelible impression on the young man; they are keys to his later works as an artist. He endured a very strict Catholic upbringing, especially a suppressive and punishing parochial school system, with its dogma of guilt and demand for humility. Omnipresent in school, in church, were pictures and statues of Christ's flagellation, the crowning with thorns, the crucifixion, as well as graphic depictions of the stoning of St. Stephen, St. Sebastian's arrow-pierced body, the cutting off of St. Agatha's breasts – all torments to which Christian saints were subjected – and these saints' apparent ecstasy as cherubim came flying down, offering the palm of martyrdom.

In total contrast to this plethora of paintings of agony was Helnwein's first elated encounter with the pictorial universe of Walt Disney. Though scorned and considered dangerous by school authorities, here was a beam of light. Later, in 1984, claiming that he had learned more from Disney than from Leonardo da Vinci, the artist visited Carl Barks in California to pay homage to the inventor of Donald Duck and Uncle Scrooge McDuck. And when Gottfried Helnwein first saw a picture of

Wand. Seine verbundene linke Hand ruht auf einem Comic-Heft, während der andere, ausgezehrte Arm mit bandagierter Hand zu seiner Rechten baumelt. Eine grauenhafte Wunde klafft quer über das Gesicht, von der Nase über das Kinn zum Hals. Die Augen sind hervorgetreten. Keine Regung oder Emotion spiegelt sich auf dem puppenhaften Kindergesicht wider.

Was, so muß sich der Betrachter fragen, veranlaßte den Künstler, sich Bildern von Leid, Qual und Tod zuzuwenden? Während der Nachkriegsjahre, als Helnwein in Wien aufwuchs, sprach niemand von der Brutalität der Nazizeit. Jegliche Erinnerung wurde unterdrückt und Österreichs bedingungslose Kollaboration geleugnet. Das Land sah sich vielmehr selbst als »erstes Opfer des Faschismus«. Gottfried fiel es schwer, dieses niederdrückende Schweigen des österreichischen Kleinbürgertums zu akzeptieren – er war ein rebellisches Kind, interessiert an sozialen und politischen Fragen sowie an der jüngsten Vergangenheit.

Zwei Erfahrungen wurden zur bleibenden Erinnerung für den jungen Mann; sie sind die Schlüssel zu seinen späteren Werken. Er erfuhr eine strenge, katholische Erziehung und ein auf Unterdrückung und Bestrafung basierendes konfessionelles Schulsystem, mit seinem Dogma der Schuld und dem Aufruf zur Bescheidenheit. Bilder und Statuen von der Geißelung Christi, der Dornenkrönung und der Kreuzigung sowie grafische Darstellungen der Steinigung des Hl. Stephanus, des pfeilgespickten Körpers des Hl. Sebastian oder der abgeschnittenen Brüste der Hl. Agatha waren allgegenwärtig.

In krassem Gegensatz zu dieser Flut an Todeskampfdarstellungen steht die Bilderwelt Walt Disneys. Obwohl von Schulautoritäten verunglimpft und als jugendgefährdend eingestuft, war sie ein Lichtblick. Später, 1984, besuchte der Künstler Carl Barks in Kalifornien, um dem Erfinder von Donald Duck und dem Geizhals Onkel Dagobert Tribut zu zollen, und behauptete, er habe mehr von Disney als von Leonardo da

tandis que l'autre bras amaigri et sa main couverte de pansements pendent à sa droite. Une horrible cicatrice traverse son visage du nez au menton et descend jusqu'au cou, et qui plus est, les yeux de la fillette sont proéminents. Aucune expression, aucune émotion ne se dégage de son enfantin visage de poupée.

On en vient à ce demander ce qui a pu pousser cet artiste à se consacrer à des images de souffrance, de torture et de mort. Pendant les années d'après-guerre, alors que Helnwein grandit à Vienne, personne ne parle de la brutalité de la période nazie. On a perdu la mémoire et l'Autriche nie sa collaboration inconditionnelle en tentant désormais de faire figure de « première victime du fascisme ». Ce pesant silence de la petite bourgeoisie autrichienne est difficilement supportable pour Gottfried – c'est un enfant rebelle qui s'intéresse aux problèmes sociaux et politiques et aux évènements récents.

Deux expériences laissent une impression indélébile sur le jeune homme, des expériences clés pour ses œuvres à venir. Il subit une éducation catholique très stricte, dans une école paroissiale extrêmement répressive, qui a pour dogme d'inculquer la culpabilité et l'humilité. Les images et les statues montrant la flagellation du Christ sont omniprésentes, tout comme le couronnement d'épines, la crucifixion, les représentations picturales de la lapidation de saint Etienne, le corps de saint Sébastien transpercé de flèches, l'amputation des seins de sainte Agathe.

Le monde picturale de Walt Disney contraste radicalement avec ces abondantes représentations de l'agonie chez Helnwein. Bien que méprisé et considéré comme dangereux par les autorités scolaires, c'est comme un rayon de soleil. Plus tard, en 1984, quand l'artiste rendra visite à Carl Barks en Californie pour rendre hommage au père de Donald Duck et d'oncle Picsou, il déclarera avoir davantage appris de Walt Disney que de Léonard de Vinci. Helnwein est ensuite émerveillé en voyant pour la

Elvis Presley on a chewing-gum card, he was enchanted.

In the continuing debate about high and low art, Helnwein completely rejects the argument that popular art forms – jazz, movies, comic books, rock'n'roll – corrupt the true and transcendental aesthetic experience. He claims that in fact the split between high and low art is elitist and totally artificial – that Disney, like Picasso, initiated a break with classical ideals of beauty and made a new visual art with authentic emotional meaning: "Good comics, for me, is sacred art," he once said.[3]

Helnwein is an artist who often uses his own work for themes and images; he continues to be preoccupied with Disney creatures. In 1993 he made a crayon drawing of Pablo Picasso (after Brassaï's famous photograph) gazing at a grouchy little Donald Duck in his hand. As part of the same series, we see *The Temptation of Joseph Beuys* (1993), with Beuys seated in quiet contemplation as he looks at a jubilant comic-strip character (see page 153), and *Mozart's Skull* of the same year, with Donald Duck and a human skull. In 1995 he made several large renderings of Donald Duck in blue monochrome, followed by a Mickey Mouse (1996), which measures over three meters across. The artist's ongoing preoccupation with the Mouse and the Duck is worth noting. He admires the animated creatures' vitality and multiplicity of expression, and does not seem concerned about the strangely asexual notions of the Disney families nor with the capitalist entrepreneurship of the Duck family, nor the exploitation of the imagination of the young and impressionable by the synthetic Hollywood dream machine.[4]

It is true, of course, that major artists have for a long time been involved in popular art, often at the beginning of their careers. Toulouse-Lautrec and Pierre Bonnard were among the finest designers of art nouveau travel posters. Both Matisse and Picasso designed French travel posters.

Vinci gelernt. Und als Helnwein erstmals ein Bild von Elvis Presley auf einem Kaugummipapier sah, war er davon hingerissen.

Innerhalb der fortdauernden Debatte um hohe und leichte Kunst weist Helnwein das Argument zurück, daß populäre Kunstformen – Jazz, Filme, Comics, Rock'n'Roll – die wahre und transzendentale ästhetische Erfahrung verderben. Die Spaltung in Hoch- und Trivialkunst sei elitär und absolut künstlich, Disney wie Picasso brachen mit den klassischen Schönheitsidealen und schufen eine neue visuelle Kunst von wahrhaftiger emotionaler Bedeutung. »Für mich sind gute Comics eine heilige Kunst«, sagte er einmal[3].

Helnwein zitiert häufig sein eigenes Werk in der Themen- und Motivwahl; weiterhin beschäftigt er sich mit Disneys Figuren. 1993 fertigte er eine Bleistiftzeichnung von Pablo Picasso an (nach Brassaïs berühmter Fotografie), der einen griesgrämigen kleinen Donald Duck in seiner Hand anstarrt. Zu derselben Bilderserie gehören *Die Versuchung des Joseph Beuys,* worauf der sitzende Beuys in stiller Kontemplation eine frohlockende Comic-Figur betrachtet (s. S. 153), und *Mozarts Schädel,* mit Donald Duck und einem menschlichen Schädel (beide von 1993). 1995 schuf Helnwein mehrere großformatige Arbeiten mit Donald Duck, monochrom blau, und Micky Maus (1996). Die fortdauernde Beschäftigung des Künstlers mit der Maus und der Ente ist beachtenswert. Er bewundert die Vitalität und die facettenreichen Ausdrucksformen der animierten Kreaturen. Helnwein scheint sich weder über die sonderbar asexuelle Anmutung der Disney-Familien zu wundern noch um das kapitalistische Unternehmertum der Duck-Familie oder die Ausbeutung der Vorstellungskraft der Menschen durch die synthetische Traummaschine Hollywoods[4].

Viele bedeutende Künstler haben sich über längere Zeit hinweg, meist zu Beginn ihrer Karriere, der populären Kunst verschrieben. Toulouse-Lautrec und Pierre Bonnard gehörten zu den besten Gestaltern von

première fois le portrait d'Elvis Presley sur une tablette de chewing-gum.

Dans l'éternelle polémique sur les arts majeurs et mineurs, Helnwein récuse tous les arguments qui reprochent aux arts populaires – jazz, cinéma, bandes dessinées, rock'n'roll – d'entacher l'expérience esthétique véritable et transcendante. Il déclare qu'en réalité, l'abîme entre les arts majeurs et mineurs est élitiste et complètement artificiel – que Disney, tout comme Picasso, sont à l'origine de la rupture avec les idéaux classiques de la beauté et ont donné naissance à un nouvel art ayant une réelle signification émotionnelle. Il dit même un jour : « Pour moi, une bonne bande dessinée, c'est de l'art sacré »[3].

Helnwein reprend souvent ses propres œuvres pour traiter de nouveaux thèmes et images tout en continuant à s'intéresser aux créatures de Disney. En 1993, il réalise au crayon un portrait de Picasso (d'après la célèbre photographie de Brassaï) en train d'observer un petit Donald Duck grognon posé sur sa main. Dans la même série, on retrouve *La Tentation de Joseph Beuys* (1993) qui montre Beuys assis et absorbé dans sa méditation, regardant un personnage de bande dessinée débordant de joie (voir p. 153), ainsi que *Le Crâne de Mozart,* avec Donald Duck et un crâne humain qui date de la même année. En 1995, il réalise plusieurs grands portraits du célèbre canard en camaïeu de bleus, puis, un de Mickey (1996). Cet intérêt constant que l'artiste porte à la fameuse souris et au canard mérite d'être signalé. Il admire la vitalité de ces créatures animées et leurs multiples expressions, il ne semble concerné ni par le caractère étrangement asexué des familles inventées par Disney ni par l'esprit capitaliste du clan Duck, ou par l'exploitation de l'imaginaire des gens par les artifices de la machine à rêves hollywoodienne[4].

Bon nombre d'artistes majeurs ont longtemps œuvré dans les arts populaires, le plus souvent au début de leur carrière. Toulouse-Lautrec et Pierre Bonnard comptaient

Giacomo Balla, preceded by James Ensor, incorporated graffiti in his paintings. Kurt Schwitters, master of detritus, used everything from used train tickets to comic strips in his Merz collages, and Richard Lindner spent many years as an illustrator and art director before turning to painting. Andy Warhol designed shoe advertisements; James Rosenquist made big billboards for Times Square; Lyonel Feininger, followed by Öyvind Fahlstrom and Robert Crumb, actually produced comic strips; and Roy Lichtenstein based his early work on the comics, while Claes Oldenburg in the early 1970s designed the Maus Museum in honor of the great animator. Helnwein then clearly belongs to a viable tradition in modern art, a tradition in total opposition to the formalist and puritanical construct of a critic like Clement Greenberg, who juxtaposed avant-garde with kitsch, proclaiming that a work of art must transcend the chaos of modern life.

The very essence of postmodernism is the interconnectedness that erases boundaries between different aspects of culture, whether high or low, in favor of creating polymorphous paradigms of multicultural values. Rarely, however, has an artist so thoroughly inverted Walter Benjamin's misgivings about lack of authenticity and the aura of uniqueness of a work of art in the era of mechanical reproduction. Helnwein has done this by embracing all the possibilities of technological processes to bring art to the widest possible public. To this end, he uses offset lithography, posters, magazine covers, photographs, and large murals in the public area. By his carefully calculated appearance and dress he even makes his own person into a popular idol.

Jugendstil-Reiseplakaten. Matisse und Picasso entwarfen französische Reiseplakate. Giacomo Balla fügte wie bereits James Ensor Graffiti in seine Gemälde ein. Kurt Schwitters, der Meister des Abfalls, verwandte alles mögliche für seine Merz-Collagen, vom Bahnticket bis hin zu Comic-Strips, und Richard Lindner war zunächst Illustrator und Art Director, bevor er sich der Malerei zuwandte. Andy Warhol entwarf Werbung für Schuhe, James Rosenquist fertigte große Reklametafeln für den Times Square, und Lyonel Feininger, später auch Öyvind Fahlstrom und Robert Crumb, produzierten Comic-Strips. Auf diesem Medium basierten auch Roy Lichtensteins frühe Werke; Claes Oldenburg entwarf in den frühen 70er Jahren das Maus-Museum zu Ehren des großen Animators. Helnwein läßt sich also klar in eine Tradition innerhalb der modernen Kunst einordnen, die das genaue Gegenteil der formalistischen und puritanischen Kritiken etwa eines Clement Greenberg ist, der die Avantgarde neben dem Kitsch ansiedelte und dabei ausrief, daß ein Kunstwerk das Chaos des modernen Lebens übersteigen müsse.

Die Essenz der Postmoderne liegt in der Verwischung der Grenzen zwischen den verschiedenen Aspekten der Kultur, ob Hoch- oder Massenkultur, um polymorphe Paradigmen multikultureller Werte zu schaffen. Dennoch hat selten ein Künstler so deutlich Walter Benjamins Bedenken gegenüber dem Mangel an Authentizität und der Aura der Einmaligkeit eines Kunstwerks im Zeitalter seiner technischen Reproduzierbarkeit widerlegt. Helnwein schöpfte alle technischen Möglichkeiten aus, um Kunst einer möglichst breiten Öffentlichkeit zugänglich zu machen. Er arbeitete dabei mit Offset-Lithographien, Plakaten, Zeitschriften-Covern, Fotografien und großen Wänden auf öffentlichen Plätzen. Durch sein sorgfältig kalkuliertes Auftreten und seine ausgewählte Kleidung macht er sogar seine eigene Person zu einem populären Idol.

parmi les meilleurs créateurs d'affiches d'agences de voyage Art nouveau. Matisse et Picasso peignaient eux aussi ce genre d'affiches en France. Précédé par James Ensor, Giacomo Balla incorporait des graffitis à ses tableaux. Dans ses collages Merz, Kurt Schwitters, le maître de la récupération, tirait profit de tout, du vieux billet de train aux bandes dessinées. Richard Lindner fut d'abord illustrateur, puis directeur artistique avant de se tourner vers la peinture. Warhol dessinait des publicités pour chaussures, James Rosenquist réalisait de grandes affiches pour Times Square. Lyonel Feininger, puis Öyvind Fahlstrom et Robert Crumb faisaient des bandes dessinées, quant à Roy Lichtenstein, il s'en inspira dans ses premières œuvres, tandis qu'au début des années 70, Claes Oldenburg, imaginait un musée en l'honneur de la célèbre souris. Helnwein appartient de toute évidence à une tradition présente dans l'art moderne, qui s'oppose radicalement aux thèses formalistes et puritaines d'un critique tel que Clement Greenberg, qui, juxtaposant avant-garde et kitsch, proclame que l'œuvre d'art doit transcender le chaos de la vie moderne.

La véritable essence du postmodernisme réside dans les transversales qui gomment les frontières entre les différents aspects de la culture, qu'elle soit supérieure ou inférieure, au bénéfice de l'émergence des paradigmes polymorphes des valeurs multiculturelles. Il est toutefois rare qu'un artiste ait inversé de manière aussi conséquente les doutes exprimés par Walter Benjamin quant à l'absence d'authenticité et à l'aura du caractère unique de l'œuvre d'art à l'ère de la reproduction à la machine. Or, Helnwein réalise cette inversion en exploitant toutes les possibilités technologiques pour rendre l'art accessible à un large public. A ces fins, il utilise la lithographie offset, l'affiche, les couvertures de magazines, la photographie et les larges murs des lieux publics. Par une apparence et une tenue où rien n'est laissé au hasard, il fait de sa propre personne, une idole populaire.

Early Years, Education and Rebellion

Gottfried Helnwein looks back at his education in a Catholic Gymnasium as a catastrophe, and his goal has been largely to undermine and destroy the repressive system based on the hateful intolerance instilled by the Christian religion, which he considers the primary source of fascism. He completely despised and rejected the school system and his only desire was to paint. He abandoned school and was admitted to the Experimental Institute of Higher Graphic Instruction in 1965 – an institution that was anything but experimental; instruction proved to be totally traditional and conformist. In rebellion against these constraints, Helnwein cut his hand with a razor blade and with his own blood drew a picture of Adolf Hitler, which outraged the school administration and made the young artist aware for the first time of the potency of a picture. Soon thereafter he was dismissed from the school.

Rejecting the art tradition of the Establishment and believing in the primitive power of Trivial Art as a counter-aesthetic concept, Helnwein wanted to be admitted to the Vienna Academy of Art, where he could work autonomously in the great ateliers. He had heard of Rudolf Hausner, on the Academy's faculty, and also the oldest member of the school of fantastic realism, one of the major trends in Viennese art in the postwar period. The other original artists of this group were Arik Brauer, Ernst Fuchs, Wolfgang Hutter, and Anton Lehmden. They had worked in the rubble of the destroyed and divided city, finding the substance of their art in dream, imagination, and fantasy. Most were students of Albert Paris Gütersloh at the Vienna Academy; they also looked at the work of Albrecht Altdorfer and other Renaissance masters of the Danube school. They admired Persian miniature painting and were very much aware of the

Kinderjahre, Erziehung und Auflehnung

Im Rückblick beurteilt Helnwein seine Erziehung an einem katholischen Gymnasium als Katastrophe. Sein Ziel war es stets, das repressive System, das auf der haßerfüllten Intoleranz der katholischen Kirche basiert, weitgehend zu unterminieren und zu zerstören; im Katholizismus sieht er auch die Hauptquelle des Faschismus. Er verachtete das Schulsystem; sein Sehnen und Streben galt allein dem Malen. Er verließ die Schule und ging 1965 an die Höhere Graphische Bundeslehr- und Versuchsanstalt – die Ausbildung erwies sich jedoch als traditionell und konformistisch. In Auflehnung gegen diese Einschränkungen schnitt sich Helnwein mit einer Rasierklinge in die Hand und malte mit seinem eigenen Blut ein Porträt von Hitler. Die Schulverwaltung reagierte entsetzt, und der junge Künstler begriff zum ersten Mal die Wirkungskraft eines Bildes. Kurz darauf wurde er der Schule verwiesen.

Helnwein lehnte die künstlerische Tradition der bürgerlichen Gesellschaft ab und glaubte an die primitive Kraft der Trivialkunst als kontra-ästhetisches Konzept. Er wollte an die Wiener Akademie der Bildenden Künste, wo er unabhängig arbeiten konnte. Er hatte vom Akademieprofessor Rudolf Hausner gehört, dem ältesten Mitglied der Schule des Phantastischen Realismus, einer der Hauptströmungen der Wiener Nachkriegskunst. Die anderen Gründungsmitglieder waren Arik Brauer, Ernst Fuchs, Wolfgang Hutter und Anton Lehmden. Sie hatten zwischen den Trümmern der geteilten Stadt gearbeitet und die Substanz ihrer Kunst in Träumen, in der Vorstellungskraft und der Phantasie gefunden. Die meisten von ihnen waren Studenten von Albert Paris Gütersloh an der Wiener Akademie; sie widmeten sich dem Werk Albrecht Altdorfers und anderer Renaissancemeister der Donauschule. Sie bewunderten persische Miniaturen und verspürten den Einfluß der

Années de Jeunesse, Education et Rébellion

Rétrospectivement, Helnwein juge catastrophique l'éducation que dispensait son lycée catholique. Son but est alors de saper et de détruire ce système répressif basé sur l'intolérance et la haine inculquées par la religion catholique, et qu'il considère comme étant la source essentielle du fascisme. Il refuse le système scolaire dans son ensemble, son seul désir est de peindre. Il quitte donc l'école et entre en 1965 à l'Institut expérimental d'enseignement supérieur des arts graphiques – les méthodes pédagogiques s'y avèrent conformistes et des plus traditionnelles. En signe de révolte contre ces contraintes, Helnwein s'entaille la main avec une lame de rasoir et dessine un portrait d'Hitler avec son propre sang. L'indignation avec laquelle réagit l'administration scolaire lui fait pour la première fois prendre conscience du pouvoir de l'image. Peu de temps après, il est renvoyé de cet institut.

Rejetant les traditions artistiques du système établi et croyant au pouvoir primitif de l'art trivial en tant que concept anti-esthétique, Helnwein désire entrer à l'Académie des Beaux Arts de Vienne où il pourra travailler avec davantage d'autonomie. Il a entendu parler du professeur d'académie Rudolf Hausner, l'aîné des membres de l'école du réalisme fantastique, l'une des tendances artistiques majeures dans la Vienne de l'après-guerre. Ce groupe réunit d'autres artistes originaux comme Arik Brauer, Ernst Fuchs, Wolfgang Hutter et Anton Lehmden. Ils ont œuvré dans les ruines de la ville divisée, puisant la substance de leur art dans le rêve, l'imaginaire et le fantastique. La plupart ont été les élèves d'Albert Paris Gütersloh aux Beaux-Arts de Vienne et s'inspirent des œuvres d'Albrecht Altdorfer et autres maîtres de la Renaissance danubienne. Ils admirent les miniatures persanes, sont très attentifs au surréalisme, et en particulier à Max Ernst, Salvador Dalí et René Magritte. Mais plutôt que de puiser

Self-Portrait/Selbstbildnis/Autoportrait, 1987
Photograph

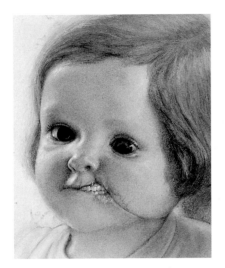

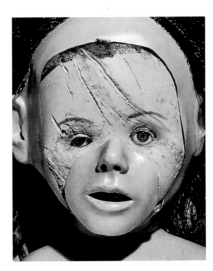

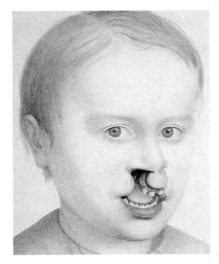

Helnwein
Colored pencil and watercolor, 1972

Cindy Sherman
Photograph, 1995

Medical drawing/Medizinische
Zeichnung/Dessin médical, 19th century
Photograph, 1996

surrealists, particularly Max Ernst, Salvador Dalí, and René Magritte. But rather than searching for the unconscious and the "pure psychic automatisms" without recourse to conscious thought advocated by André Breton, they explored personal symbols and actually have a greater affinity with symbolist painters of the fin de siècle. By the early 1960s this group, together with Friedensreich Hundertwasser, whose work is distantly related to theirs, had achieved international recognition.

At this time the international tachist movement, dominant among the Academy faculty, was represented in Vienna by artists largely sponsored by Monsignor Mauer at the Galerie St. Stephan: Austrian artists such as Wolfgang Hollegha, Josef Mikl, Markus Prachensky and the early Arnulf Rainer.

Rainer, an artist whom Helnwein holds in high esteem, was also at the time connected to the group that became known as Wiener Aktionismus. Sigmund Freud's city, sometimes referred to as the breeding ground of neurosis, gave birth to this group of artists – Günter Brus, Otto Mühl, Hermann Nitsch, Rudolf Schwarzkogler – who felt that the tachism, or action painting, they

Surrealisten, von Max Ernst, Salvador Dalí und René Magritte. Aber anstatt nach dem Unbewußten und den »reinen psychischen Automatismen« zu suchen, ohne das bewußte Denken eines André Breton, entdeckten sie eine persönliche Symbolsprache und hegten eine stärkere Affinität zu den Malern des Symbolismus der Jahrhundertwende. Anfang der 60er Jahre hatte die Künstlergruppe zusammen mit Friedensreich Hundertwasser, dessen Werk nur entfernt mit dem ihrigen verwandt ist, internationale Anerkennung gefunden.

Zu dieser Zeit wurden die Wiener Repräsentanten des Tachismus, die dominierende Strömung an der Akademie, von Monsignore Mauer von der Galerie St. Stephan gefördert: österreichische Künstler wie Wolfgang Hollegha, Josef Mikl, Markus Prachensky und der junge Arnulf Rainer. Rainer, ein von Helnwein hochgeschätzter Künstler, unterhielt gleichzeitig Verbindungen zu jener Gruppe, die unter dem Namen Wiener Aktionismus bekannt wurde. In der Stadt Sigmund Freuds, auch als Brutstätte der Neurose bezeichnet, entstand diese Kunstrichtung, mit Günter Brus, Otto Mühl, Hermann Nitsch und Rudolf Schwarzkogler. Sie empfanden Werke des Tachismus oder des

dans l'inconscient et dans les « automatismes psychiques » sans avoir recours à la pensée consciente, tel que le prônait André Breton, ils explorent la symbolique individuelle et ont en vérité de plus grandes affinités avec les peintres symbolistes de la période fin de siècle. Au début des années 60, ce groupe, où l'on trouve aussi Friedensreich Hundertwasser, dont les travaux sont toutefois très éloignés des leurs, est reconnu dans le monde entier.

A cette époque, un mouvement international, le tachisme, règne en maître sur l'Académie ; ses représentants à Vienne sont des artistes parrainés par Monseigneur Mauer de la galerie St Stephan, des artistes autrichiens comme Wolfgang Hollegha, Josef Mikl, Markus Prachensky et le jeune Arnulf Rainer. Rainer, un artiste qu'Helnwein estime beaucoup, entretient alors des relations avec un autre groupe qui deviendra célèbre sous le nom d'Actionnistes viennois. La ville de Sigmund Freud, parfois considérée comme le terreau de la névrose, engendre ce groupe d'artistes réunissant Günter Brus, Otto Mühl, Hermann Nitsch et Rudolf Schwarzkogler, qui considèrent que le tachisme, ou l'action painting, est susceptible de conduire à une action directe

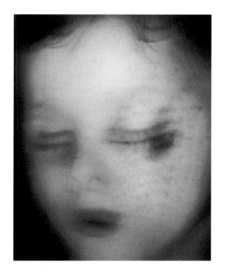

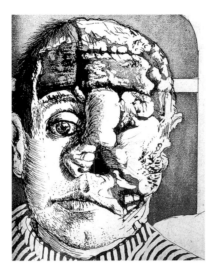

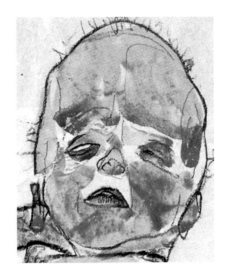

Helnwein
Photograph, 1996

Otto Dix
Etching, 1924

Egon Schiele
Watercolor and charcoal, 1910

saw in the galleries could lead to direct and actual life action on the part of the artists, an attitude they shared with other artists in Europe (Mathieu, Klein), Japan (Gutai) and the USA (Happenings, Performances). Kristine Stiles has described the confrontational and cathartic aspects of these artist-actions:

"Systematically assaulting repressive sexual mores, hypocritical religious values, the overt destruction of war, and the covert physical and psychological violence of the family, they created confrontational, often sadomasochistic and misogynistic, actions aimed at visualizing pain as a means of catharsis for healing. Scandalous in form and content, their art led repeatedly to arrest, fines, and imprisonment."[5]

One artist, Schwarzkogler, who used bandaged figures for performances dealing with castration, wounding, and healing, died in his twenties in a fall, perhaps intentional, from his apartment window.

The Aktionists came to the attention of the art world (and the police) only in the early 1970s, after Nitsch began his bloody performances of the "Orgies Mysteries Theater" in Schloss Prinzenhof near Vienna. The young Gottfried Helnwein was

Action painting als Aufforderung zu Live-Aktionen, eine Auffassung, die sie mit anderen Künstlern in Europa (Mathieu, Klein), Japan (Gutai) und den USA (Happenings, Performances) teilten. Kristine Stiles hat die auf Konfrontation gerichteten und kathartischen Aspekte dieser Aktionen beschrieben: »Eine systematisch verletzende repressive Sexualmoral, scheinheilige religiöse Werte, die offene Zerstörung des Krieges und die verdeckte physische und psychische Gewalt in der Familie, sie alle provozierten auf Auseinandersetzung gerichtete, oft sadomasochistische und frauenfeindliche Aktionen, die Schmerz als einen kathartischen Beitrag zur Heilung zu visualisieren versuchen. Skandalös in Form und Inhalt, zog ihre Kunst immer wieder Verhaftungen, Geldbußen und Gefängnisstrafen nach sich.«[5]

Einer der Künstler, Schwarzkogler, der bandagierte Gestalten in seinen Kastrations-, Verletzungs- und Heilungsaktionen einsetzte, starb noch vor Vollendung seines 30. Lebensjahres an den Folgen eines – vielleicht absichtlichen – Sturzes aus dem Fenster seiner Wohnung.

Die Wiener Aktionisten erlangten die Aufmerksamkeit der Kunstwelt (und der Polizei) lediglich in den frühen 70er Jahren,

et actuelle de la part des artistes, une attitude qu'ils partagent avec d'autres artistes européens (Mathieu, Klein), japonais (Gutai) et américains (happenings et représentations). Kristine Stiles résume l'aspect de confrontation et les aspects cathartiques de ces actions comme suit : « Attaquant systématiquement les mœurs sexuelles répressives, l'hypocrisie des valeurs religieuses, la destruction manifeste provoquée par la guerre, ainsi que la violence physique et psychique exercée dans la famille sans que personne ne le soupçonne, ils organisaient des confrontations, souvent de caractère sadomasochiste et misogyne destinées à visualiser la souffrance en tant que moyen purgatif de guérison. Scandaleux par sa forme et son contenu, l'exercice de cet art leur vaut régulièrement des arrestations, des amendes et des incarcérations. »[5]

L'un d'eux, Schwarzkogler, utilise dans ses représentations des personnages avec des bandages qui évoquent la castration, la blessure et la guérison ; il meurt alors qu'il a une vingtaine d'années d'une chute, peut-être intentionnelle, de la fenêtre de son appartement.

Les Actionnistes n'attirent l'attention du monde de l'art (et de la police) qu'au début

not aware of these events. As a result of his rebellious attitude towards traditional art he had isolated himself from the art world. He had never looked at an art book or magazine, never gone to a museum to see an exhibition – but he had decided that he did want to go to the Academy and develop his own kind of art.

To gain admission in 1969 he presented a painting titled *Osterwetter*. Painted in soft colors and evoking a melancholy mood, it pictured two children who look very much like dolls; they have been playing with a knife with which one has killed the other. Surely, this imagery must have had its source in the pictures of bloody martyrdom that the artist was raised with in the church. This initial painting, rather naive in execution, was praised highly by Rudolf Hausner, who at once accepted Helnwein in his class. Hausner, the only professor at the Academy who was not an abstract painter, permitted his students total freedom, explaining:

"Nothing falsifies the teaching process more than the attempt to project the work of the teacher on the student. As I find myself in a permanent state of self-analysis in my work, I am not likely to confuse it with that of the student. I therefore never speak about my work. The relationship is solely predicated on the special condition of the student; and I work with him on nothing but his personal development."[6]

Helnwein for the first time in his life felt free to do and work as he pleased. Yet he still objected to the school's heavy authoritarian atmosphere and hierarchic organization. He must by now have been aware of the wave of student rebellion which had spread from Berkeley to New York, Paris and Prague in 1969. Swept up by the spirit of the time, he and a few friends, wanting to affirm themselves, organized their own carefully planned "Anarchist Aktion" against the Academy's antiquated admission system. They used fire extinguishers, stink bombs, and profuse

nachdem Nitsch auf Schloß Prinzenhof bei Wien mit seinen blutigen Ritualspielen des »Orgien-Mysterien-Theaters« begonnen hatte. Der junge Helnwein nahm keine Notiz von diesen Ereignissen. Aus seiner rebellischen Haltung gegenüber der traditionellen Kunst heraus hatte er sich von der Kunstwelt isoliert. Er hatte nie ein Kunstbuch oder eine Kunstzeitschrift gelesen, nie ein Museum oder eine Ausstellung besucht – aber er hatte beschlossen, auf die Akademie zu gehen und seine eigene Kunst zu entwickeln.

Um die Zulassung zu erhalten, reichte er 1969 ein Gemälde mit dem Titel *Osterwetter* ein. Die weichen Farben vermitteln eine melancholische Stimmung. Dargestellt sind zwei puppenähnliche Kinder, von denen eines das andere beim Spiel mit einem Messer getötet hat. Das Sujet dieses Bildes lehnt sich an die blutigen Märtyrerszenen in der Kirche aus der Kindheit des Künstlers an. Dieses erste Bild, ziemlich naiv in der Ausführung, wurde von Rudolf Hausner hochgelobt, so daß er Helnwein sofort in seine Klasse aufnahm. Hausner, der einzige Professor der Akademie, der kein abstrakter Maler war, ließ seinen Studenten absolute Freiheit: »Nichts verfälscht den Vorgang ärger als der Versuch, in die Anliegen des Schülers die des Lehrers zu projizieren. Da ich mich durch meine Arbeit in einer Art permanenter Selbstanalyse befinde, neige ich nicht dazu, mich mit dem Schüler zu verwechseln. Daher rede ich mit ihm nie über meine Arbeit. Das Arbeitsverhältnis ist ausschließlich durch die speziellen Konditionen des Schülers bestimmt – ich arbeite mit ihm an nichts anderem als an seiner Entwicklung zu sich selbst.«[6]

Zum ersten Mal in seinem Leben konnte Helnwein tun und lassen, was er wollte. Dennoch nahm er immer noch Anstoß an der stark autoritär geprägten Atmosphäre und der hierarchischen Organisation der Kunsthochschule. Zu diesem Zeitpunkt muß er bereits auf die Welle der Studentenproteste aufmerksam geworden sein, die 1969 von Berkeley nach New York, Paris und Prag

des années 70, quand Nitsch commence à organiser les performances sanglantes de l'« Orgies Mysteries Theater » au château de Prinzenhof, près de Vienne. Le jeune Helnwein ignore tout de ces manifestations. Son attitude de rebelle en marge de l'art traditionnel l'a isolé du milieu. Jamais il n'a lu un livre ou un magazine d'art, et jamais il ne va au musée voir une exposition, mais il a décidé d'entrer à l'Académie et de développer sa propre méthode de travail.

En 1969, pour passer le concours d'admission, il présente une peinture appelée *Osterwetter* réalisée avec des couleurs pastel qui évoquent la mélancolie. Elle représente deux enfants qui ressemblent fortement à des poupées. En jouant avec un couteau, l'un d'eux a tué l'autre. Ces images puisent leur source dans les tableaux des martyres sanguinolents des églises avec lesquels l'artiste a grandi. Cette première peinture, plutôt naïve dans son exécution, reçoit maints éloges de Rudolf Hausner qui accepte immédiatement Helnwein dans sa classe. Hausner, le seul professeur de l'Académie des Beaux-Arts à ne pas être un peintre abstrait, laisse à ses élèves l'entière liberté de s'exprimer : « Rien ne falsifie davantage le processus d'apprentissage qu'un enseignant qui tente de projeter son propre travail dans celui de l'étudiant. Comme en travaillant, je me trouve dans un état d'auto-analyse permanente, je ne risque pas de le confondre avec celui des élèves. C'est pourquoi je ne parle jamais de mon œuvre. La relation entre nous est seulement déterminée par la singularité de l'étudiant ; je ne travaille avec lui, mais uniquement à son développement individuel. »[6]

Pour la première fois de sa vie, Helnwein se sent libre de faire ce qui lui plaît, même s'il continue de désapprouver l'atmosphère autoritaire de l'école. C'est sans doute à cette époque qu'il s'intéresse à la révolte estudiantine qui, telle une vague, déferle de Berkeley à New York, pour atteindre Paris et Prague en 1969. Emporté par l'esprit de l'époque, il se joint à quelques amis voulant,

Giants/Giganten/Géants, 1993
Colored pencil on paper, 33 × 24 inches, 84 × 62 cm
Private Collection

Egon Schiele
Watercolor and pencil, 1913

smoke; they burnt doors, threw windows into the schoolyard. Though nobody was injured, general panic ensued, and the resulting publicity revealed the students' objections.

As part of his continuing protest against the establishment, and to remind Austria of the recent past, toward which the country maintained a policy of official denial, Helnwein once more painted a portrait of Hitler and entered it in a student show, together with early watercolors of bandaged children. But the Hitler painting engendered many admiring responses from the public – hardly surprising given the nation's complicit silence about the Nazi era.

In 1972 Helnwein, still a student, performed his first Aktion pieces, art-theater works documented with photographs. Like much of his other art, they focused on children who were often bandaged and had wounds inflicted with surgical instruments. These Aktion events are part of a modernist tradition: art as acts of defiance against the Establishment.

Art-theater goes back to futurist "scenographics," to Dada events in Zurich, to Mayakovsky's revolutionary Agit-props and on to the performances of the 1960s.

übergeschwappt war. Vom Zeitgeist aufgerüttelt suchten er und einige seiner Freunde nach Selbstbestätigung und organisierten ihre eigene, sorgfältig geplante »Anarchistenaktion« gegen das antiquierte Aufnahmeverfahren der Akademie. Sie setzten Feuerlöscher, Stinkbomben und dicke Rauchschwaden ein, verbrannten Türen und warfen Fenster in den Hof der Kunsthochschule. Obwohl niemand verletzt wurde, brach eine allgemeine Panik aus, und die daraus resultierende Publicity brachte den Studentenprotest an die Öffentlichkeit.

Als Ausdruck seines anhaltenden Protests gegen das Establishment und um Österreich an seine jüngste Vergangenheit zu erinnern, gegenüber der das Land eine Politik des offiziellen Leugnens verfolgte, malte Helnwein ein weiteres Porträt von Hitler und zeigte es zusammen mit einigen frühen Aquarellen von bandagierten Kindern bei einer Studentenveranstaltung. Tatsächlich erntete das Hitler-Gemälde viel Bewunderung beim Publikum, was angesichts des komplizenhaften Schweigens der Nation über die Nazizeit kaum überrascht.

1972 inszenierte der Student Helnwein seine ersten Aktionen, Werke aus dem Bereich Kunst-Theater, die in Fotografien fest-

comme lui, s'affirmer ; ils organisent et préparent soigneusement leur propre « action anarchiste » contre le système archaïque d'admission à l'Académie. Ils prennent des extincteurs, lancent des boules puantes, font de la fumée, brûlent des portes et jettent les fenêtres dans la cour de l'école. Bien qu'il n'y ait pas de blessé, la panique est générale, et le battage qui en résulte, révèle un malaise estudiantin.

S'inscrivant dans la contestation permanente du système, et voulant rappeler à l'Autriche son passé récent, alors que le pays s'obstine dans une politique de reniement officiel, Helnwein réalise une fois encore un portrait d'Hitler qu'il présente lors d'une exposition de travaux d'étudiants, en même temps que d'anciennes aquarelles avec les enfants couverts de pansements. Mais le portrait d'Hitler engendre une réaction positive du public – ce qui n'est guère surprenant étant donné le silence complice de la nation quant à son passé nazi.

En 1972, alors qu'il est encore étudiant, Helnwein se produit dans ses propres actions, des représentations d'art-théâtre documentées par des photographies. Comme la plupart de ses travaux, elles se focalisent sur des enfants souvent couverts de ban-

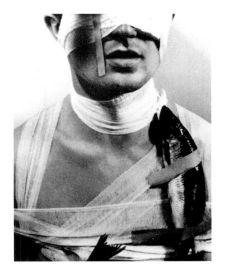

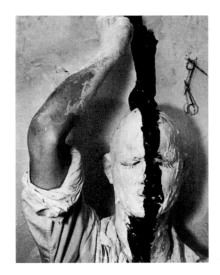

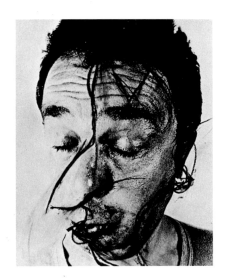

Rudolf Schwarzkogler
Aktion, 1965

Günter Brus
Aktion, 1965

Arnulf Rainer
Oil-crayon on photograph, 1971

Unlike the slightly earlier Viennese Aktionist artists, Helnwein did not use children's bodies as aesthetic (or anti-aesthetic) objects, or as part of physical-sexual display. His intent was to provoke a sense of outrage against the odious and generally accepted treatment of the child as society's easy victim. He continued his Aktion performances until 1976, when he performed Aktion *Always Prepared*. Here he appeared lying in the street with a bandaged head; a passing woman or child tried to assist him, but most passers-by walked on apathetically, ignoring the presumed accident victim at their feet.

gehalten sind. Wie bei einem Großteil seiner Werke standen im Mittelpunkt des Geschehens bandagierte und verwundete Kinder, die mit chirurgischen Instrumenten verletzt worden waren. Seine Aktionskunst gehört zur modernistischen Tradition: Kunst als Ausdruck der Mißbilligung des Establishments.

Das Kunst-Theater geht auf futuristische »Szenographien«, Dadaisten-Veranstaltungen in Zürich, Majakowskis revolutionäre Agitprops und Performances der 60er Jahre zurück. Anders als die Wiener Aktionisten benutzte Helnwein die Kinderkörper nicht als ästhetische (oder anti-ästhetische) Objekte oder als Bestandteil physisch-sexueller Zurschaustellung; er wollte vielmehr ein Gefühl der Empörung gegen die verabscheuungswürdige und allgemein tolerierte Behandlung von Kindern als wehrlose Opfer provozieren. Er fuhr mit der Aktionskunst bis 1976 fort, als er die Aktion *Allzeit bereit* durchführte. Dabei lag er mit verbundenem Kopf auf der Straße; eine Passantin oder ein Kind versuchten, ihm Hilfe zu leisten, doch die meisten gingen teilnahmslos vorüber und ignorierten das angebliche Unfallopfer zu ihren Füßen.

dages, qui présentent des blessures infligées par des instruments chirurgicaux. Ces actions s'inscrivent dans une tradition moderne d'après laquelle l'art est un défi lancé à l'establishment.

L'art-théâtre remonte aux « scénographies » futuristes, aux manifestations Dada de Zurich, à l'agit-prop révolutionnaire de Maïakovski et aux happenings des années 60. A l'inverse des actionnistes viennois, Helnwein n'utilise pas les corps d'enfants comme des objets esthétiques (ou anti-esthétiques), ni comme des images physiques et sexuelles. Son intention est de provoquer la réprobation contre les traitements odieux et généralement tolérés que subissaient les enfants et qui constituaient des victimes dociles pour la société. Il continuera ce genre d'actions jusqu'en 1976, année de la performance appelée *Toujours prêt*. Il se produit alors allongé dans la rue, la tête bandée ; une femme qui passe par là, parfois un enfant, tentent de lui porter assistance, mais la plupart des gens poursuivent leur chemin, ignorant la victime de l'accident présumé qui gît à leurs pieds.

Self-Portrait with Cyril/Selbstbildnis mit Cyril/Autoportrait avec Cyril, 1982 ▷
Photograph

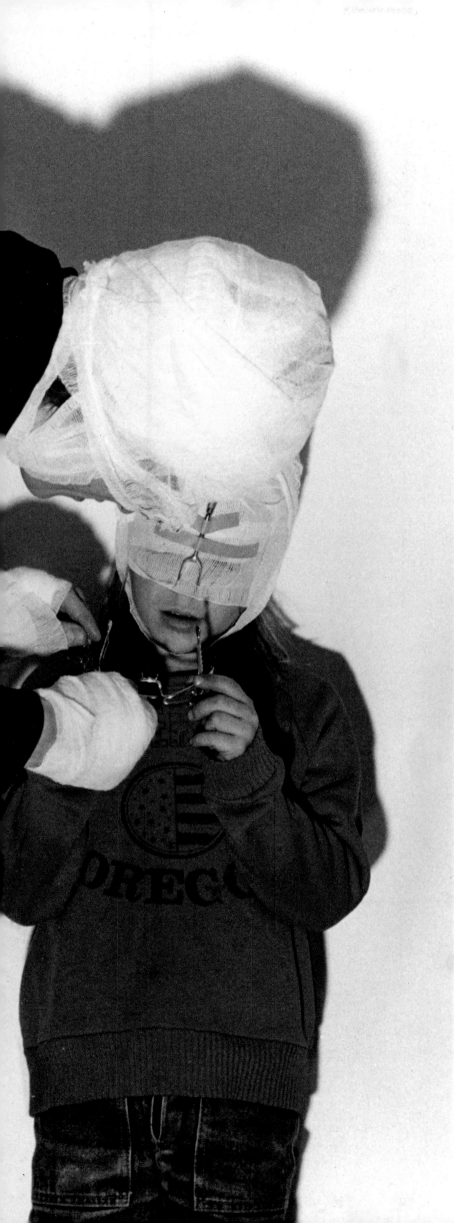

Self-Portraits

The artist also saw himself as victim and martyr. As early as 1970 he had started to paint and photograph himself in an ongoing series of self-portraits, some of them life-size with bandages around his head and forks and surgical instruments piercing his mouth or cheek. Frequently the distortions of these tormented images make it difficult to recognize Helnwein's face. He appears as a screaming man, mirroring the frightening aspects of life: a twentieth-century Man of Sorrows. His frozen cry, showing the artist in a state of implacable trauma, recalls Edvard Munch's *Scream* and Francis Bacon's screaming popes. The cry in Helnwein's self-portraits is so loud that the viewer not only sees the paintings – he seems to hear them too.

Some of Helnwein's grimacing faces also recall the grotesque and wild physiognomic distortions – quite possibly also self-portraits – by the eccentric eighteenth-century Viennese sculptor Franz Xaver Messerschmidt. They could also be seen as part of the Austrian pictorial tradition that resurfaced in the perturbed and distorted expressionist faces painted by Oskar Kokoschka and Egon Schiele before World War I, reappearing in the exaggerated wild mimicry in Arnulf Rainer's *Face Farces*.

Helnwein's related desire for self-exposure is manifested in a long series of self-portraits as victim and victimizer. The earliest, a photograph from 1970, prepared the ground for a watercolor on cardboard in 1977. Depicting the artist's bust and head standing in splendid isolation against a background of a vast blue sky, it has the connotation of a modern icon. These self-portraits continued, altered in many versions. They served as magazine covers and posters. Later the artist incorporated his self-portraits into some of his fragmented and ambiguous triptychs of the 1980s and 1990s. In a series entitled *Untermensch* (Sub-Human)[7], referring

Selbstporträts

Der Künstler sah auch sich selbst als Opfer und Märtyrer. 1970 hatte er angefangen, sich selbst in einer fortlaufenden Reihe von Selbstporträts zu malen und zu fotografieren; einige in Lebensgröße, mit verbundenem Kopf, mit von Gabeln und medizinischen Instrumenten durchbohrten Lippen oder Wangen. Häufig erschweren die Verzerrungen dieser gequälten Bildnisse, Helnweins Gesicht wiederzuerkennen. Er erscheint als schreiender Mann, der die furchterregende Seite des Lebens widerspiegelt: eine Leidensgestalt des 20. Jahrhunderts. Sein gefrorener Schrei zeigt den Künstler in einem Zustand unerbittlichen Traumas und ruft Edvard Munchs *Der Schrei* und Francis Bacons schreiende Päpste in Erinnerung. Der Schrei in Helnweins Selbstporträts ist so durchdringend, daß der Betrachter die Gemälde nicht nur sieht – er scheint sie auch zu hören.

Einige von Helnweins Grimassen erinnern an die grotesken und wilden physiognomischen Verrenkungen des exzentrischen Wiener Bildhauers Franz Xaver Messerschmidt aus dem 18. Jahrhundert – höchstwahrscheinlich ebenfalls Selbstbildnisse. Sie können auch als ein Teil der österreichischen ikonographischen Tradition angesehen werden, die in den verstörten und verzerrten expressionistischen Gesichtern der Malerei Oskar Kokoschkas oder Egon Schieles vor dem Ersten Weltkrieg wieder auftauchte und abermals in den übertrieben wilden *Face Farces* Arnulf Rainers erschien.

Helnweins Bedürfnis nach Zurschaustellung seiner selbst manifestiert sich in einer Serie von Selbstporträts als Opfer und Täter. Das früheste von ihnen, eine Fotografie von 1970, diente als Vorlage für ein Aquarell auf Karton von 1977. Es zeigt die Büste und den Kopf des Künstlers, die sich vom weiten blauen Himmel im Hintergrund abheben, und vermittelt die Konnotation einer modernen Ikone. Die Serie setzte er in mannigfaltiger Abwandlung

Autoportraits

L'artiste se considère aussi comme victime et martyr. Dès 1970, il commence à se peindre et à se photographier pour une série suivie d'autoportraits, dont certains en grandeur nature, sur lesquelles il se représente la tête bandée, avec des fourchettes et des instruments chirurgicaux lui perçant la bouche et les joues. Souvent, ces images tourmentées et déformées, ne permettent guère de reconnaître les traits d'Helnwein. Il y apparaît comme un homme hurlant, reflétant les aspects terrifiants de la vie : une représentation de l'Homme de douleur du 20e siècle. Son cri glacé dans un implacable état traumatique, rappelle *Le Cri* d'Edvard Munch ainsi que les papes hurlants de Francis Bacon. Dans les autoportraits d'Helnwein, le cri retentit d'une manière si assourdissante que le spectateur voit non seulement les tableaux mais croit aussi les entendre.

Certains de ces visages grimaçants renvoient aux déformations grotesques et sauvages de la physionomie – et probablement aussi aux autoportraits de Franz Xaver Messerschmidt, un sculpteur excentrique viennois du 18e siècle. Mais ils participent sans doute de cette tradition picturale autrichienne qui réapparaissait avec les visages expressionnistes perturbés et déformés que peignaient Oskar Kokoschka et Egon Schiele avant la Première Guerre mondiale, puis qui resurgira avec les mimiques exagérées des *Face Farces* d'Arnulf Rainer.

Le désir évident chez Helnwein de s'exposer lui-même se manifeste dans une longue série d'autoportraits où il se représente à la fois comme victime et comme bourreau. Le plus ancien, une photographie de 1970, prépare le terrain pour une aquarelle sur carton de 1977. Il montre la tête et le buste de l'artiste campé dans un splendide isolement devant un immense ciel bleu en arrière-plan – autant de connotations à l'icône moderne. Ces autoportraits successifs sont déclinés en plusieurs versions. Ils servent de

Self-Portrait with Smiling-Aid (detail)/*Selbstbildnis mit Schmunzelhilfe* (Detail)/*Autoportrait avec prothèse à sourire* (détail), 1972
Photograph, 15 × 10¼ inches, 38 × 24 cm
Niederösterreichisches Landesmuseum, Vienna

The Mulatto-Girl Erika in her House (detail)/*Die Mulattin Erika in ihrem Haus* (Detail)/*La mulâtre Erika dans sa maison* (détail), 1977
India ink on paper, approx. 10 × 16 inches, 25 × 40 cm
Private Collection, Austria

Rembrandt
The Golfer/Der Golfspieler/Le joueur de golf, 1654
Etching

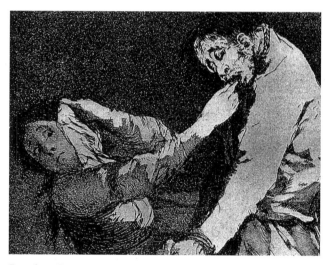

Francisco Goya
*Caprichos "A caza de dientes" (Hunting for Teeth/Auf der Jagd
nach Zähnen/La chasse aux dents),* 1797/98
Etching and aquatint

Alfred Kubin
Head in the Swamp/Kopf im Sumpf/Tête dans la boue, 1945
Ink on paper

"A work of art is as good or bad as the reaction to it," Helnwein says. And he is a master not only of provoking such reaction but also in creating the ambivalence and openness in his pictures for the widest possible, frequently contradictory, democratic range of interpretations. He dislikes providing rational picture captions for and unequivocal explanations of his paintings, which would tie down their reception in a one-sided way. Such "artistic artificial limbs" and "travel routes for the head and the heart" mostly anticipate the experience of the observer and confirm him in his attitude of passive consumption. This restraint also explains Helnwein's love of the exquisitely absurd and vague picture titles of his pen and ink drawings and some water colours of recent years. The purpose of a work of art can only be "the I" of the observer, his experience of self.

» Ein Kunstwerk ist so gut oder schlecht wie die Reaktion darauf«, versichert Helnwein. Und er ist ein Meister nicht nur im Provozieren von Reaktionen, sondern im Ambivalentmachen und Offenhalten des Bildes für ein möglichst breites, häufig sich widersprechendes demokratisches Deutungsspektrum. Er gibt ungern rationale Bildlegenden, eindeutige Erklärungen zu seinen Bildern, die ihre Rezeption einseitig festlegen. Derlei » Kunstprothesen « und » Reiserouten für Kopf und Herz« greifen meist dem Betrachter vor und bestärken ihn in seiner passiven Konsumhaltung. Diese Zurückhaltung erklärt auch Helnweins Vorliebe für die ausgesucht absurden, vagen Bildtitel seiner Federzeichnungen und mancher Aquarelle der letzten Jahre. Das Ziel des Kunstwerks könne nur das » eigene Ich« des Betrachters, die Selbsterfahrung sein.

«Une œuvre est bonne ou mauvaise en fonction de la réaction qu'elle suscite» affirme Helnwein. Quant à lui, il est passé maître non seulement dans l'art de provoquer des réactions, mais aussi dans la manière de rendre le tableau ambivalent et ouvert offrant un éventail d'interprétations démocratiques avec de fréquentes contradictions. Il n'aime pas donner de titres rationnels, des explications univoques qui figeraient la réception de ses œuvres d'une façon partiale. Ce genre de «prothèses esthétiques» et d' «itinéraires pour la tête et le cœur» s'emparent du spectateur et le confortent dans une attitude consommatoire passive. Cette réserve explique aussi la prédilection d'Helnwein pour les titres délibérément absurdes et vagues de ses dessins à la plume et de certaines aquarelles des dernières années. L'œuvre d'art ne peut viser que le «moi personnel» du spectateur, être une expérience vécue.

Peter Gorsen

India ink, 1977   Colored pencil, 1987

again to Nazi racial theory and practice, he created many versions of his persona as bloodied martyr, as Nazi officer, as romantic hero, warrior, tank commander, mummy, guerrilla fighter, night wanderer, and concealed witness.

Always self-assertive and preoccupied with his own image, Helnwein relates to the self-transformations by Cindy Sherman and her various invented guises, disguises, disfigurements, and appropriated images she uses to refer to her own persona. In a cibachrome photograph of 1987 entitled *Icarus,* Helnwein wears a uniform, a green headband, and dark glasses with blood running down his face as he holds out his arm, beckoning the viewer. By 1988, in individual canvases and triptychs, his face all but disappears in layers of oil and acrylic of red or white abstractions, or it may reassert itself as a metallic mechanical object (*Self-Portrait No. 12,* 1986).

fort. Diese Selbstporträts dienten als Motive für Zeitschriften-Cover und Poster. Später integrierte der Künstler sie in seine bruch-stückhaften und doppeldeutigen Triptychen aus den 80er und 90er Jahren. In der Serie *Untermensch*[7], die sich auf die Rassentheo-rien und -praxis der Nazis bezieht, schuf er zahlreiche Varianten seiner Person als blutüberströmter Märtyrer, Nazi-Offizier, romantischer Held, Krieger, Panzerkom-mandant, Mumie, Guerilla-Kämpfer, Nacht-wanderer und verborgener Zeuge.

Stets selbstbewußt und mit seinem eigenen Image beschäftigt, sind Helnweins Darstel-lungen vergleichbar mit den Rollenspielen von Cindy Sherman. Ihre unterschiedlichen Gestalten, Verkleidungen, Verunstaltungen und Images verweisen auf ihre eigene Per-son. Auf der Cibachrome-Fotografie *Ikarus* von 1987 trägt Helnwein eine Uniform, ein grünes Stirnband und eine dunkle Brille, Blut rinnt über sein Gesicht, während er den Arm appellierend ausstreckt. 1988 schließlich verschwindet sein Gesicht unter Schichten von Öl und Acryl in roten und weißen Abstraktionen, oder es behauptet sich als ein metallisches mechanisches Objekt (*Selbstporträt Nr. 12,* 1986).

couvertures de magazines et de posters. Plus tard, l'artiste les inclura dans les triptyques fragmentés et ambigus des années 80 et 90. Dans une série intitulée *Sous-homme*[7], qui se réfère à la théorie et à la pratique racistes des nazis, il crée plusieurs variantes le re-présentant lui-même en martyr ensanglan-té, officier nazi, héros romantique, guerrier, capitaine d'un blindé, momie, guérillero, somnambule et témoin masqué.

Affirmant toujours sa personnalité et pré-occupé par sa propre image, Helnwein se rapproche de Cindy Sherman qui se méta-morphose, s'invente des costumes, des dé-guisements et s'approprie des images qu'elle utilise pour renvoyer à sa propre personne. Sur un cliché cibachrome de 1987 intitulé *Icare,* Helnwein porte un uniforme, un bandeau vert au front et des lunettes sombres, le sang inonde son visage tandis qu'il tend le bras en faisant un signe au spectateur. Vers 1988, son visage disparait presque entièrement sous des couches d'huile et d'acrylique dans des abstractions rouges ou blanches, à moins qu'il ne soit évoqué à nouveau sous la forme d'un objet mécanique en métal (*Autoportrait nº 12,* 1986).

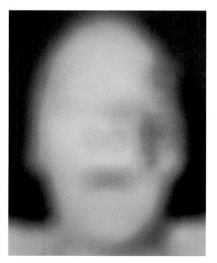

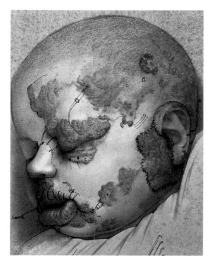

Photograph, 1996

Watercolor and india ink on lithograph,
1971

Oil and pastel, 1989

Drawings and Watercolors

Toward the end of his academic studies, Helnwein produced line drawings in pencil. *Boys, The Intrusion, Me and You,* and *Dr. Dotter* (all of 1972) are caricatures, funny people with long noses and droll expressions, which indicate his sources in the comic strip. Then a major change becomes evident in his work. In 1975 he began a series of extraordinary drawings in which he established his personal calligraphy. Hair-thin lines create thorny thickets on the page, often resulting in networks of spider webs of myriad penciled marks. They are drawn, scratched, and, at times, scraped on transparent and/or smooth paper. The result often resembles carefully executed etchings. The hard and brittle lines also create dramatic light effects, and in some of these visionary drawings, the light source appears to be within a person or object.

Generally drawings make us more aware of the physical act of making a picture than does painting, but rarely is the process of structuring and restructuring as visible as it is in Helnwein's drawings of the 1970s. The result is a mysterious set of works depicting people often engaged in bewildering

Zeichnungen und Aquarelle

Gegen Ende seiner Akademieausbildung schuf Helnwein Federzeichnungen. *Knaben, Der Eingriff, Ich und Du* und *Dr. Dotter* (alle von 1972) sind Karikaturen. Sie zeigen clowneske Figuren mit überlangen Nasen und drolligem Gesichtsausdruck – hier wird der Comic als Inspirationsquelle deutlich. Dann macht sich ein bedeutender Wandel in seinem Werk bemerkbar. 1975 begann er eine Serie von außergewöhnlichen Zeichnungen, die seine persönliche Kalligraphie begründen sollten. Haarfeine Linien bilden dornige Dickichte auf dem Papier. Die unzähligen Bleistiftstriche, die auf transparentes und/oder weiches Papier gezeichnet, gekratzt und manchmal geschrammt sind, werden zu spinnwebenähnlichen Netzwerken. Diese Technik ähnelt häufig sorgfältig ausgeführten Radierungen. Die harten und spröden Striche lassen dramatische Lichteffekte entstehen. In einigen dieser visionären Zeichnungen scheint die Lichtquelle eine Person oder ein Objekt zu sein.

Zeichnungen lenken die Aufmerksamkeit des Betrachters im allgemeinen stärker auf die Technik der Ausführung als Gemälde, und selten wurde der Prozeß des Strukturierens und Restrukturierens so augenfällig

Dessins et Aquarelles

Vers la fin de ses études universitaires, Helnwein réalise des dessins à la plume. *Garçons, L'Intrusion, Moi et Toi* et *Docteur Dotter* (datant tous de 1972) sont des caricatures, de drôles de personnages aux longs nez et à l'expression comique qui puisent leur source dans la bande dessinée. Puis un changement évident s'opère dans son œuvre. En 1975, il commence une série d'extraordinaires dessins dans lesquels il crée son style d'écriture personnel. Des traits fins comme des cheveux évoquant des broussailles épineuses, forment souvent un réseau de toiles d'araignée faite d'innombrables traits de crayon. Ces traits sont dessinés, grattés, et parfois gravés sur du papier transparent et/ou mou. Le résultat ressemble la plupart du temps à des gravures exécutées avec minutie. Les lignes à la fois dures et fragiles génèrent des effets de lumière spectaculaires ; sur certains de ces dessins visionnaires, la source de lumière semble se situer à l'intérieur de la personne ou de l'objet.

En général, les dessins attirent davantage que la peinture l'attention sur la technique-même de l'exécution de l'image ; le processus qui la structure et la restructure est

activities. They are placed or confined in rectangular empty rooms. Many of them are equipped with strange fixtures and implements, or are subjected to perplexing actions. Some are wearing bishops' miters, or bandages, or masks that hide their faces. There are pipes and troughs and pits into which a person is likely to fall or be submerged. Above all, there is a mysterious light that reveals and conceals figures.

At first glance, the events depicted in these drawings do not seem as strange as they become on longer perusal. Like surrealist art, these drawings cannot be subjected to the rules of logic. They depict nightmares and dreams, danger and threat. It seems most fitting that Helnwein was commissioned in 1979 to furnish illustrations for a German edition of Edgar Allan Poe's macabre tales.[8] The exquisite drawings in this book, with their sensitive treatment of blacks, whites, and grays, have a chiaroscuro effect reminiscent of Rembrandt's etchings. Helnwein's drawings are essays in black humor and personal satire. W. H. Auden once remarked that satire is both angry and optimistic, postulating evil and also its potential arrogation. Helnwein's drawings embody both a sense of gruesome phantasmagoria and possible hope. To find historical precedents, we must look at Goya's *Caprichos*. Here the Spanish artist of the Enlightenment pictured man's incongruities, injustices, stupidities, and cruelties, hoping that these depictions might help people to replace superstition with reason. Closer to home are the visionary and hallucinatory drawings by the Austrian artist Alfred Kubin, known for his fictive, baffling, and, at times, violent drawings. An original member of the Blue Rider group, he was banished by the Nazis as punishment for being a "degenerate artist", but continued working in isolation. In 1959, the year of his death, the Galerie St. Stephan in Vienna mounted a memorial exhibition for Kubin, who once again became a well-known artist in Austria.

wie in Helnweins Zeichnungen aus den 70er Jahren. Das Ergebnis ist eine mysteriöse Werkgruppe, die Menschen bei seltsamen Tätigkeiten in leeren rechteckigen Räumen zeigt. Viele von ihnen sind mit seltsamen Accessoires und Apparaten ausgerüstet. Einige tragen Mitren, Verbände oder Masken, die ihre Gesichter verdecken. Es gibt Rohre, Tröge und Gruben, in die sie leicht hineinfallen könnten. Über all diesen beängstigenden Szenarien liegt ein mysteriöses Licht, das die Figuren enthüllt und verdeckt.

Auf den ersten Blick erscheinen die in den Zeichnungen dargestellten Vorgänge kaum merkwürdig. Erst bei längerer Betrachtung erschließt sich die Bildaussage. Diese Zeichnungen können ebenso wie die surrealistische Kunst nicht den Regeln der Logik unterworfen werden. Sie stellen Alpträume und Träume, Gefahr und Bedrohung dar. Daher verwundert es nicht, daß Helnwein 1979 eine deutsche Ausgabe von Edgar Allan Poes unheimlichen Geschichten illustrieren sollte[8]. Die herausragenden Zeichnungen mit ihren sensiblen Schwarz-, Weiß- und Grautönen haben einen Chiaroscuro-Effekt, der an die Radierungen Rembrandts erinnert. Helnweins Zeichnungen sind Essays des schwarzen Humors und persönlicher Satire. W.H. Auden bemerkte einmal, daß die Satire zugleich zornig und optimistisch sei, weil sie sowohl das Böse als auch seine potentielle Inanspruchnahme postuliere. Helnweins Zeichnungen vermitteln gleichzeitig den Eindruck von schaurigen Phantasmagorien und möglicher Hoffnung. Den historischen Vorläufer findet man bei Goyas *Caprichos,* in denen der spanische Künstler der Aufklärung die menschlichen Ungereimtheiten, Ungerechtigkeiten, Dummheiten und Grausamkeiten darstellt, in der Hoffnung, die Menschen würden den Aberglauben durch den Verstand ersetzen. Ein geographisch naheliegenderes Vorbild sind die visionären und halluzinativen Zeichnungen des österreichischen Künstlers Alfred Kubin, der für seine fiktiven, rätselhaften und zum Teil gewalterfüllten Arbei-

rarement aussi visible que sur les planches d'Helnwein issues des années 70. Il en résulte un mystérieux ensemble d'œuvres représentant des personnages vaquant souvent à des occupations déconcertantes. Ils sont campés ou confinés dans des espaces rectangulaires et vides. Beaucoup d'entre eux sont équipés d'accessoires et d'appareils étranges, ou exécutent des actes déroutants. Certains portent des mitres d'évêques, des bandes ou des masques qui dissimulent leur visage. On y voit des tuyaux, des dépressions et des fosses dans lesquels les êtres semblent sur le point de tomber ou d'être submergés. Et surtout, il y a cette mystérieuse lumière qui révèle et cache les personnages.

A première vue, les événements que représentent ces dessins ne semblent pas aussi étranges qu'ils le deviennent après une observation plus approfondie. Comme pour l'art surréaliste, ces dessins n'obéissent pas aux règles de la logique. Ils décrivent des cauchemars et des rêves, le danger et la menace. Il semble donc pertinent qu'en 1979 Helnwein ait été chargé de dessiner les illustrations d'une édition allemande des contes macabres d'Edgar Allan Poe[8]. Par le traitement sensible des noirs, blancs et gris, les magnifiques dessins de ce livre rappellent les clairs-obscurs des gravures de Rembrandt. Les dessins d'Helnwein sont à la fois des essais d'humour noir et d'autodérision. W. H. Auden notait un jour que la satire exprime à la fois la colère et l'optimisme puisqu'elle postule le mal, ainsi que son attribution potentielle. Les dessins d'Helnwein incarnent à la fois un imaginaire macabre et un possible espoir. Pour trouver des précédents historiques, il nous faut revenir aux *Caprichos* de Goya. L'artiste espagnol du siècle des lumières y représentait les incongruités, les injustices, les stupidités et les cruautés humaines dans l'espoir que ces descriptions amènent les gens à renoncer à la superstition pour lui préférer la raison. Plus proches de nous, les dessins visionnaires et hallucinatoires de l'artiste autrichien Alfred Kubin, célèbre pour ses dessins

Arno Breker Holding a Picture of Joseph Beuys/
Arno Breker tenant un portrait de Joseph Beuys, 1988
Silver print, 39 × 26 inches, 99 × 66 cm
Musée de l'Elysée, Lausanne, Switzerland

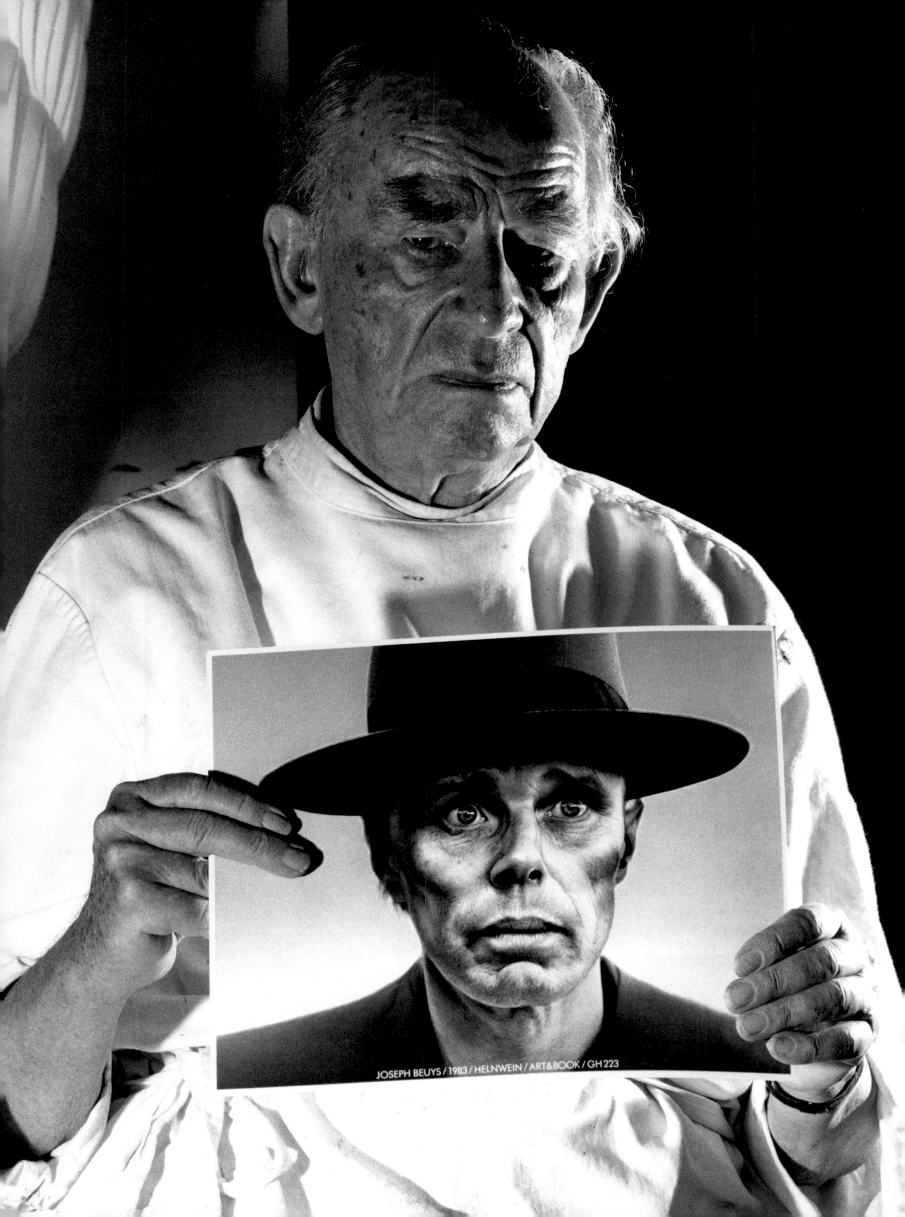

JOSEPH BEUYS / 1983 / HELNWEIN / ART&BOOK / GH 223

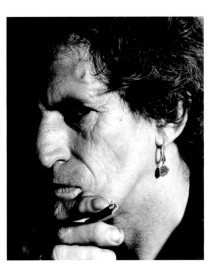

Keith Richards, 1990
Silver print

Intimately related to Helnwein's Aktion pieces of the early 1970s were his series of watercolors, such as the previously mentioned *Life not Worth Living* and the earlier *Embarrassing*. He devised a unique dry watercolor technique that employed the minimum of water (the opposite of the typical wet watercolors done by Emil Nolde, for example). Helnwein applied pigment with the thinnest brush and was able to achieve illusionistic light effects by scratching with a razor blade into the paint. In *Mean Child* (1970, cf. p. 62), possibly the earliest work in the series, he presents a frontal head of a girl, eyes staring at the viewer, blood emerging from her mouth and a gash across her cheek. Various parts of her face are labeled with captions: "Lewd", "Improper", "Careless", "Happy to Be Punished", or "Talking about Sex". This watercolor by the 22-year-old artist evokes a sense of melancholy that pervades much of his work. The theme of the girl as victim is seen in disquieting watercolors such as *Little Correction* (1971), *Embarrassing* (1971), and *The Intrusion* (1971, cf. p. 70). The last depicts a young blonde girl strapped to a table while an enormous shiny metal tube is forced into her mouth.

ten bekannt ist. Ursprünglich war er Mitglied der Gruppe der Blauen Reiter; er wurde von den Nazis als »entarteter Künstler« diffamiert und verbannt. Im Exil setzte er seine Arbeit jedoch fort. In seinem Todesjahr 1959 organisierte die Galerie St. Stephan in Wien eine Gedenkausstellung für Kubin, der dadurch in Österreich wieder zu einem bekannten Künstler wurde.

Eng verwandt mit Helnweins Aktionen der frühen 70er Jahre sind seine Aquarelle, wie *Lebensunwertes Leben* und *Peinlich*. Er entwickelte eine »trockene« Aquarelltechnik, bei der nur ein Minimum an Wasser verwendet wird (im Gegensatz zu den »nassen« Aquarellen Emil Noldes). Helnwein trug die Farbe mit dem dünnsten Pinsel auf und brachte illusionistische Lichteffekte hervor, indem er mit einer Rasierklinge über die Farbe schabte. *Gemeines Kind* (1970, vgl. S. 62), wahrscheinlich die früheste Arbeit dieser Serie, zeigt in Frontalansicht das Gesicht eines Mädchens. Seine Augen starren den Betrachter an, während aus seinem Mund Blut austritt und über seine Wange eine Narbe verläuft. Einzelne Gesichtsteile sind mit Kommentaren versehen: »Unkeusches gedacht, getrieben, erduldet«, »Unpassendes erwähnt«, »Unachtsamkeit

fictifs, déconcertants et quelquefois violents. Membre dès le début du groupe du Cavalier bleu, Kubin fut proscrit par les nazis et classé parmi les « artistes dégénérés », mais continua à travailler dans l'isolement. En 1959, l'année de sa mort, la galerie St Stephan de Vienne organisera une rétrospective en son honneur, et Kubin connut ainsi un regain de notoriété en Autriche.

Une série d'aquarelles, dont *Indigne de vivre* et *Gênant* citées précédemment, est étroitement liée aux actions d'Helnwein du début des années 70. Il invente une technique unique d'aquarelle à sec qui utilise le minimum d'eau (à l'inverse des aquarelles très « mouillées » qu'employait Emil Nolde p. ex.). Helnwein applique le pigment avec un pinceau extrêmement fin et réussit à donner des effets de lumière illusionnistes en grattant la peinture avec une lame de rasoir. Dans *Méchante enfant* (1970, voir p. 62), probablement la première œuvre de la série, il présente de manière frontale la tête d'une petite fille dont les yeux fixent le spectateur ; du sang s'écoule de sa bouche et une balafre traverse sa joue. Plusieurs parties de son visage comportent des commentaires : « obscène », « incorrecte », « négligente », « contente d'être punie », ou

Charles Bukowski, 1991
Silver print

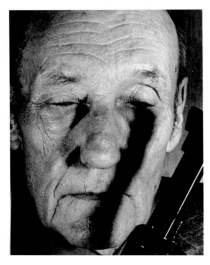

William S. Burroughs, 1990
Silver print

Andy Warhol, 1983
Silver print

Helnwein's drawing of a man thrusting a girl's mouth open with strong hands is seen hanging on the wall behind the main scene of cruelty. One of the most successful pictures in the series is *Sunday's Child* (1972, cf. p. 73): Here an apparently happy, smiling blonde girl, her tongue playfully sticking out, holds some chocolates in her hand as she stands in front of a store that has food ads on its window, much as one would see at such a store or in a pop painting. A cute little duckling holding an ice cream cone smiles as it walks along the sidewalk. As you look more closely, you see that the child wears the identifying armband of the blind, and that blood runs down her leg. We do a double-take: what does it mean? Is she menstruating early in life? Was she raped? As Helnwein so often does, here he provokes shock, horror, and the dread of violence.

In his extensive interview with Andreas Mäckler, Helnwein remarked:

"I am aware that individuals on this planet are badly abused and maltreated, that they are deeply injured and suppressed, and that it is all covered up with optimistic propaganda. A long time before I began painting, I had the impression that

gebilligt«, »sich über Züchtigungen gefreut«, »arztgespielt« und »über Geschlechtliches gesprochen, gespottet & gelacht«. Dieses Aquarell des 22jährigen Künstlers erzeugt eine melancholische Stimmung, die einen Großteil seines Werkes durchdringt. Das Motiv des Mädchens als Opfer ist auch auf anderen beunruhigenden Aquarellen dargestellt, wie *Kleine Korrektur* (1971), *Peinlich* (1971) und *Der Eingriff* (1971, vgl. S. 70). Letzteres zeigt ein kleines blondes Mädchen, das auf einem Tisch liegend festgegurtet ist, während ein gewaltiges glänzendes Metallrohr in seinen Mund hineingezwängt ist. Eine Zeichnung von einem Mann, der mit starken Händen den Mund eines Mädchens aufreißt, ist im Hintergrund des eigentlichen grausamen Vorgangs als Wandbild zu sehen. Eines der eindrucksvollsten Bilder dieser Aquarellserie ist *Sonntagskind* (1972, vgl. S. 73): Dargestellt ist ein scheinbar glückliches, lächelndes, blondes Mädchen, das frech seine Zunge herausstreckt und in der linken Hand eine Tafel Schokolade hält. Es steht vor einem Geschäft, an dessen Fenster sich Lebensmittelwerbung befindet, wie in der Realität oder auf einem Pop-Art-Gemälde. Ein niedliches Entenküken schleckt an einem Eis und

« parlant de sexe ». Cette aquarelle peinte à l'âge de 22 ans, évoque une mélancolie qui domine toute l'œuvre. Le thème de l'enfant victime se retrouve dans des aquarelles troublantes comme *Petite correction* (1971), *Gênant* (1971) et *L'Intrusion* (1971, voir p. 70). Cette dernière représente une petite fille blonde attachée à une table tandis qu'un énorme tube de métal luisant est enfoncé dans sa bouche. Un autre dessin d'Helnwein montrant un homme forçant de ses mains une enfant à ouvrir la bouche, est accroché au mur, à l'arrière-plan de cette scène atroce. *L'Enfant du dimanche* (1972, voir p. 73) est l'une des œuvres les plus célèbres de la série : une fillette blonde souriante qui semble heureuse, tire malicieusement la langue, elle tient du chocolat dans sa main gauche et se trouve devant un magasin où des publicités pour des produits alimentaires ont été collées sur la vitrine, tout ceci exactement représenté comme dans la vie réelle ou dans un tableau pop'art. Un adorable petit canard tenant une glace marche sur le trottoir en souriant. Mais si l'on regarde l'ensemble plus attentivement, on constate que l'enfant porte un brassard l'identifiant comme aveugle et que du sang coule le long de ses jambes. On a alors une

mankind is in a bad state, that nobody lives without pain even if this is repressed, and that there is evidently a longing to overcome this and to rise above it. Especially my early pictures deal with these concerns and hold them up to the viewer."[9]

The artist was also preoccupied with the image of a young girl with bandaged head and hand. She appears in a series of watercolors done in the softest of muted colors, with a predominant pale, grayish blue. *Beautiful Victim I* (1974, cf. p. 61) shows the girl lying on the floor in sunlight. In *Beautiful Victim II* (1974, cf. p. 71), she stands by a window, and in the last work of the series, *Red Mouth* (1978, cf. p. 83), we see her with forehead and chin in surgical dressing, stretched out on a white bolster and wearing a white shirt and red lipstick. Her eyes closed, she seems to be sleeping, dreaming, or suffering. This poignant picture resonates with intimations of deep pain. It is work of great sadness, reminding us of Nietzsche's remark that the "authenticity of the creative artist can supply meaning to the despair and absurdity of existence".

watschelt den Bürgersteig entlang. Doch das Kind trägt eine Blindenbinde am Arm und Blut läuft zwischen seinen Beinen herunter. Zwei Erklärungen sind möglich: Hat seine Menstruation vorzeitig eingesetzt? Wurde es sexuell mißbraucht? Wie so oft provoziert Helnwein Schock, Abscheu und die Furcht vor Gewalt.

In einem Interview mit Andreas Mäckler bemerkte Helnwein: »Ich bin mir dessen bewußt, daß auf diesem Planeten Individuen schwer mißbraucht und malträtiert, tief verletzt und unterdrückt werden, und daß all dies mit optimistischer Propaganda vertuscht wird. Lange bevor ich zu malen begann, hatte ich den Eindruck, daß die Menschheit sich in einem schlechten Zustand befindet, daß niemand ohne Schmerzen lebt, und daß es offensichtlich eine Sehnsucht gibt, dies zu überwinden. Speziell in meinen frühen Bildern geht es um diese Anliegen, die dem Betrachter vor Augen gehalten werden.«[9]

Der Künstler beschäftigte sich wiederholt mit dem Motiv des kleinen Mädchens mit verbundenem Kopf und bandagierter Hand. Es erscheint in einer Serie von Aquarellen, die in den weichesten und gedämpftesten Farben gemalt sind, wobei ein blasses, gräuliches Blau dominiert. *Beautiful Victim I* (1974, vgl. S. 61) zeigt das Mädchen im Sonnenlicht auf dem Boden liegend. In *Beautiful Victim II* (1974, vgl. S. 71) steht es am Fenster, und in der letzten Arbeit dieser Reihe, *Roter Mund* (1978, vgl. S. 83), sind Stirn und Kinn verbunden. Es ist auf eine weiße Nackenrolle gebettet, seine Augen sind geschlossen. Diese ergreifende Arbeit ist von großer Traurigkeit, die an Nietzsches Bemerkung erinnert, daß die »Wahrhaftigkeit des schaffenden Künstlers der Verzweiflung und Absurdität der Existenz Bedeutung verleihen kann«.

perception double : la fillette a-t-elle des menstruations précoces ? A-t-elle été violée ? Comme souvent chez Helnwein, il veut ici choquer, provoquer l'effroi et la peur de la violence.

Dans une interview avec Andreas Mäckler, Helnwein explique : « J'ai conscience que sur cette planète, on abuse gravement des individus, on les maltraite et les blesse, on les opprime, et que tout ceci est camouflé par une propagande optimiste. Longtemps avant de commencer à peindre, j'avais l'impression que l'humanité était en piteux état, que personne n'est épargné de la souffrance, même si on essait de l'ignorer et qu'il y a de toute évidence une envie de la surpasser et de la transcender. Mes premières œuvres, en particulier, traitent de ce sujet et l'exhibent sous les yeux des spectateurs. »[9]

L'artiste est également hanté par l'image d'une fillette à la tête et à la main bandée. Elle apparaît sur une série d'aquarelles réalisées avec les plus douces des couleurs sourdes où prédomine un gris-bleu pale. *Belle victime I* (1974, voir p. 61) montre la petite fille allongée sur le sol dans les rayons du soleil. Dans *Belle victime II* (1974, voir p. 71), elle se tient près d'une fenêtre, puis dans la dernière œuvre de la série, *Bouche rouge* (1978, voir p. 83), on la retrouve étendue sur un traversin blanc, portant une chemise blanche et du rouge à lèvre tandis que son front et son menton sont couverts de pansements chirurgicaux. Elle a les yeux fermés, elle semble dormir, rêver, ou souffrir. Cette image poignante évoque une profonde douleur. C'est une œuvre immensément tragique qui nous renvoie aux paroles de Nietzsche qui pensait que « l'authenticité de l'artiste créateur, peut donner du sens au désespoir et à l'absurdité de l'existence ».

Photographs, Theater Designs

Helnwein, who had been using the camera to document his street actions and for self-portraiture, concentrated on photography as a major medium in his work in the early 1980s. He decided to take photographic portraits of icons of contemporary culture, both high and low, that he was particularly interested in. In 1982 he went to London to meet with the Rolling Stones, with whom he had identified when a youth in Vienna; there he took a somber photograph of Mick Jagger.

In his early photographic portraits, Helnwein's personal style becomes evident. His portraits are not idealized images like those of Edward Steichen, or grandly composed portraits, like those of Arnold Newman, who both photographed artists, composers, and writers in relation to their work. They also differ from Robert Mapplethorpe's smooth and highly finished portraits, but do relate to the incisive and poignant portraits by Richard Avedon.

Helnwein does not do his own darkroom work, nor does he manipulate the printed images, but takes advantage of the camera as an instrument for observation. He was able to examine the faces of his sitters in isolation and to focus on specific details.

Susan Sontag, in her frequently quoted essay "On Photography", sees the medium as "a powerful instrument for depersonalizing the world."[10] This may well be true in the case of war photographs, which she cites as an example. It certainly does not apply to portraitists like Avedon and Helnwein. Photography equipped Helnwein with a means of constructing a picture in a manner different from painting, and permitted new possibilities in the visual relationship between artist and model: the photographer can become a participant and an observer. Helnwein made an outstanding series of photos of Andy Warhol in 1983, four years before the artist's early death.

Fotografien, Bühnenbilder

Helnwein, der die Kamera schon zur Dokumentation seiner Straßenaktionen und für seine Selbstporträts eingesetzt hatte, wandte sich der Fotografie als Hauptmedium in den frühen 80er Jahren zu. Er entschloß sich, Porträtfotos von Idolen der zeitgenössischen Hoch- und Massenkultur aufzunehmen, für die er sich besonders interessierte. 1982 ging er nach London, um die Rolling Stones zu treffen, mit denen er sich als Jugendlicher in Wien identifiziert hatte; dort nahm er ein düsteres Foto von Mick Jagger auf.

Bereits in seinen frühen Porträtfotografien wird Helnweins persönlicher Stil deutlich. Seine Bildnisse sind nicht idealisiert wie die von Edward Steichen oder großartig komponiert wie jene von Arnold Newman. Beide Fotografen nahmen Künstler, Komponisten und Schriftsteller im Zusammenhang mit ihrem Werk auf. Sie unterscheiden sich auch von Robert Mapplethorpes sanften und perfektionistischen Porträts. Eher sind sie in der Nähe von Richard Avedons prägnanten und scharfsinnigen Porträts angesiedelt.

Helnwein entwickelt seine Aufnahmen nicht selbst in der Dunkelkammer, er manipuliert auch nicht die Abzüge. Er macht sich die Kamera als ein Instrument zur Beobachtung zunutze. Er studiert die Gesichter seiner Modelle genau und hebt die charakteristischen Details hervor.

Susan Sontag bezeichnet dieses Medium in ihrem Essay »On Photography« als »ein mächtiges Instrument zur Entpersönlichung der Welt«[10]. Das mag im Fall von Kriegsfotografien, die sie als Beispiel anführt, stimmen. Aber es trifft ganz bestimmt nicht auf Porträtisten wie Avedon und Helnwein zu. Die Fotografie ermöglichte Helnwein eine Bildkonstruktion, die sich von der Malerei unterscheidet, und erlaubte neue Möglichkeiten im visuellen Verhältnis zwischen Künstler und Modell: der Fotograf kann gleichzeitig in die Rolle des Teilneh-

Photographies, Travaux pour le Théâtre

Au début des années 80, Helnwein, qui utilisait déjà l'appareil photographique pour fixer ses actions dans les rues et ses autoportraits, se consacre davantage à la photographie, qui devient l'un de ses supports favoris. Il décide de faire des portraits photographiques des idoles de la culture contemporaine, majeure et mineure, qui l'intéressent le plus. En 1982, il se rend à Londres pour y rencontrer les Rolling Stones à qui il s'identifiait pendant sa jeunesse à Vienne ; il prend alors une photo sombre de Mick Jagger.

L'originalité du style d'Helnwein se révèle dès ses premiers portraits photographiques. Ce ne sont pas des images idéalisées comme celles d'Edward Steichen ou composées avec maints artifices comme chez Arnold Newman qui, tous deux photographiaient des artistes, des compositeurs et des écrivains en rapport avec leur travail. Il se démarque aussi des portraits minutieux et délicats de Robert Mapplethorpe, se rapprochant plutôt de la technique de portrait incisive et poignante de Richard Avedon.

Helnwein ne travaille pas lui-même en chambre noire, il ne manipule pas les images imprimées, mais tire parti des avantages de l'objectif comme d'un outil d'observation. Il étudie méticuleusement les visages de ses modèles et se focalise sur des détails spécifiques.

Dans « On Photography », un essai de Susan Sontag, celle-ci considère la photographie comme un « puissant instrument de dépersonnalisation du monde »[10]. Ceci vaut peut-être pour les photographes de guerre qu'elle mentionne à titre d'exemples, mais ne s'applique certainement pas à des portraitistes comme Avedon et Helnwein. La photographie donna à Helnwein la possibilité de composer une image d'une autre manière que sa peinture, elle ouvre d'autres possibilités quant à la relation visuelle entre l'artiste et son modèle : le photographe est

Selection (Ninth November Night)/Selektion (Neunter November Nacht)/Sélection (La Nuit du neuf novembre), 1988 ▷
100 meter-long (300 ft) installation at the Museum Ludwig in Cologne/100-Meter-lange-Installation
am Museum Ludwig in Köln/Installation de 100 m de longueur au Musée Ludwig à Cologne
Scanachrome on vinyl, each picture 146 × 98 inches, 370 × 250 cm

slush in the early morning hours in a deserted Times Square. It became one of the painter's most popular works.

In 1990, Helnwein made a large assemblage of paintings based on photographs. Called *48 Portraits* (cf. p. 310), it depicts 48 women of achievement. Done in muted reds, it is the artist's response to Gerhard Richter's well-known *48 Portraits* of twenty years earlier, in black and white, and limited solely to males.

Helnwein's reputation in Austria became confirmed when Walter Koschatzky, director of the Albertina, mounted a major solo exhibition in 1985 for the 37-year-old artist at Vienna's great graphics museum. But the following year Helnwein left Austria, that tightly wrapped country where he had always felt alienated, and settled in a castle in the foothills of the Eifel Mountains south of Cologne.

Two years earlier, the Municipal Museum in Munich had organized a Helnwein solo show that attracted over 100,000 visitors. One of them was Peter Zadek, one of Germany's most original and provocative theater directors, who asked him to make a poster for John Hopkins's "Loosing Time" for the Hamburger Schauspielhaus. In 1988, he made his controversial "Lulu" poster, which showed a little man dressed in a heavy overcoat gazing at a girl's naked crotch. A minor scandal ensued when the mayor of Hamburg protested, accusing Zadek and Helnwein of pornography. Also in 1988, however, the artist began designing sets and costumes for a series of brilliant productions by the choreographer and director Hans Kresnik, including "Macbeth", "King Lear", and "Oedipus" in Heidelberg, and "Marat/Sade" in Stuttgart. His vanguard designs for "Carmina Burana" for the Munich Staatsoper, however, were rejected on grounds of being too radical for the Bavarian capital. In 1996 Helnwein did the designs for a great production of "Pasolini" in Hamburg.

Es wurde eines der bekanntesten Werke Helnweins.

1990 schuf der Künstler eine große Bilderserie, basierend auf Fotografien. Er nannte sie *48 Porträts* (vgl. S. 310), und sie zeigt 48 berühmte Frauen. In gedämpften Rottönen gehalten, sind sie Helnweins Antwort auf Gerhard Richters bekannte *48 Porträts* in Schwarzweiß, die nur Männer zeigen und 20 Jahre zuvor geschaffen wurden.

Helnweins Ansehen in Österreich festigte sich, als Walter Koschatzky, Leiter der Albertina, 1985 eine große Einzelausstellung für den 37jährigen Künstler in Wiens Grafikmuseum organisierte. Ein Jahr später verließ Helnwein Österreich, dieses verschanzte Land, in dem er sich stets ausgegrenzt gefühlt hatte, und ließ sich auf einem Schloß am Rand der Eifel südlich von Köln nieder.

Zwei Jahre zuvor hatte das Stadtmuseum in München eine Einzelausstellung organisiert, die über 100 000 Besucher anzog. Einer von ihnen war Peter Zadek, einer der originellsten und provozierendsten Theaterregisseure Deutschlands, der Helnwein bat, ein Plakat zu John Hopkins' »Verlorene Zeit« für das Hamburger Schauspielhaus zu gestalten. 1988 entwarf der Künstler sein kontrovers diskutiertes Theaterplakat zu »Lulu«. Es zeigt einen kleinen Mann in einem schweren Mantel, der den nackten Unterleib eines Mädchens anstarrt. Der Skandal brach aus, als der Bürgermeister von Hamburg Zadek und Helnwein der Pornographie beschuldigte. Dennoch begann der Künstler im selben Jahr mit dem Entwurf von Bühnenbildern und Kostümen für eine Reihe von brillanten Inszenierungen des Choreographen und Regisseurs Hans Kresnik, u. a. für »Macbeth«, »König Lear« und »Ödipus« in Heidelberg und »Marat/Sade« in Stuttgart. Seine Avantgarde-Entwürfe für die »Carmina Burana« an der Münchner Staatsoper wurden jedoch mit der Begründung abgelehnt, daß sie zu radikal für die bayerische Hauptstadt seien. 1996 stattete Helnwein die Inszenierung »Pasolini« in Hamburg aus.

tir de photographies qu'il appelle *48 Portraits* (voir p. 310). Ce cycle représentait 48 femmes marquantes. Peinte avec des rouges sourds, cette série répond aux fameux *48 Portraits* en noir et blanc et ne représentant que des hommes que Gerhard Richter réalisa 20 ans plus tôt.

En Autriche, la notoriété d'Helnwein se confirme quand en 1985, Walter Koschatzky, le directeur de l'Albertina, organise une grande exposition personnelle au Musée d'arts graphiques de Vienne consacrée à l'artiste, alors âgé de 37 ans. Pourtant l'année suivante, Helnwein quittera l'Autriche, ce pays guindé à l'esprit étriqué où il avait toujours ressenti une certaine aliénation, pour s'installer dans un château aux pieds du massif de l'Eifel, au sud de Cologne.

Deux ans auparavant, le Musée municipal de Munich avait organisé une exposition personnelle de Helnwein qui avait attiré plus de 100 000 visiteurs. L'un d'eux était Peter Zadek, l'un des metteurs en scène de théâtre allemands les plus originaux et les plus provocateurs. Zadek demande alors à Helnwein de dessiner l'affiche de « Loosing Time » de John Hopkins qui doit être jouée au Schauspielhaus de Hambourg. En 1988, Helnwein réalise l'affiche très controversée pour « Lulu », où l'on voit un petit homme vêtu d'un lourd manteau fixant l'entrejambe d'une fille nue. Le scandale éclate alors, et le maire de Hambourg accuse Zadek et Helnwein de pornographie. Mais en dépit de ces incidents, dès 1988, l'artiste crée des décors et des costumes pour une série de brillantes productions du chorégraphe et metteur en scène Hans Kresnik, entre autres pour « Macbeth », le « Roi Lear » et « Œdipe » à Heidelberg, puis pour « Marat/Sade » à Stuttgart. Mais les décors d'avant-garde qu'il imagine pour la mise en scène des « Carmina Burana » à l'Opéra de Munich seront refusés parce que considérés comme trop radicaux pour la capitale bavaroise. En 1996, Helnwein réalisera la scénographie de la grande production « Pasolini », à Hambourg.

◁ *White Christmas* (48 sculptures)/*Noël blanc* (48 sculptures), 1992
Plaster, silkpaper and pollen
Installation at the Leopold Hoesch Museum in Düren, Germany

EARLY WORKS
FRÜHE ARBEITEN
PREMIERES ŒUVRES
1970–1988

Aktion Sorgenkind/Action enfance en détresse, Vienna, 1972

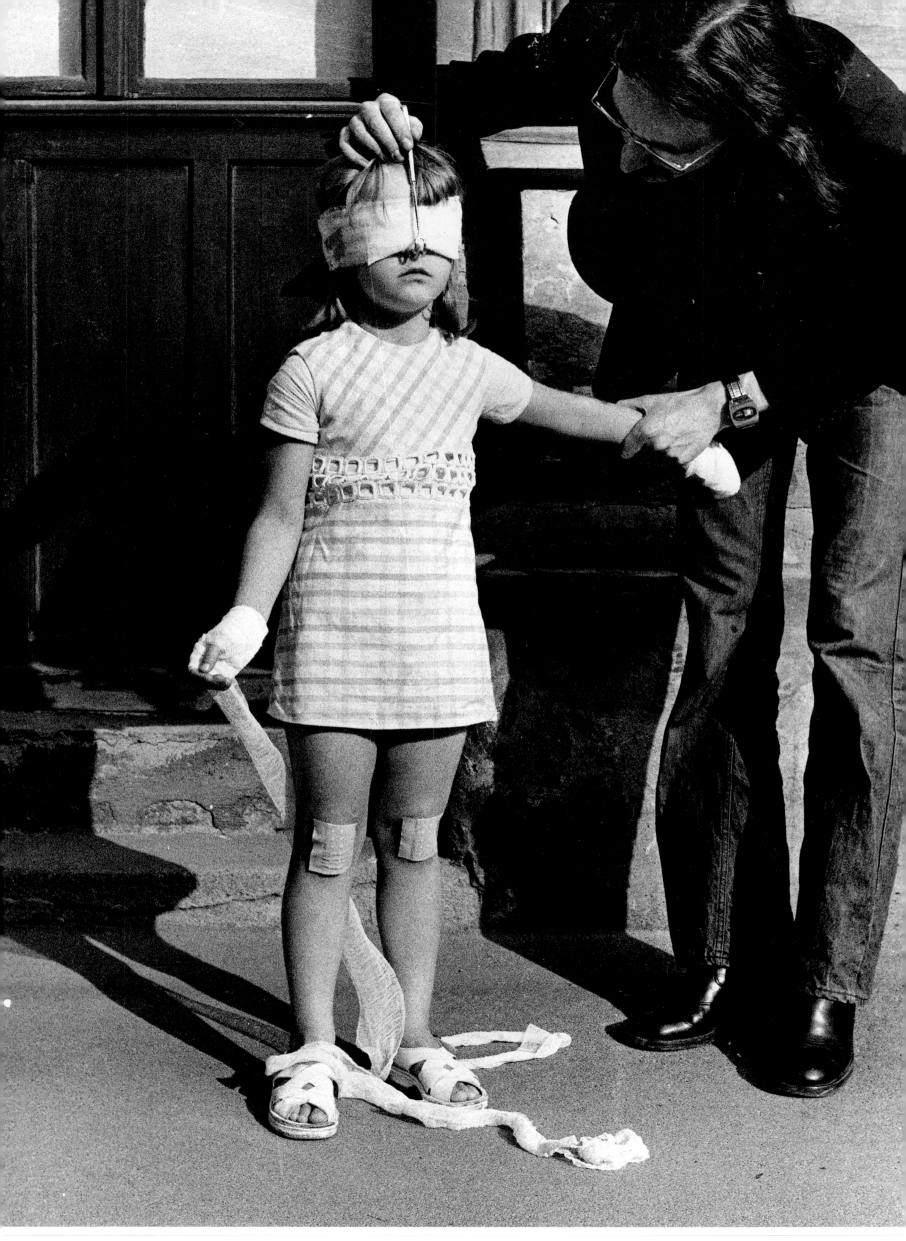

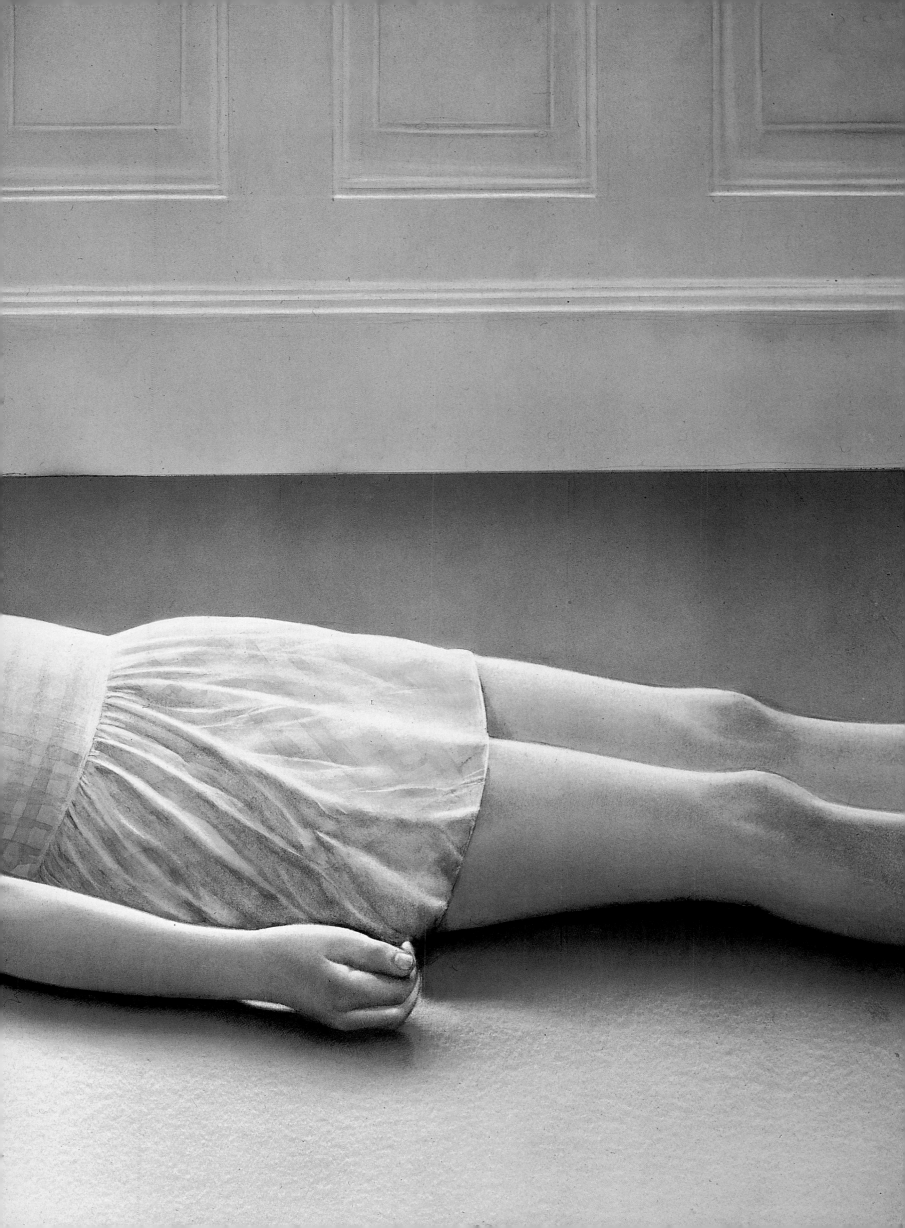

Amadeus, and Mercedes, were mounted on the columns and exhibited in the church for the duration of the installation. *Kindskopf* is now permanently placed in the State Russian Museum in St. Petersburg.

At about the same time the painter made *White Christmas* (1992, cf. p. 42/43), one of his rare works in three dimensions. Done in plaster with pollen sprayed on the surface, it is a group of 48 children without faces. They are not merely standing in space, but appear to crowd in on the unsuspecting viewer.

Helnwein works on many programs simultaneously. In the late 1980s he also began a series of large triptychs. The triptych, which frequently served as the sacred altarpiece in northern medieval churches, was revived as an art form in the late nineteenth century by artists such as Hans von Marées and found its culmination in the nine great triptychs by Max Beckmann. Helnwein's *The Silent Glow of the Avant-Garde I* (1986, cf. p. 232) relates to this German tradition. Its centerpiece is a reproduction of Caspar David Friedrich's *The Sea of Ice* (1823/24), a painting that referred directly to the wreck of the ship "Hope" in its attempt to discover the passage to the North Pole. But in keeping with Friedrich's existential and religious pessimism, the work alludes more generally to the manifestation of fate and destructive forces in nature. Gottfried Helnwein included his own image, with blood on headband and shirt, on either side of the ship, which has been destroyed by blocks of ice. It responds to Friedrich's romantic painting in which human endeavor is vanquished by nature, with a contemporary version of defeat.

Caspar David Friedrich, a professor at the Dresden Academy, was closely associated with the Dresden circle of Romantic poets. More than a century later, in February 1945, Dresden, one of the world's most beautiful cities, was destroyed by Allied firebombing. Helnwein used a picture of the devastated

an der Stelle, die einst den Mönchen vorbehalten war. An den Pfeilern der Kirche waren Gemälde von drei Kindern Helnweins, Ali Elvis, Amadeus und Mercedes, angebracht. Sie blieben dort für die Dauer der Installation ausgestellt. *Kindskopf* gehört nun zur Sammlung des Staatlichen Russischen Museums in St. Petersburg.

Etwa zur selben Zeit schuf Helnwein *White Christmas* (1992, vgl. S. 42/43), eines der wenigen dreidimensionalen Werke. Es ist aus Gips gefertigt, auf dessen Oberfläche Blütenstaub gesprüht wurde, und zeigt eine Gruppe von 48 gesichtslosen Kindern, die sich um den nichtsahnenden Betrachter zu versammeln scheinen.

Helnwein arbeitet immer an mehreren Projekten gleichzeitig. In den späten 80er Jahren begann er auch mit einer Serie großformatiger Triptychen. Das Triptychon besteht aus drei Tafeln und diente in den mittelalterlichen Kirchen Nordeuropas häufig als Altarbild. Im ausgehenden 19. Jahrhundert wurde es von Künstlern wie Hans von Marées als Kunstform wiederbelebt und gipfelte in den neun großen Triptychen von Max Beckmann. Helnweins *Das stille Leuchten der Avantgarde I* (1986, vgl. S. 232) bezieht sich auf diese deutsche Tradition. Die Mitteltafel ist eine Wiedergabe von Caspar David Friedrichs *Das Eismeer* (1823/24). Friedrichs Gemälde schildert die Havarie des Schiffs »Hoffnung«, das den Seeweg zum Nordpol entdecken sollte. In Einklang mit dem existentiellen und religiösen Pessimismus des Romantikers spielt Helnweins Werk auf die Erscheinungsformen des Schicksals und die zerstörerischen Kräfte der Natur an. Helnwein fügte nämlich zu beiden Seiten des Schiffs, das an Eisbergen zerschellt, eine Abbildung seiner selbst mit blutigem Stirnband und Hemd ein. Diese Selbstporträts beziehen sich auf Friedrichs romantisches Gemälde, auf dem menschliches Streben von der Natur bezwungen wird, in einer modernen Version dieser Niederlage.

Caspar David Friedrich, Professor an der Dresdner Akademie, stand in engem

temps 1991. Cette œuvre de six mètres de hauteur est placée au fond de la nef dans la grande arche, à l'endroit qui jadis séparait les moines des autres membres de la congrégation. Des tableaux représentant trois des quatre enfants de l'artiste, Ali Elvis, Amadeus et Mercedes, sont accrochés aux colonnes et exposés dans l'église pendant la durée de l'installation. *Kindskopf* fait maintenant partie de la collection permanente du Musée national russe de St Pétersbourg.

A peu près à la même période, le peintre exécute *White Christmas* (1992, voir p. 42/43), l'une de ses rares œuvres en trois dimensions. C'est un groupe de 48 enfants sans visage, en plâtre avec du pollen saupoudré sur la surface. Les personnages ne sont pas simplement répartis dans l'espace, mais semblent entrer en foule et se diriger vers un spectateur qui ne se doute de rien.

Helnwein travaille sur plusieurs projets en même temps. A la fin des années 80, il entame également une série de grands triptyques. Ce genre souvent utilisé pour les retables et l'art sacré dans les églises médiévales du nord de l'Europe avait connu un regain d'intérêt à la fin du 19e siècle avec des artistes comme Hans von Marées, pour culminer avec les neuf grands triptyques de Max Beckmann. *L'Eclat discret de l'avantgarde I* de Helnwein (1986, voir p. 232) renvoie à cette tradition allemande. Son panneau central reproduit *La Mer glacée* de Caspar David Friedrich (1823/24), un tableau qui se réfère directement au naufrage du « Espoir », un navire qui avait tenté d'ouvrir le passage vers le pôle nord. Reflet du pessimisme existentiel et religieux de Friedrich, l'œuvre fait plus généralement allusion aux manifestations du destin et des forces destructrices de la nature. Gottfried Helnwein y inclut sa propre image, la tête bandée et la chemise couverte de sang encadrant de chaque côté le navire détruit par les blocs de glace. Il répond au tableau romantique de Friedrich où le peintre voit les tentatives humaines anéanties par la

Embarrassing (detail)/*Peinlich* (Detail)/*Gênant* (détail), 1971
Colored pencil, pencil, watercolor and india ink on cardboard

city as the center panel of the triptych *Song of the Deputies* (1996). The side panels show self-portraits of the artist with a bandage over his head and eyes, and a harrowing clamp between his tongue and nose.

The blue monochrome lends a new sense of magical distance to his work; the color became predominant during the last decade. An ingenious *Annunciation* of 1991 (cf. p. 302) depicts a young girl sitting on her bed and watching a TV screen from which, as in Woody Allen's "Purple Rose of Cairo", the white shadow of an angel emerges, beckoning toward the presumptive virgin. In *Night III* (1990, cf. p. 271), also a monochrome but created and developed on a computer then transferred to canvas by an ink-jet process before being overpainted with acrylic and oil, the child stands in front of the television set while two chilling men, whose faces have been rubbed out to make them indistinct, sit next to her. *Night II* (cf. p. 281) of the same year shows soldiers running in the dark of night toward their own death. The portrait of his son, *Ali* (1991, cf. p. 260), is a poignant image of a solitary figure. The different tones of blue provide a mysterious glow to the child's body and his head, with its closed eyes. In the same year Helnwein painted two large canvases, *Fire-Man* (cf. p. 171) and *Ice-Man* (cf. p. 170), in blue monotone, both based on photographs of men who were wounded in World War I. He painted these disfigured faces with an out-of-focus blur that creates images of powerful presence.

Occasionally the artist made use of color, as in the huge triptych, six meters in width, *Vienna Panorama* (1995). It shows the artist surrounded by his paints, solvents, and brushes, as he paints a grand panorama of his native city.

For eight years, from 1988 to 1996, the artist worked on a large blue monochrome, *Turkish Family II* (cf. p. 274), with seven people occupying the same room and appearing to sit for their photo. This social comment plumbs the deep division between

Kontakt zum Dresdner Kreis romantischer Dichter. Mehr als ein Jahrhundert später, im Februar 1945, wurde Dresden, eine der schönsten Städte der Welt, von den Alliierten zerstört. Helnwein setzte ein Bild der dem Erdboden gleichgemachten Stadt als Mitteltafel des Triptychons *Lied der Abgesandten* (1996) ein. Die Seitentafeln zeigen Selbstbildnisse des Künstlers, mit Mullbinden um Kopf und Augen und einer entsetzlichen Klemme zwischen Zunge und Nase.

Die monochrom blaue Farbgebung verleiht seinem Werk eine neue magische Distanz und dominiert während der 90er Jahre. *Die Verkündigung* von 1991 (vgl. S. 302) zeigt kunstvoll ein junges Mädchen, das auf seinem Bett sitzend auf den Fernsehschirm schaut, aus dem, wie in Woody Allens »Purple Rose of Cairo«, der weiße Schatten eines Engels heraustritt und die vermeintliche Jungfrau heranwinkt. Auch *Nacht III* (1990, vgl. S. 271) ist monochrom blau gehalten. Es ist auf einem Computer erarbeitet und mit einem Tintenstrahldrucker auf die Leinwand übertragen worden, bevor es mit Acryl und Öl übermalt wurde. Dargestellt ist ein Kind vor einem Fernsehapparat, während zwei frostig wirkende Männer, deren Gesichter bis zur Unkenntlichkeit ausradiert wurden, neben ihr sitzen. *Nacht II* (vgl. S. 281) aus demselben Jahr zeigt Soldaten, die in der Dunkelheit der Nacht in den Tod laufen. Das Porträt seines Sohnes, *Ali* (1991, vgl. S. 260), ist die ergreifende Darstellung eines einsamen Menschen. Die verschiedenen Blautöne überziehen Körper und Kopf des Kindes mit einem mysteriösen Schimmer. Im selben Jahr malte Helnwein zwei großformatige, monoton blaue Leinwandgemälde, *Feuermensch* (vgl. S. 171) und *Eismensch* (vgl. S. 170), die beide auf Fotografien von Männern basieren, die im Ersten Weltkrieg verwundet wurden. Er malte die entstellten Gesichter verschwommen, wodurch die starke Präsenz der Bilder noch unterstrichen wurde.

nature, en lui ajoutant une version contemporaine de la défaite.

Caspar David Friedrich, professeur à l'Académie des Beaux-Arts de Dresde, entretenait des liens étroits avec le cercle de poètes romantiques de la ville. Plus d'un siècle plus tard, en février 1945, Dresde, une des plus belles cités du monde, était détruite par les bombardements alliés. Helnwein utilisera une photo de la ville en ruines comme panneau central pour le triptyque *Chant des suppléants* (1996). Les panneaux latéraux montrent des autoportraits de l'artiste avec un bandage lui couvrant la tête et les yeux, ainsi qu'une terrifiante agrafe entre sa langue et son nez.

Les monochromes bleus confèrent à son œuvre une sorte de nouvelle distance magique. Pendant les années 90, la couleur dominera. Une ingénieuse *Annonciation* de 1991 (voir p. 302) représente une jeune fille assise sur son lit en train de regarder un écran de télévision d'où émerge la silhouette blanche d'un ange qui rappelle « La Rose Pourpre du Caire » de Woody Allen et fait un signe en direction de la présumée vierge. Dans *Nuit III* (1990, voir p. 271), un autre monochrome, mais réalisé et remanié par ordinateur, puis transféré sur toile grâce à un procédé d'impression par jet d'encre avant d'être repeint à l'acrylique et à l'huile, l'enfant se tient face au téléviseur tandis que deux hommes qui donne le frisson et dont les visages ont été effacés pour les rendre méconnaissables, sont assis à côté d'elle. *Nuit II* (voir p. 281), de la même année, montre des soldats courant dans l'obscurité de la nuit à la rencontre de leur propre mort. Le portrait de son fils *Ali* (1991, voir p. 260) est un tableau poignant représentant la solitude. Les différents tons de bleu créent l'illusion d'une étrange lueur émanant du corps et du visage de l'enfant aux yeux fermés. La même année, Helnwein peint deux grandes toiles d'un bleu uniforme intitulées *Homme de feu* (voir p. 171) et *Homme de glace* (voir p. 170), inspirées de photographies de blessés de la Première Guerre

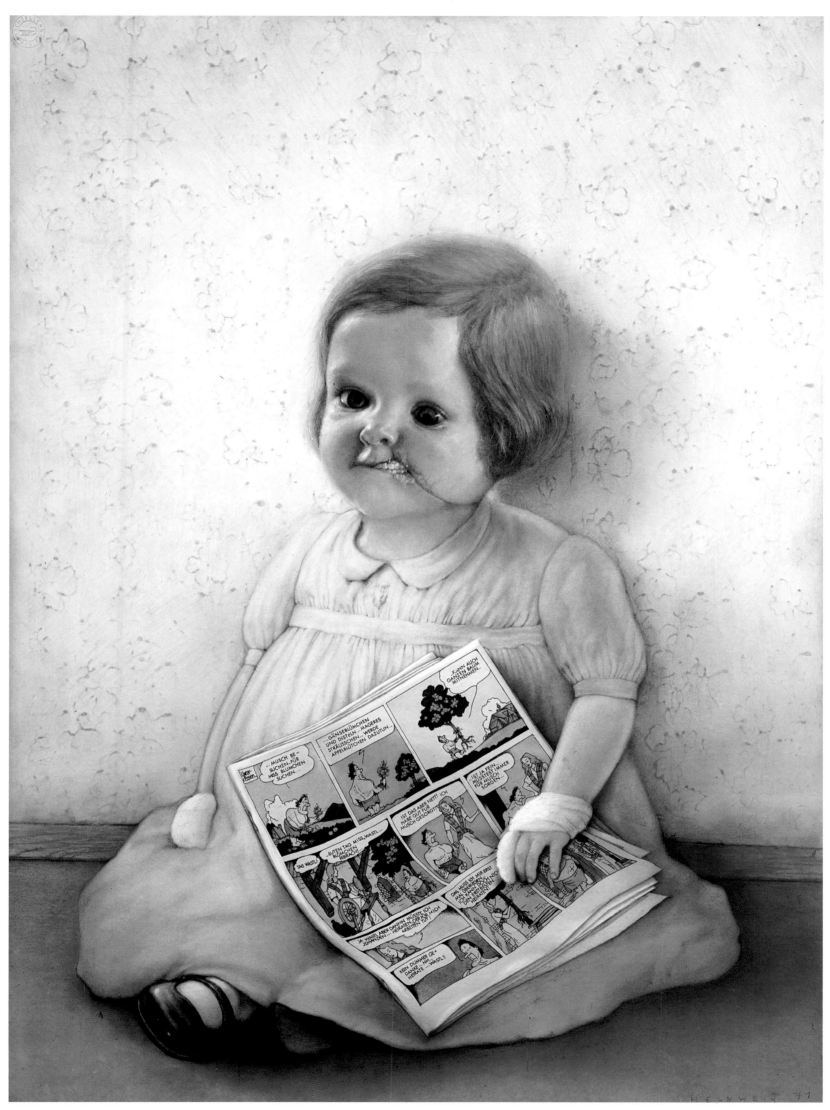

Embarrassing/Peinlich/Gênant, 1971
Colored pencil, pencil, watercolor and india ink on cardboard, 25³⁄₅ × 13⁴⁄₅ inches, 60 × 35 cm
Private Collection, Germany

The Intrusion/Der Eingriff/L'Intrusion, 1971
Watercolor, colored pencil and pencil on cardboard, 21⅕ × 24⅖ inches, 54 × 62 cm
Wolfgang Payer, Berlin

Beautiful Victim II/Belle victime II, 1974
Watercolor on cardboard, 40 × 28⅘ inches, 102 × 73 cm
Courtesy Klaus Kiefer Gallery, Essen

the Germans and the immigrant Turkish Gastarbeiter (guest workers). There is a Turkish woman with four children – the boys wearing Mickey Mouse caps – on one side of the room, looking at the viewer as if he were behind the camera, while two German ladies, appearing very suburban in their short skirts, literally look down their noses at the immigrant family. To add to the confounding of this disparate group, there are three computers, their screens placed at random in the room.

Working with totally different subjects, Helnwein made the triptych *3 Poets* in 1994. They are portraits of Goethe, Heine, and Thomas Mann. The former two are based on famous painted portraits of the poets, the latter on a well-known photograph of Mann. It seems that Helnwein wanted to recapture the images of the classicist, the idealist, and the rationalist among great German writers.

Between 1994 and 1996 Helnwein made a series of perhaps a hundred dark-blue monochromes, which he entitled *Fire* (cf. p. 355–363). These paintings, done in oil and acrylic and based on photographs of writers, painters, poets, composers, scientists, film makers, political activists, actors, philosophers, and pop stars, are depictions of the rebels of the twentieth century who were going against the current of the established culture of their time. These portraits are painted in the darkest blue, with a veil over the faces, making them exceedingly difficult to detect, even in daylight. They create a sense of ineffable ambiguity, and it takes time and attention to raise the faces into recognition of their identity. The obscurity of the images makes for a significant continuity between the invisible and the visible in these paintings.

With enough distance from his childhood, both in time and feeling, Helnwein was eventually able to respond to his religious upbringing in a different way. Instead of martyrs, he now avails himself of themes like the Virgin mourning over

Gelegentlich setzte der Künstler Farben ein, wie in dem riesigen, sechs Meter breiten Triptychon *Wiener Panorama* (1995). Es zeigt den Künstler umgeben von seinen Farben, Lösungsmitteln und Pinseln beim Malen einer Ansicht seiner Geburtsstadt.

Acht Jahre lang, von 1988 bis 1996, arbeitete Helnwein an einem großen, monochrom blauen Gemälde, *Türkenfamilie II* (vgl. S. 274). Dargestellt sind sieben Personen in einem Raum, die anscheinend für ein Foto posieren. Dieses Bild soll die tiefe Spaltung zwischen Deutschen und türkischen Gastarbeitern kritisieren. Man sieht auf der einen Seite des Zimmers eine türkische Frau mit vier Kindern – die Jungen tragen Micky-Maus-Ohren, und alle schauen den Betrachter an, als stünde er hinter der Kamera. Zwei deutsche Frauen, die in ihren kurzen Röcken unteres Vorstadtniveau verkörpern, schauen im wahrsten Sinne des Wortes auf die Einwandererfamilie herab. Um die Verwirrung innerhalb dieser ungleichen Gruppe zu verstärken, stehen dort drei Computer, deren Bildschirme wahllos in den Raum gerichtet sind.

Mit einer ganz anderen Thematik setzte sich Helnwein auseinander, als er 1994 das Triptychon *3 Dichter* malte. Dargestellt sind Goethe, Heine und Thomas Mann. Die ersten beiden Bildnisse basieren auf berühmten Porträts der Dichter, das letzte auf einer bekannten Fotografie von Thomas Mann. Anscheinend wollte der Künstler den Klassizisten, Idealisten und Rationalisten unter den großen deutschen Schriftstellern einfangen.

Zwischen 1994 und 1996 malte Helnwein eine Serie von etwa 100 monochrom dunkelblauen Bildern, die er *Feuer* (vgl. S. 355–363) betitelte. Die Gemälde in Öl und Acryl basieren auf Fotografien von Schriftstellern, Malern, Dichtern, Komponisten, Wissenschaftlern, Filmemachern, politischen Aktivisten, Schauspielern, Philosophen und Popstars. Es sind Darstellungen der Rebellen des 20. Jahrhunderts, die gegen den Strom der etablierten Kultur ihrer Zeit schwammen. Die Porträts sind in einem dunklen

mondiale. Il réalise ces visages défigurés en estompant les détails pour générer un flou qui donne des images d'une extraordinaire intensité.

Parfois, il a recours à la couleur, comme dans *Panorama de Vienne* (1995), un immense triptyque de six mètres de large qui montre l'artiste entouré de ses tableaux, solvants et pinceaux, et en train de peindre un vaste panorama de sa ville natale.

Pendant huit ans, de 1988 à 1996, il travaille à un grand monochrome bleu intitulé *Famille turque II* (voir p. 274), représentant sept personnes dans une même pièce et semblant poser pour une photo. Ce commentaire social met le doigt sur la profonde division entre la population allemande et les immigrés turcs, appelés Gastarbeiter (travailleurs invités). On y voit une femme turque et quatre enfants – les garçons portant des casquettes à l'effigie de Mickey Mouse –, dans un coin de la pièce, fixant le spectateur comme s'il était derrière l'objectif, alors que deux Allemandes très banlieusardes, en jupes courtes, regardent la famille immigrée de haut. Pour augmenter la confusion générée par ce groupe hétérogène, trois ordinateurs et leurs écrans sont répartis au hasard dans la pièce.

Travaillant sur des sujets radicalement différents, Helnwein réalise en 1994 le triptyque intitulé *3 Poètes*, représentant des portraits de Goethe, Heine et Thomas Mann. Les deux premiers sont tirés de tableaux célèbres représentant les écrivains, tandis que le dernier reprend une photo très connue de Mann. Il semble qu'Helnwein veuille saisir les images du classicisme, de l'idéalisme et du rationalisme parmi de grands écrivains allemands.

Entre 1994 et 1996, il se consacre à une série comprenant une centaine de monochromes bleus foncés qu'il appelle *Feu* (voir p. 355–363). Ces peintures à l'huile et à l'acrylique reproduisent des photographies d'écrivains, peintres, poètes, compositeurs, scientifiques, réalisateurs de cinéma, activistes politiques, acteurs, philosophes et

Sunday's Child/Sonntagskind/L'Enfant du dimanche, 1972
Watercolor, colored pencil and pencil on cardboard, 40 × 28⅘ inches, 102 × 73 cm
Private Collection, Germany

Christ's dead body or the Madonna and Child – always with the purpose of making the viewer re-examine the authority of traditional values.

The large *Pieta Lutz* (1994) depicting a father with his son stretched out on his lap, is a painting of close friends of the artist. As its name implies, it also reflects on Christian iconography. Here we have a masculine Pieta with homoerotic connotations questioning the archetypal Christian symbolism. Related to this painting is the series of dark-blue Madonna paintings. This group actually began with works in pencil, like *Virgin with Pinocchio after Bronzino,* and another drawing of the Madonna with a mutilated Christ Child, after a painting by Mantegna. In 1996, again using the computer-painting and ink-jet method, Helnwein painted a series of Madonnas in which he adopted images of the Virgin and Child taken from well-known paintings by Leonardo or Caravaggio and transferred them onto the canvas, then overpainting the image with oil and acrylic, leaving it all in monochrome darkness. In these works, the paint subsumes and becomes coexistent with the photograph; it becomes a new signifier, which inverts the familiar images. The Madonna paintings no doubt presented themselves quite intuitively to this former Catholic, and they led to Helnwein's significant *Epiphany I (Adoration of the Magi)* of 1996 (cf. p. 304/305). This large (210 × 333 cm) painting in blue monochrome depicts the Adoration of the Magi. But the Madonna is a young maiden of pure Aryan blood, and presents a Christ Child who looks like a young Adolf Hitler, and the Wise Men all wear well-tailored SS and Reichswehr uniforms, Nazi officials decorated with the Iron Cross. They stand attentively, with approving respect, next to the Virgin. The most prominent Nazi holds a document in his hands, while the soldier on the right seems to examine the child, perhaps to see whether he is circumcised. It is a powerful and very enigmatic painting,

Blau gehalten, das die Gesichter geradezu verschleiert. Erzeugt wird so ein Eindruck von unbeschreiblicher Doppeldeutigkeit. Die vielsagende Kontinuität zwischen dem Unsichtbaren und dem Sichtbaren auf diesen Bildern basiert auf der Düsterheit der Bildnisse.

Mit genügend Distanz zu seiner Kindheit, in zeitlicher wie auch in emotionaler Hinsicht, war Helnwein nunmehr in der Lage, seine katholische Erziehung auf eine andere Weise zu verarbeiten. An die Stelle des Märtyrertums treten nun Themen wie die über den Tod Christi trauernde Jungfrau oder die Madonna mit Kind – immer in der Absicht, den Betrachter die Gültigkeit traditioneller Werte überdenken zu lassen.

Die große *Pieta Lutz* (1994) zeigt einen Vater, dessen Sohn ausgestreckt auf seinem Schoß liegt. Dargestellt sind enge Freunde des Künstlers. Wie der Name »Pieta« bereits besagt, bezieht sich dieses Bild auf die christliche Ikonographie. Helnwein zeigt aber eine männliche Pieta mit homoerotischen Konnotationen, die den archetypischen christlichen Symbolismus in Frage stellt. In Beziehung zu diesem Gemälde steht die Serie der dunkelblauen Madonnen-Gemälde. Diese Werkgruppe basiert auf Bleistiftarbeiten wie der *Jungfrau mit Pinocchio nach Bronzino* und einer anderen Madonna-Zeichnung mit einem verstümmelten Christuskind, nach einem Gemälde von Mantegna. 1996 malte Helnwein eine Reihe von Madonnen, wobei er wieder die Motive digitalisierte und mit Ink-jet auf die Leinwand übertrug. Er übernahm Bildnisse der Jungfrau mit Kind aus bekannten Gemälden von Leonardo und Caravaggio, die er anschließend mit Öl und Acryl übermalte und in monochromer Dunkelheit beließ. In diesen Arbeiten koexistieren Farbe und Fotografie. Die Farbe wird zu einem neuen Bedeutungsträger, der das Vertraute auf den Kopf stellt. Der ehemalige Katholik nimmt die Madonnenbilder zweifelsohne intuitiv auf, und sie führen zu Helnweins bedeutender *Epiphanie I* von 1996 (vgl. S. 304/305).

pop-stars représentent des êtres rebelles qui, au 20ᵉ siècle, ont contesté les courants culturels dominant à leur époque. Ces portraits peints d'un bleu très sombre avec des visages presque voilés et difficilement identifiables, même à la lumière du jour, suscitent une indescriptible impression d'ambiguïté. Ici, l'obscurité des images contribue à une continuité significative entre l'invisible et le visible.

Avec le recul suffisant autant affectif que temporel qu'il a par rapport à son enfance, Helnwein est dès lors peut-être en mesure de réagir autrement à son éducation religieuse. Au lieu de martyrs, il a recours à des thèmes tels que la Vierge déplorant le Christ mort ou la Madone à l'enfant – toutefois toujours dans l'intention d'amener le spectateur à remettre en question le pouvoir des valeurs traditionnelles.

La grande *Pieta Lutz* (1994), représentant un père avec son fils allongé sur ses genoux, est le portrait d'amis proches de l'artiste. Comme l'indique son titre, elle renvoie également à l'iconographie chrétienne. Ici, on a à faire à une pieta masculine avec des connotations homosexuelles remettant en cause le symbolisme de l'archétype chrétien. La série de Madones peintes en bleu foncé se réfère à ce même thème. Cet ensemble d'œuvres commence par des travaux au crayon comme *Vierge et Pinocchio d'après Bronzino* et un autre dessin de la Madone avec un Enfant Jésus mutilé, inspiré d'un tableau de Mantegna. En 1996, utilisant de nouveau l'ordinateur et la méthode du jet d'encre, Helnwein peint une série de Madones où il reprend le motif de la Vierge à l'Enfant de célèbres tableaux de Léonard ou du Caravage, avant de les transférer sur toile pour les repeindre à l'huile et à l'acrylique, laissant le tout dans des monochromes sombres. Dans ces œuvres, la peinture coexiste avec la photographie ; elle prend une nouvelle signification tout en inversant les images qui nous sont familières. Les Madones s'imposent sans aucun doute de manière intuitive à cet ancien catholique et

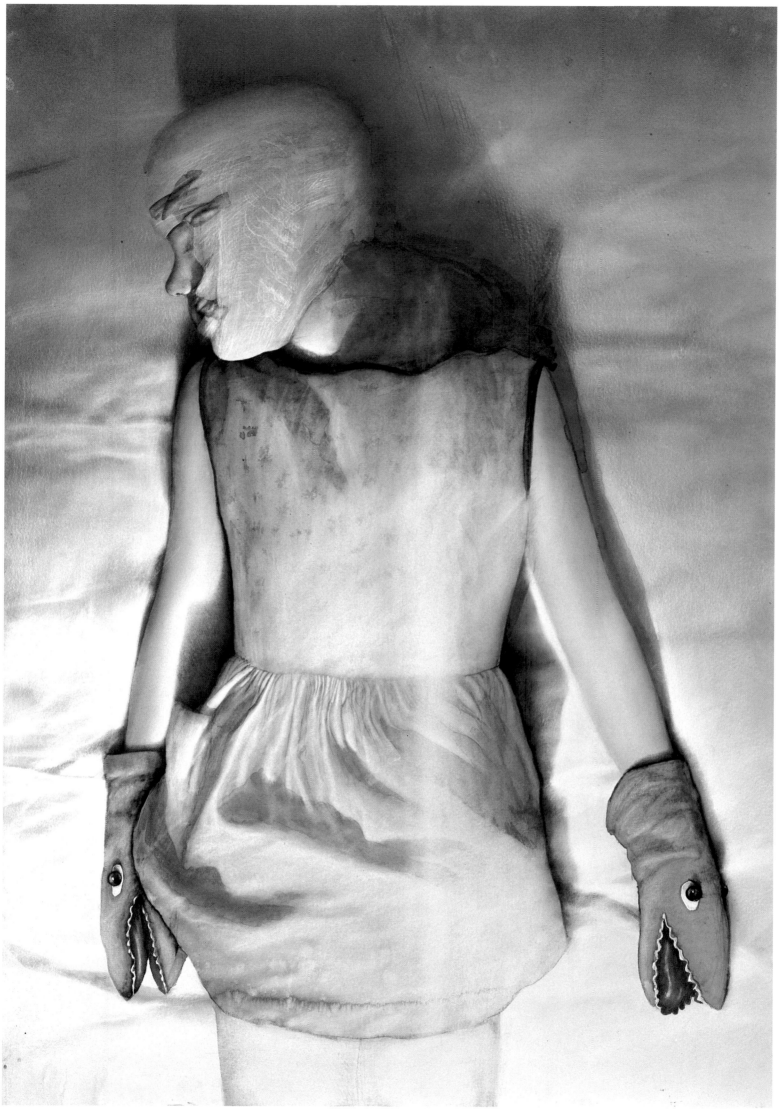

Crocodile Rock, 1978
Watercolor on cardboard, 35²⁄₅ × 23³⁄₅ inches, 90 × 60 cm
Private Collection, Austria

Leid macht stark/La souffrance endurcit, 1974
Watercolor on cardboard, 28⅘ × 18⅘ inches, 73 × 48 cm
Traute Winkelbauer, Vienna   76

Child of Light/Lichtkind/Enfant lumière, 1976
Watercolor on cardboard, 35²/₅ × 23³/₅ inches, 90 × 60 cm

77

Private Collection, Austria

Easy Rider, 1972
Watercolor on cardboard, 8²⁄₅ × 7³⁄₅ inches, 21,4 × 19,5 cm
Private Collection, Austria

78

The Song I/Das Lied I/La chanson I, 1981
Watercolor on cardboard, 63 × 45⅗ inches, 160 × 116 cm
Private Collection, Austria

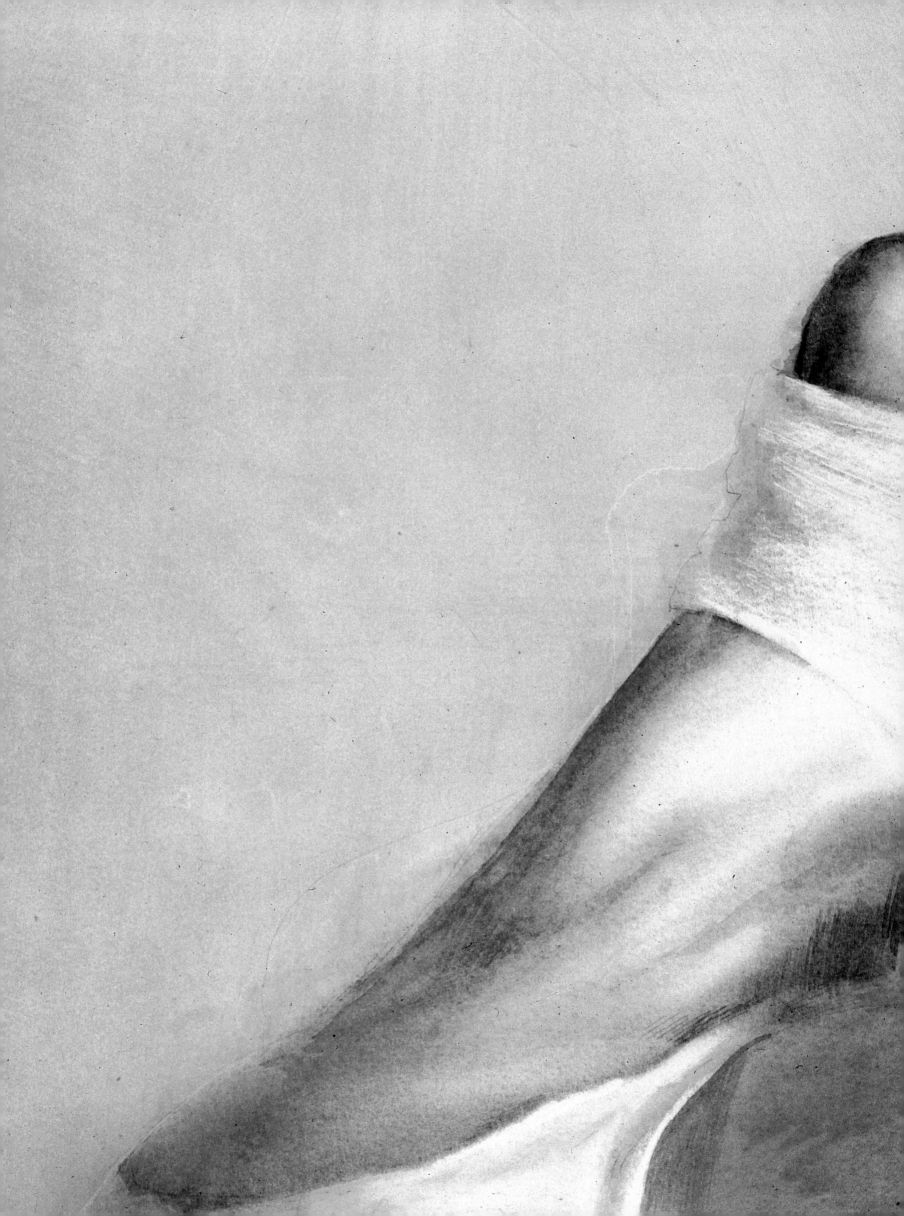

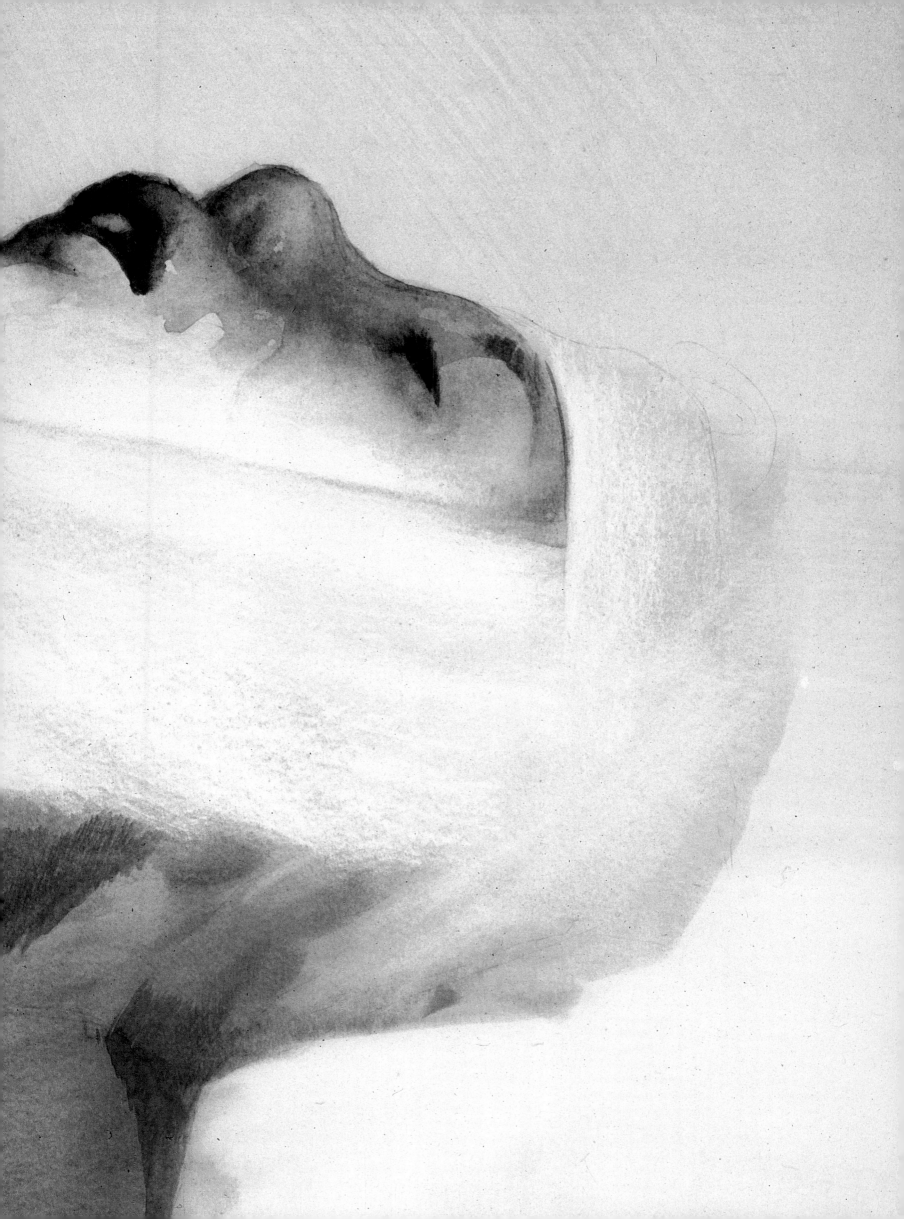

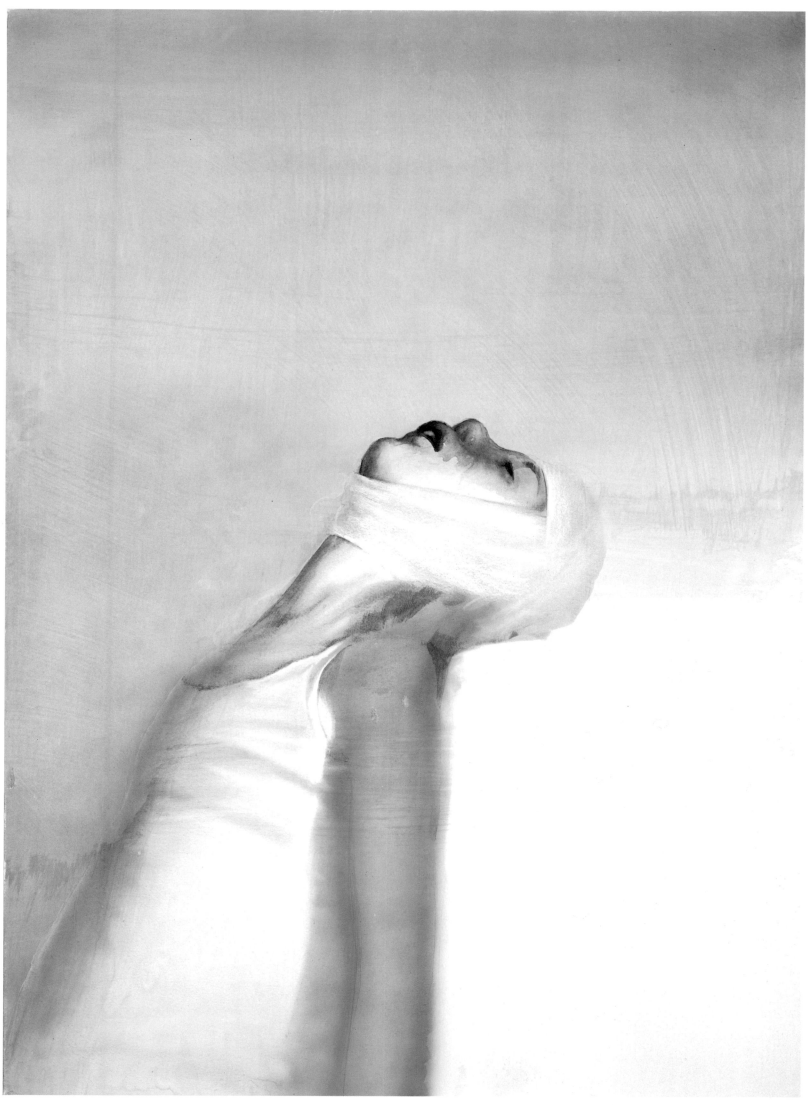

Red Mouth/Roter Mund/Bouche rouge, 1978
Watercolor on cardboard, 38⅗ × 28 inches, 98 × 71 cm
Private Collection, Vienna

LE ZINGEL SE PÊCHE DANS LA SAÔNE

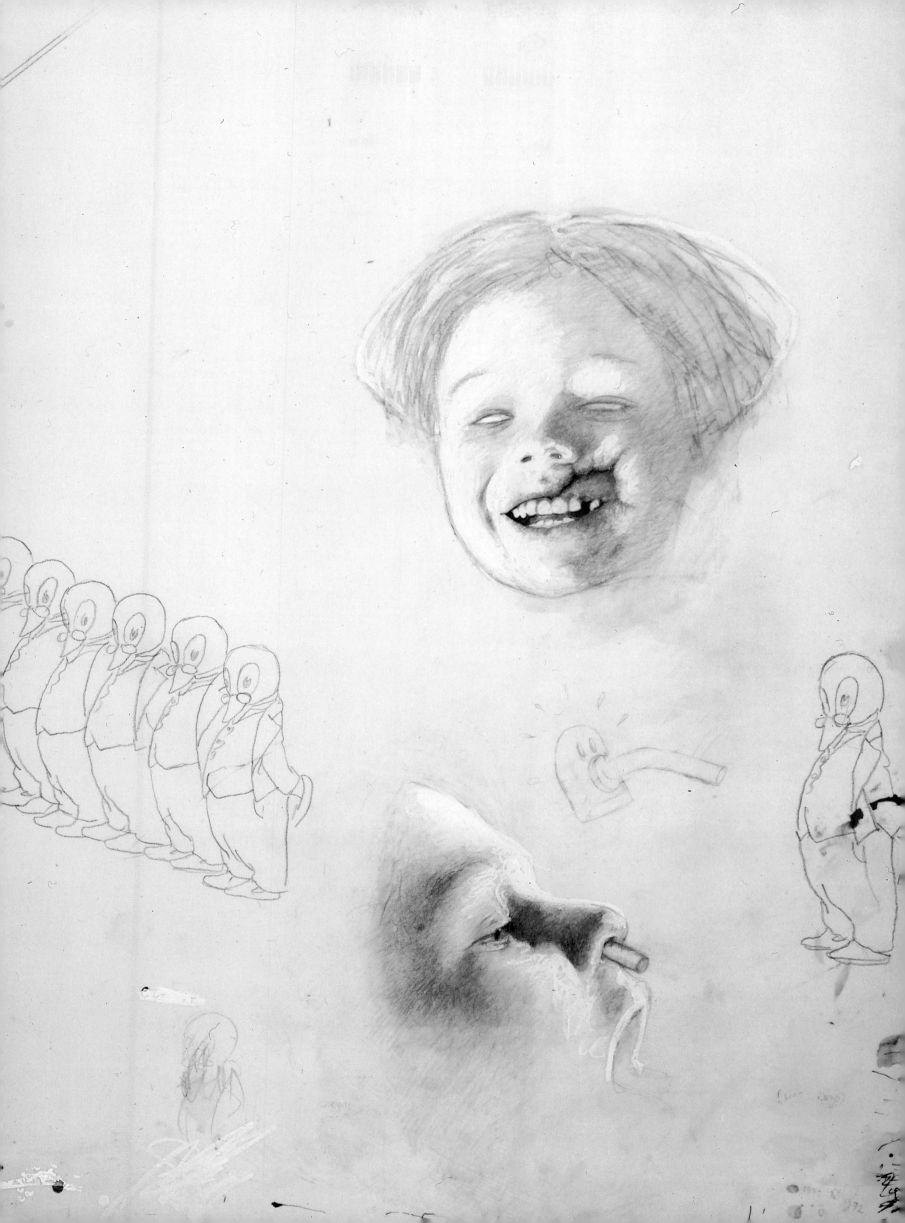

Heart of Glass/Das gläserne Herz/Le cœur de verre, 1987
Colored pencil on paper, 31 × 23³⁄₅ inches, 80 × 60 cm
Private Collection, Germany

◁ Untitled/Ohne Titel/Sans titre, 1991
Pencil, pastel, india ink and watercolor on paper, 22²⁄₅ × 27³⁄₅ inches, 57 × 70 cm
Kurt and Veronika Fliegerbauer, Germany

Untitled/Ohne Titel/Sans titre, 1986
Watercolor on cardboard, 39²⁄₅ × 27½ inches, 100 × 70 cm

Mother, Is It you? I/Mutter, du hier? I/Maman, toi ici? I, 1971
Oil on paper and wood, 15⅘ × 11⅘ inches, 40 × 30 cm
Bank Austria Collection, Vienna

HELNWEIN

The Revelation/Die Offenbarung/La Révélation, 1979
Watercolor on cardboard, 20 × 14⅗ inches, 51 × 37cm
Kurt and Veronika Fliegerbauer, Germany

The Incident (detail)/*Der Zwischenfall* (Detail)/*L'Incident* (détail), 1979
Watercolor on cardboard

96

Earthquake/Erdbeben/Tremblement de terre, 1977
Watercolor on cardboard, 14 × 21⅖ inch, 36,9 × 54,3 cm
Raymond Glücksmann, Switzerland

done with the eyes and brush of a realist painter.

In 1998 Helnwein expects to enlarge this work to enormous size and display a version of it at the Königsplatz, the grand neo-Grecian square that also served as the center for Nazis' mass meetings and ostentatious rituals, and which Hitler called the "community space for the *Volk*."

Much like Joseph Beuys, who opened new, unexpected, and far-reaching spheres for art, Gottfried Helnwein has made works that extend beyond the art scene into the social and political realm. Like his predecessor, he has moved beyond the realm of pure aesthetics, engaging his art into the everyday world. Furthermore, his principal interest is not to express personal feelings and emotions, but to make statements that go beyond the individual. He wants to see his work not trapped on the walls of museums and galleries, but revealed in the public domain. He expects his work to intervene in the social sphere and to have a direct impact on the life of his time. For this to occur, the viewer must, of course, respond to the artist's work, which is, after all, only half of the process of communication. Helnwein's paintings and photographs, so acute in their message, indeed facilitate our participation as viewers, which is necessary to complete the transmission. Using a profusion of media, Gottfried Helnwein leads us into an area of controversial reflection.

Dieses großformatige (210 × 333 cm), monochrom blau gehaltene Gemälde zeigt die Anbetung der Heiligen Drei Könige. Die Madonna ist nun aber eine Jungfrau reinen arischen Blutes und präsentiert ein dem jungen Adolf Hitler ähnelndes Christuskind, während die drei Weisen aus dem Morgenland gutgeschnittene SS- und Reichswehr-Uniformen tragen, Nazi-Funktionäre, die mit dem Eisernen Kreuz ausgezeichnet wurden. Sie stehen aufmerksam und respektvoll neben der Jungfrau. Der Nazi im Vordergrund hält ein Dokument in seiner Hand, während der Soldat auf der rechten Seite das Kind zu untersuchen scheint, vielleicht um nachzuschauen, ob es beschnitten ist. Es ist ein kraftvolles und rätselhaftes Gemälde, ausgeführt von einem Maler des Realismus.

1998 hat Helnwein vor, dieses Werk enorm zu vergrößern und auf dem Königsplatz in München zu installieren, einem Platz im neugriechischen Stil, der für die Massenversammlungen und protzigen Rituale der Nazis gedient hatte und den Hitler den »Platz der Volksgemeinschaft« nannte.

Ähnlich wie Beuys, der der Kunst neue, Räume öffnete, hat Helnwein Werke geschaffen, die bis in die soziale und politische Sphäre ragen. Wie sein Vorgänger hat er sich über die reine Ästhetik hinausbegeben und seine Kunst in alle Lebensbereiche übertragen. Sein Hauptinteresse besteht darin, allgemeingültige Aussagen zu treffen. Er möchte seine Arbeiten nicht als Gefangene von Museen und Galerien, sondern in der Öffentlichkeit enthüllt sehen. Er will, daß seine Werke auf das Leben seiner Zeit direkt einwirken. Der Betrachter muß auf die Arbeiten des Künstlers in irgendeiner Form reagieren, was erst die Hälfte des Kommunikationsprozesses ausmacht. Helnweins Gemälde und Fotografien mit ihren scharfsinnigen Botschaften erleichtern dem Betrachter seine aktive Beteiligung, was für eine vollständige Übermittlung notwendig ist. Gottfried Helnwein setzt zahlreiche Ausdrucksmittel ein und führt uns auf ein Gebiet der kontroversen Reflexion.

conduisent à *Epiphanie I* de 1996 (voir p. 304/305). Ce grand tableau (210 × 333 cm) en monochrome bleu représente l'Adoration des Mages. Mais la Madone est une jeune vierge au sang aryen pure qui présente un enfant Jésus ressemblant à Adolf Hitler jeune ; quant aux Rois mages, ils portent tous d'élégants uniformes de S.S. ou de la Reichswehr des fonctionnaires nazis décorés de la Croix de Fer. Attentifs, ils se tiennent près de la Vierge exprimant respect et approbation. Le plus gradé tient un document à la main, tandis qu'à sa droite, le soldat semble examiner l'Enfant, peut-être pour vérifier s'il est circoncis. C'est un tableau à la fois bouleversant et très énigmatique, réalisé avec le regard et le pinceau d'un peintre réaliste.

En 1998, Helnwein envisage d'agrandir cette œuvre à un format monumental et d'en exposer une version sur la Königsplatz, la grande place néoclassique qui servait de coulisse aux manifestation de masse et aux rituels ostentatoires des nazis et qu'Hitler appelait « l'espace du peuple ».

Tout comme Joseph Beuys qui ouvrit à l'art de nouveaux horizons, Helnwein a créé des œuvres qui entrent dans le domaine sociale et politique. A l'instar de son prédécesseur, il évolue au-delà du domaine de l'esthétique pure, engageant son art dans le monde du quotidien. Ce qui l'intéresse avant tout est de dresser des constats qui transcendent l'individu. Il refuse de voir ses travaux pris au piège sur les murs des musées et galeries, les veut accessibles à tous dans les lieux publics. A ces fins, le spectateur doit évidemment réagir à l'œuvre d'art qui, après tout, ne représente que la moitié du processus de communication. Les tableaux et les photographies d'Helnwein, si précis dans le message qu'elles véhiculent, facilitent effectivement notre participation en tant que spectateurs, une participation nécessaire à la transmission. Utilisant une profusion de médias, Gottfried Helnwein nous entraîne dans un monde de réflexion controversée.

Good Morning, You Pig!/Guten Morgen, du Sau!/Bonjour, cochon!, 1972
Watercolor on cardboard, 34¼ × 24⅖ inches, 87 × 62 cm
Wolfgang Payer, Berlin

99

The Father with the Nose/Der Vater mit der Nase/Le nez du père, 1972
Watercolor and colored pencil on cardboard, 8⅓ × 7½ inches, 21 × 19 cm
Ilse Kisser, Vienna

◁ *The Mocking Physician/Der höhnische Arzt/Le médecin moqueur,* 1973
Watercolor on paper, 34¼ × 24⅖ inches, 87 × 62 cm
Mario Herold, Leipzig

Untitled/Ohne Titel/Sans titre, 1988
Watercolor on cardboard, 23³/₅ × 16½ inches, 60 × 42 cm
Courtesy Klaus Kiefer Gallery, Essen

103

DRAWINGS AND WORKS ON PAPER
ZEICHNUNGEN UND ARBEITEN AUF PAPIER
DESSINS ET TRAVAUX SUR PAPIER

Our Duck Bishop (detail)/*Unser Entenbischof* (Detail)/
Duck, notre evêque (détail), 1977
India ink on paper

Yes, You Two! I/Ja, ihr zwei! I/Oui, tous les deux! I, 1972
India ink on paper, approx. 7½ × 5⅛ inches, 19 × 13 cm

Yes, You Two! II/Ja, ihr zwei! Ii/Oui, tous les deux! II, 1972
India ink on paper, approx. 7½ × 5⅛ inches, 19 × 13 cm

The Drain/Die Rinne/La rigole, 1976
India ink on paper, 27½ × 19½ inches, 70 × 50 cm
Private Collection, Austria

KÖNEMANN

*****FOR IMMEDIATE RELEASE*****

A New Contemporary Art Title by Könemann

Helnwein

Edited by Josef Kiblitsky

PRICE: $39.95

ISBN: 3-8290-1448-1

FORMAT: 9 ½" x 12 ½" HC

PAGE COUNT: 424 pp.

ILLUSTRATIONS: 580

LANGUAGES: English, German, French

CONTENT: On the occasion of the great retrospective of Gottfried Helnwein in the marble palace in St. Petersburg in 1991, the Russian State Museum compiled the most comprehensive monograph yet of the works of this individualistic and much discussed artist. Published by Könemann, this is the first publication that deals with all aspects of the artistic works of Helnwein between 1970 and 1997: his graphic works as well as his watercolors, oils and mixed media pictures. This volume also covers Helnwein's photographic work, installations and works for the theater. **Helnwein** includes contributions by Klaus Honnef and Peter Selz.

PUB DATE: July 12, 1999

CONTACT: Josephine Glasmacher, Tel. 212-367-8855
jglasmacher@konemann.com

137 West 19th Street New York NY 10011 Tel 212-367-8855 Toll Free 1-888-317-8855 Fax 212-367-8866

The Warm Stream /Der warme Strahl/Le courant chaud, 1974
India ir k on paper, 17½ × 14½ inches, 43 × 37 cm

Private Collection, Austria

Notes

1   In Germany and Austria over a quarter of a million
    individuals were killed by euthanasia under Hitler's
    "Racial Hygiene" program to eliminate people with
    mental or genetic disease for the creation of a truly
    clean society. The decisions were made by physicians
    who were party members. In Germany one doctor
    responsible for these murders was Dr. Hans Sewering,
    who was never tried, became a member of the senate of
    the State of Bavaria, president of the German Chamber
    of Physicians, and in 1992, president of the World
    Medical Association. When his previous history was
    uncovered, he was forced to resign. Neither Austria nor
    Germany ever prosecuted Dr. Gross, Dr. Sewering, or
    any of the other Race Hygiene physicians.

2   Malcolm Morley, in: Udo Kultermann, *New Realism*
    (Greenich, CO: New York Graphic Society, 1972), p. 14

3   Gottfried Helnwein, in: *Malerei muss sein wie
    Rockmusik*. Discussion with Andres Mäckler (Munich:
    Verlag C. H. Beck, 1992), p. 174 (hereafter Mäckler)

4   Ariel Dorfman, *How to Read Donald Duck*, trans. David
    Kunzle (New York: International General, 1975)

5   Kristine Stiles, "Performance Art", in: Stiles and Peter
    Selz, *Theories and Documents of Contemporary Art*
    (Berkeley: University of California Press, 1996), p. 687

6   Rudolf Hausner, *Ich Adam* (Munich: Deutsches
    Taschenbuch, 1987), p. 113

7   Helnwein, *Der Untermensch* (Heidelberg: Verlag Braus,
    1988)

8   *Gottfried Helnwein zeichnet unheimliche Geschichten von
    Edgar Allan Poe* (Friedrichshafen: Kunstverlag
    Weingarten, 1987)

9   Helnwein, in: Mäckler, p. 86

10 Susan Sontag, "On Photography", in: *A Susan Sontag
    Reader* (New York: Farrar Straus/Giroux, 1963), p. 359

11 Helnwein, in: Mäckler, p. 86

12 William S. Burroughs, in: *Helnwein, Faces*
    (Schaffhausen: Edition Stemmle, 1992), p. 7

13 Norman Mailer, in: Mäckler, p. 83

14 Helnwein, in: Mäckler, p. 126

15 "Gedanken von Simon Wiesenthal", in: *Helnwein,
    Neunter November Nacht* (Köln: Museum Ludwig, 1988),
    n. p.

The Bathtub Wonder of Watras/Das Wannenwunder von Watras/Le mystère de la baignoire de Watras, 1975
India ink on paper, 24²⁄₅ × 17¹⁄₃ inches, 62 × 44 cm
Private Collection, Austria

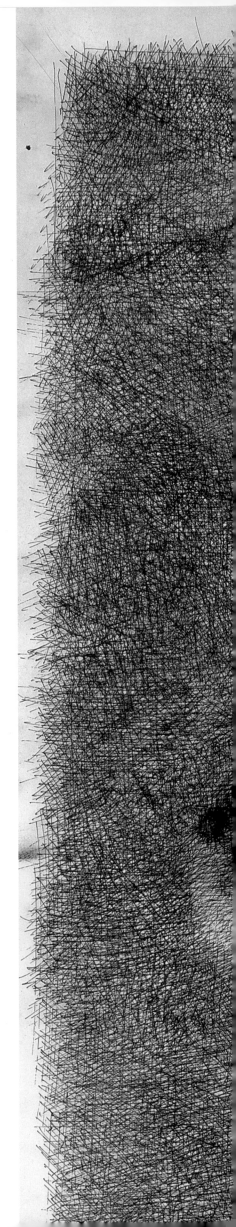

The Mine Disaster (detail)/*Das Grubenunglück* (Detail)/
Accident de la mine (détail), 1977
India ink on paper

116

King of Worms/Der Wurmkönig/Le Roi des vers, 1977
India ink on paper, 29½ × 21⅗ inches, 75 × 55 cm
Private Collection, Austria

Anna on the Upswing/Anna im Aufwind/Anna dans un vent ascendant, 1976
India ink on paper, 29½ × 21⅗ inches, 75 × 55 cm

Private Collection, Austria

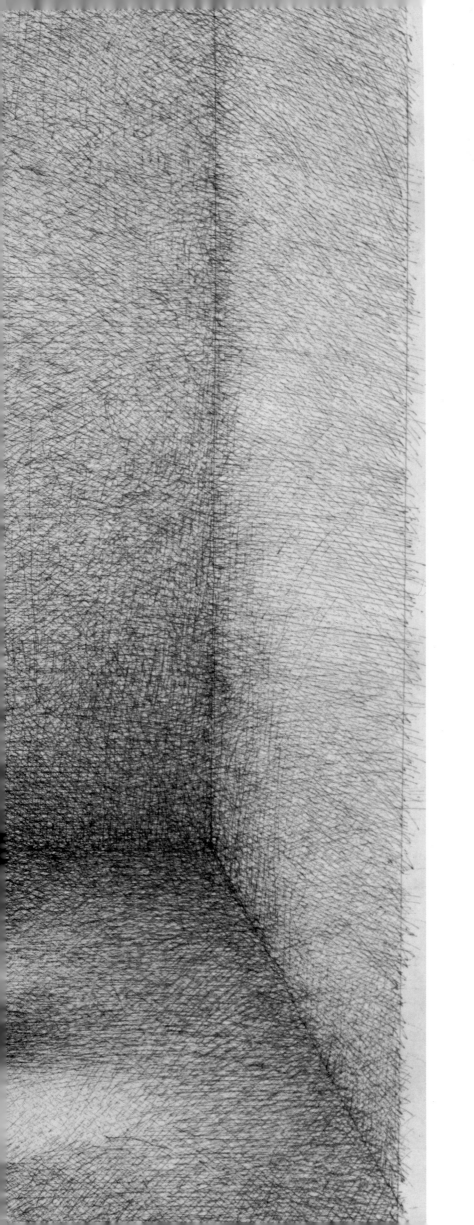

The Young Lawyer's Doom (detail)/
Das Verhängnis des jungen Anwalts (Detail)/
Le Sort du jeune avocat (détail), 1979
India ink on paper

Man without Face (detail)/
Mann ohne Gesicht (Detail)/
Homme sans visage (détail), 1985
India ink on paper

Two American Doctors Teasing a Patient (detail)/
*Zwei amerikanische Ärzte erlauben sich einen
Scherz mit einer Patientin* (Detail)/*Deux médecins
américains se permettant de plaisanter avec une
patiente* (détail), 1977
India ink on paper

Our Duck Bishop/Der Entenbischof/Duck evêque, 1977
India ink on paper, 21³⁄₅ × 29½ inches, 55 × 75 cm
Private Collection, Austria   126

*Two American Doctors Teasing a Patient/Zwei amerikanische Ärzte erlauben sich einen Scherz mit einer
Patientin/Deux médecins américains se permettant de plaisanter avec une patiente,* 1977
India ink on paper, 29½ × 21⅗ inches, 75 × 55 cm, Private Collection, Austria

Kiss of Judas I (detail)/*Judaskuss I* (Detail)/ ▷
Le Baiser de Judas I (détail), 1985
India ink on paper

Kiss of Judas II/Judaskuss II/Le Baiser de Judas II, 1985
Colored pencil on paper, 35 × 24⅘ inches, 89 × 63 cm
Courtesy Klaus Kiefer Gallery, Essen

In addition to sketches of ballet-dancing hares, booted cats, and strangled and stuffed ducks, there are studies or imaginative drawings of the heads of ill-treated children, whose mouths are grotesquely disfigured by braces and pink-colored scars. The grimaces on these mocking distorted faces signalize disobedience, opposition and turmoil, as well as a kind of childlike autonomy in the depraved world of adults. The grin found on the faces of the ill-treated children, a grotesque picture puzzle which includes both the martyrdom and subversion of mankind, is Helnwein's invention. It is manifested in the metamorphic images of injured bodies. It is an obsessive pattern which is repeated in Helnwein's pictoral representation of the world and in his staged artistic actions, serving as a metaphor for the invulnerability and invincibility deeply seated in man.

Neben Skizzen von Ballett tanzenden Hasen und gestiefelten Katzen, strangulierten und gestopften Enten finden sich Studien oder eher Wunschzeichnungen zu malträtierten Kinderköpfen, deren Münder durch Spangen und rosige Narben grauenhaft entstellt sind, aber gleichzeitig durch ihre höhnischen, Fratzen schneidenden Grimassen Ungehorsam, Widerstand, Aufruhr, so etwas wie kindliche Autonomie in der depravierten Erwachsenenwelt signalisieren. Das Feixen des malträtierten Kindes, ein groteskes Vexierbild, in das Märtyrertum und Subversion der Menschenkreatur gleichermaßen eingeflossen sind, ist ganz allein Helnweins Erfindung. Sie offenbart sich in den vielen Metamorphosen des Phantasmas vom versehrten Körper als obsessives Grundmuster seiner Bildwelt und aktionistischen Darstellungen, als Metapher einer im innersten des Menschen vorhandenen Unverletzlichkeit und Unbesiegbarkeit.

Aux croquis représentant des lièvres dansant le ballet, des chats bottés et des canards gavés et étranglés, s'ajoutent des études ou des dessins imaginés montrant des têtes d'enfants maltraités à la bouche grotesquement déformée par des prothèses et des cicatrices roses. Les grimaces sur ces visages narquois et défigurés expriment la désobéissance, l'opposition et le trouble ainsi qu'une sorte d'individualité enfantine dans le monde dépravé des adultes. Helnwein invente ce large sourire se dessinant sur les visages d'enfants maltraités, grotesque énigme en image contenant à la fois la notion de martyr et de subversion de l'humanité. Cela se manifeste dans les images métaphoriques de corps blessés. C'est un motif obsessionnel qui se répète dans les représentations picturales du monde vu par Helnwein et dans les actions qu'il met en scène pour symboliser les sentiments d'invulnérabilité et d'invincibilité profondément ancrées dans l'homme.

Peter Gorsen

BLUTENDE KNABEN

Bloody Boys/Blutende Knaben/Garçons ensanglantés, 1987
Colored pencil, 35 × 24⅘ inches, 89 × 63 cm
Private Collection, Vienna

The Original Sin/Die Erbsünde/Le Péché originel, 1987
Colored pencil on paper, 34¼ × 23⅕ inches, 87 × 59 cm
Private Collection, Germany

The Temptation/Die Versuchung/La Tentation, 1985
Colored pencil on paper, 35 × 24⅘ inches, 89 × 63 cm
H. R. Giger, Zürich

135

Triumph of Science (detail)/*Triumph der Wissenschaft* (Detail)/ ▷
Triomphe de la science (détail), 1985
Colored pencil on paper

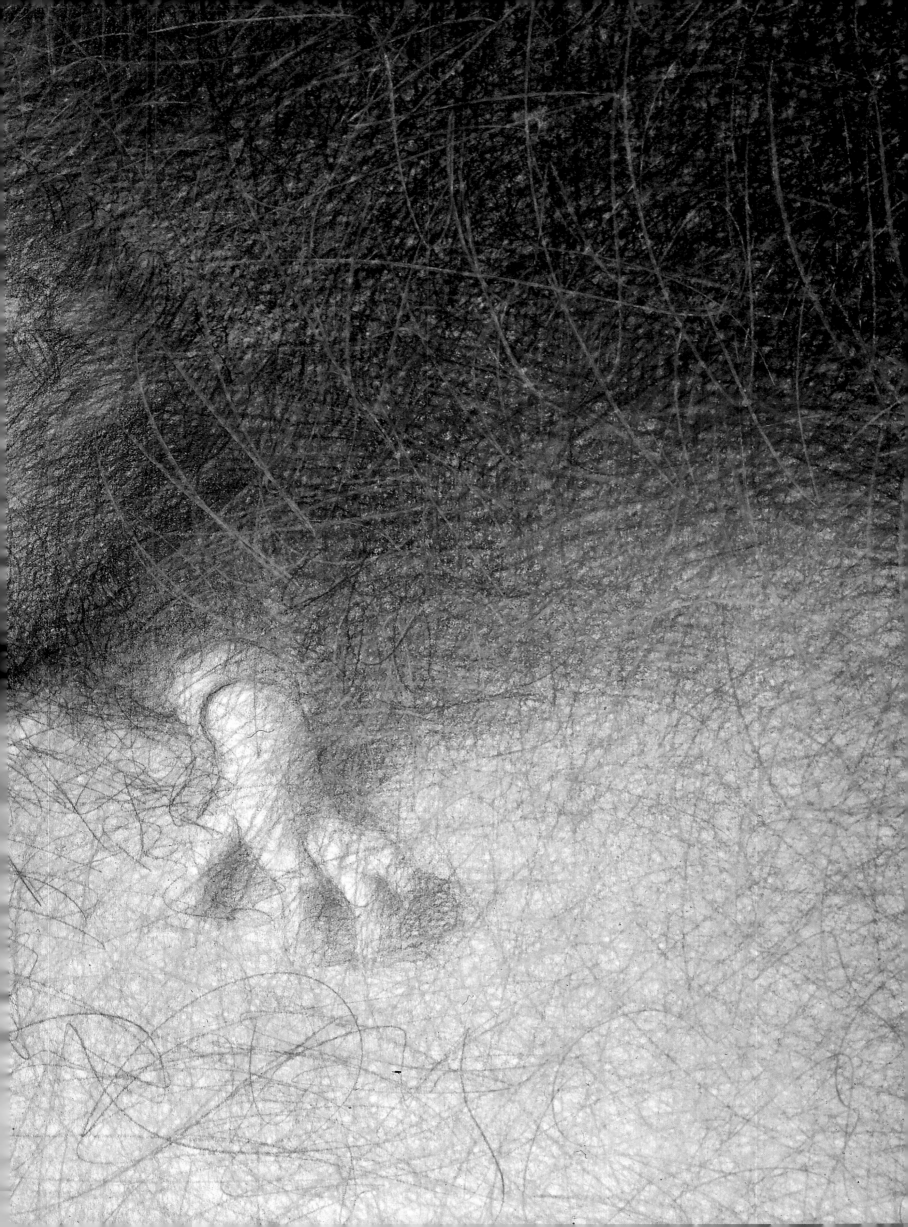

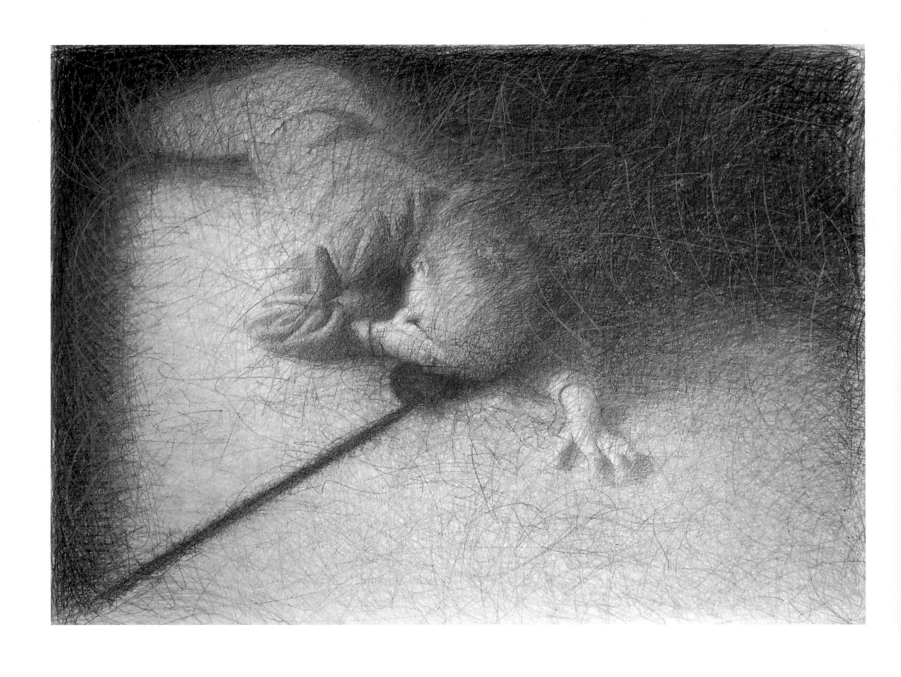

Triumph of Science/Triumph der Wissenschaft/Triomphe de la science, 1985
Colored pencil on paper, 23³⁄₅ × 33⁴⁄₅ inches, 60 × 86 cm
Peter Gorsen, Vienna

◁   Scene from the TV film "Helnwein", directed by Peter Hajek/Szene aus dem Fernsehfilm »Helnwein«,
Regie: Peter Hajek/Scène du film télévisé « Helnwein », réalisé par Peter Hajek, ORF, Vienna, 1984

Immaculate Conception/Unbefleckte Empfängnis/L'Immaculée conception, 1985
Colored pencil on paper, 3⅛½×23⅗ inches, 80×60 cm

Private Collection, Munich

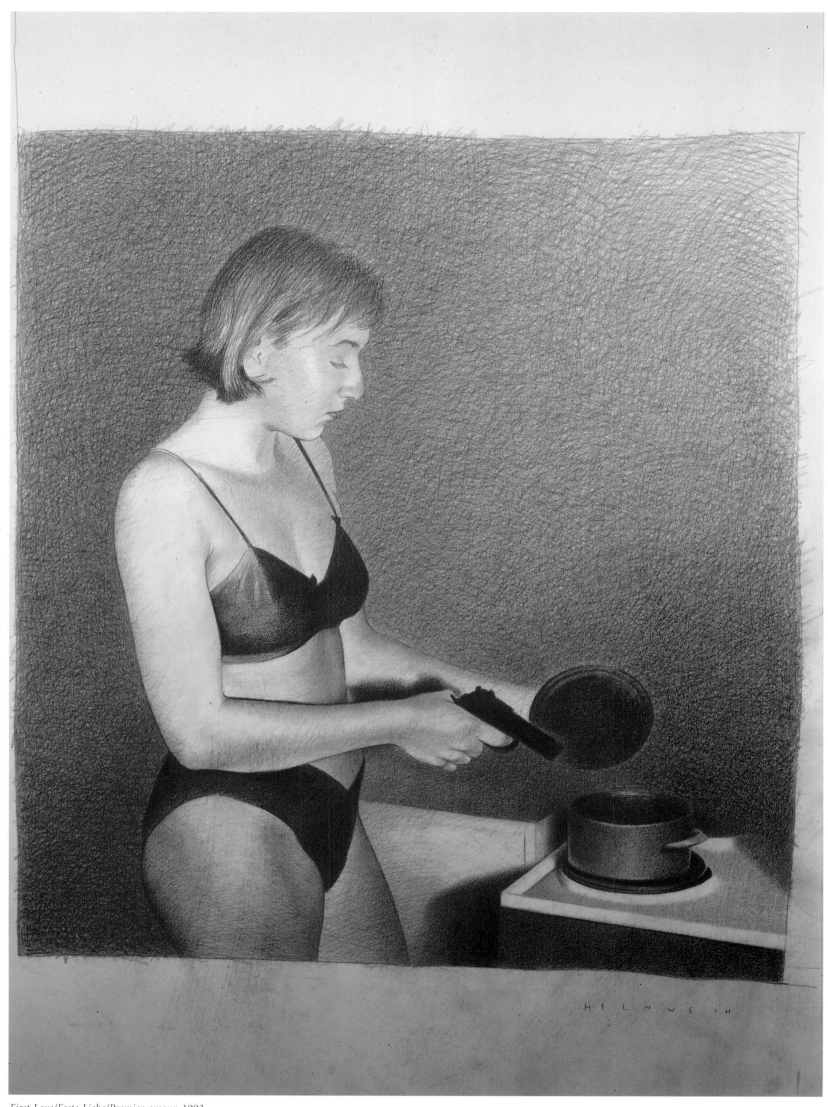

First Love/Erste Liebe/Premier amour, 1993
Colored pencil on paper, 27½ × 24 inches, 70 × 61 cm
Collection of the Artist

142

The Misfortune/Das Malheur/Le Malheur, 1987
Colored pencil on paper, 27⅕ × 24⅘ inches, 69 × 63 cm
Private Collection, Germany

The Christening Present II (Mein Herz ist klein)/Das Patengeschenk II/Le Cadeau de baptême II, 1993
Colored pencil on paper, 29 × 23⅕ inches, 74 × 59 cm
Private Collection, Cologne

The Doubting Thomas/Der ungläubige Thomas/Thomas l'incrédule, 1993
Colored pencil on paper, 32 × 23⅗ inches, 81 × 60 cm
Peter Grebner, Vienna

Untitled/Ohne Titel/Sans titre, 1993
Colored pencil on paper, 32 × 23⅗ inches, 81 × 59 cm
Peter Grebner, Vienna   146

AFTER THE LOST CARAVAGGIO - THE FAINTING MAGDALENE   HELNWEIN '93

Fainting Magdalene (after the lost Caravaggio painting)/Die ohnmächtig werdende Magdalena (nach dem verlorenen Caravaggio-Bild)/La Défaillance de sainte Madeleine (d'après le tableau perdu du Caravage), 1993
Colored pencil on paper, 30⅗ × 23⅕ inches, 78 × 59 cm, Courtesy Klaus Kiefer Gallery, Essen

The Temptation of San Antonio/Die Versuchung des San Antonio/La Tentation de Saint Antoine, 1993
Colored pencil on paper, 29 × 22½ inches, 74 × 57 cm
Private Collection, Germany

Untitled (after Bronzino) (detail)/*Ohne Titel (nach Bronzino)*
(Detail)/*Sans titre (d'après Bronzino)* (détail), 1993
Colored pencil on paper

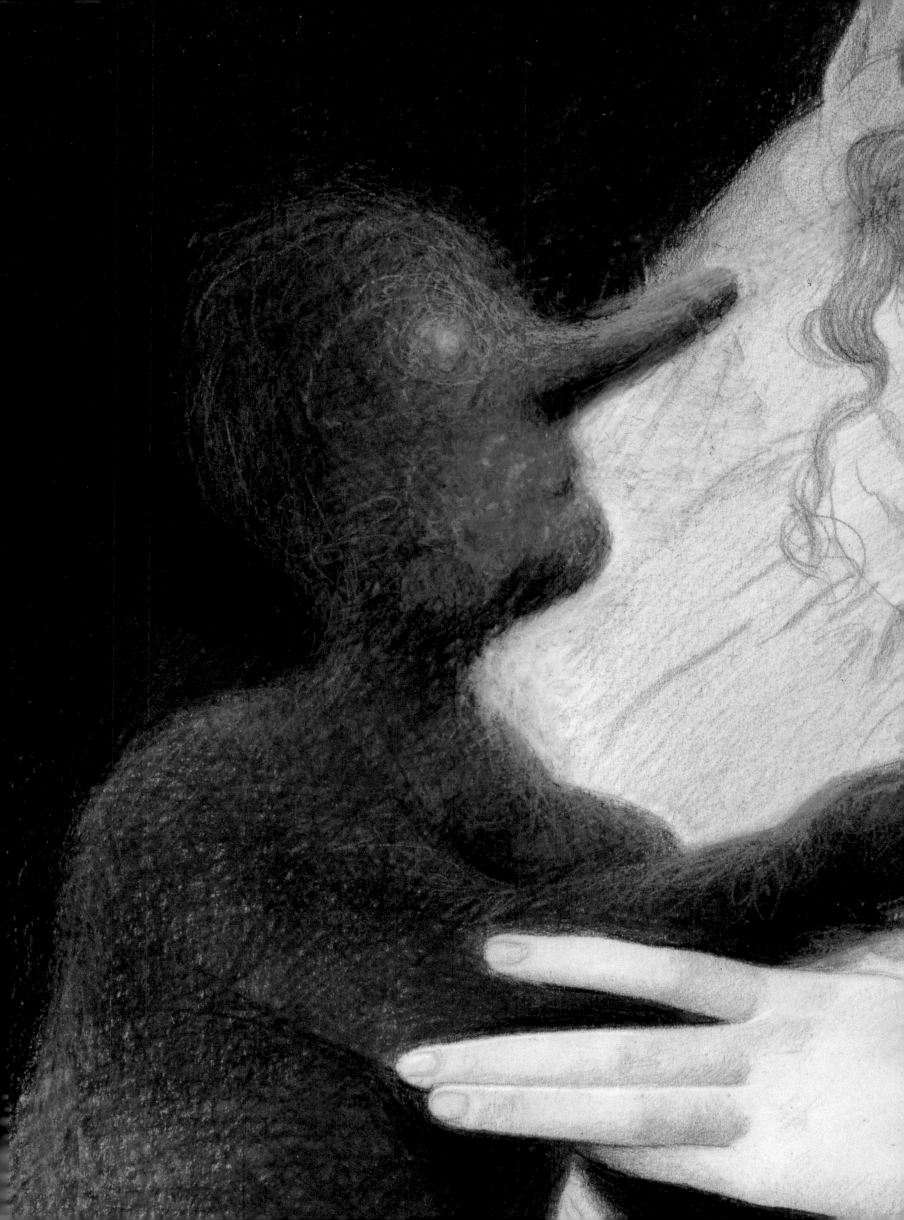

Untitled (after Bronzino)/Ohne Titel (nach Bronzino)/Sans titre (d'après Bronzino), 1993
Colored pencil on paper, 34³⁄₅ × 24²⁄₅ inches, 88 × 62 cm
Private Collection, Germany

The Disaster/Die Katastrophe/La Catastrophe, 1993
Colored pencil on paper, 34³⁄₅ × 24²⁄₅ inches, 88 × 62 cm
Martin Muller, San Francisco

152

The Temptation of Joseph Beuys/Die Versuchung des Joseph Beuys/La Tentation de Joseph Beuys, 1993
Colored pencil on paper, 27½ × 22⅖ inches, 70 × 57 cm
Courtesy Modernism Gallery, San Francisco

Self-Portrait/Selbstporträt/Autoportrait, 1993
Colored pencil on paper, 29½ × 20⅘ inches, 75 × 53 cm
Fine Arts Museums of San Francisco, Achenbach Foundation for Graphic Arts

Self-Portrait with Cyril I/Selbstporträt mit Cyril I/Autoportrait avec Cyril I, 1993
Colored pencil on paper, 22⅔ × 20½ inches, 57 × 52 cm
Private Collection, Germany

155

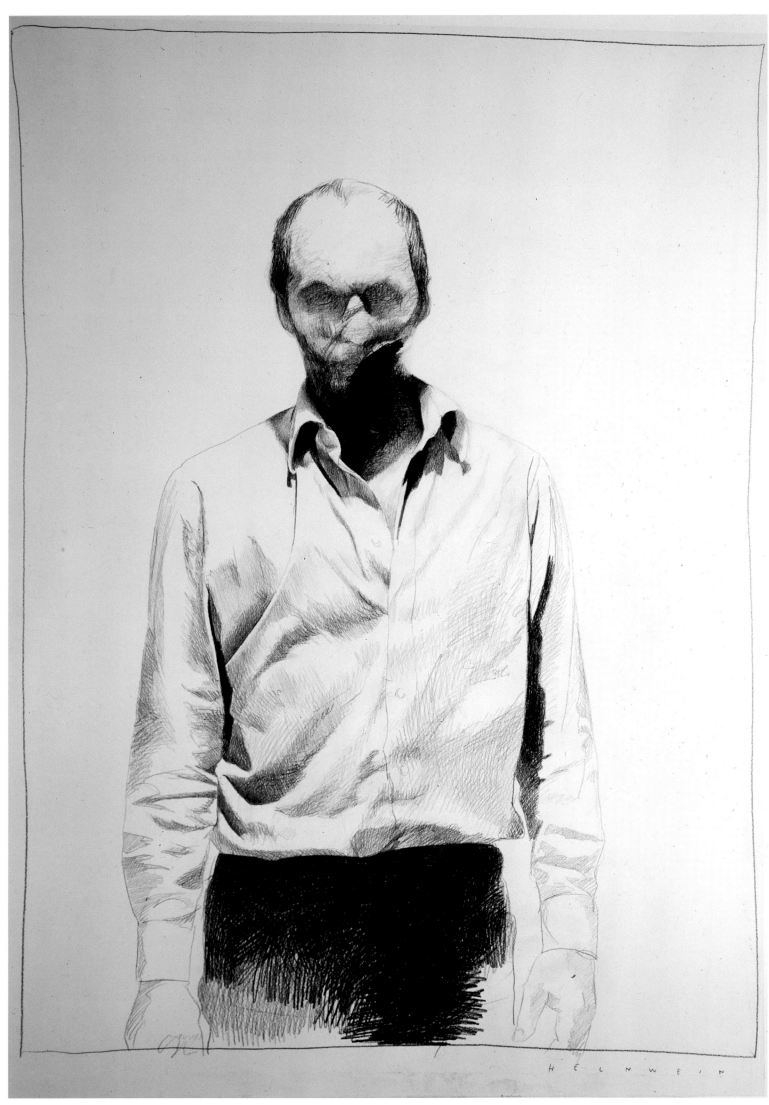

White Lie/Die Notlüge/Le Mensonge obligé, 1993
Colored pencil on paper, 33⅘ × 24⅖ inches, 86 × 62 cm
Courtesy Modernism Gallery, San Francisco   156

Peace/Friede/Paix, 1993
Colored pencil on paper, 33 × 24⅖ inches, 84 × 62 cm

Fred Poe, Little Rock, Arkansas

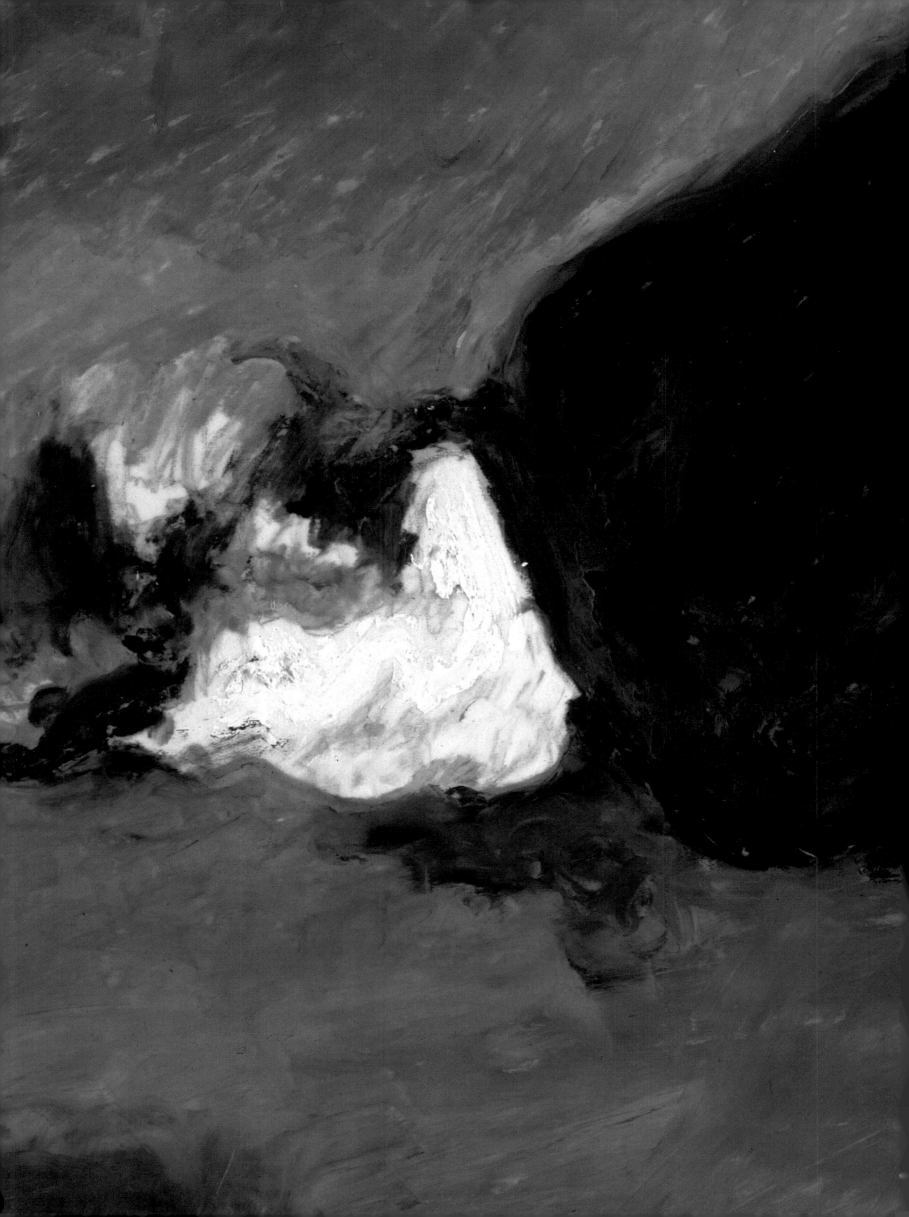

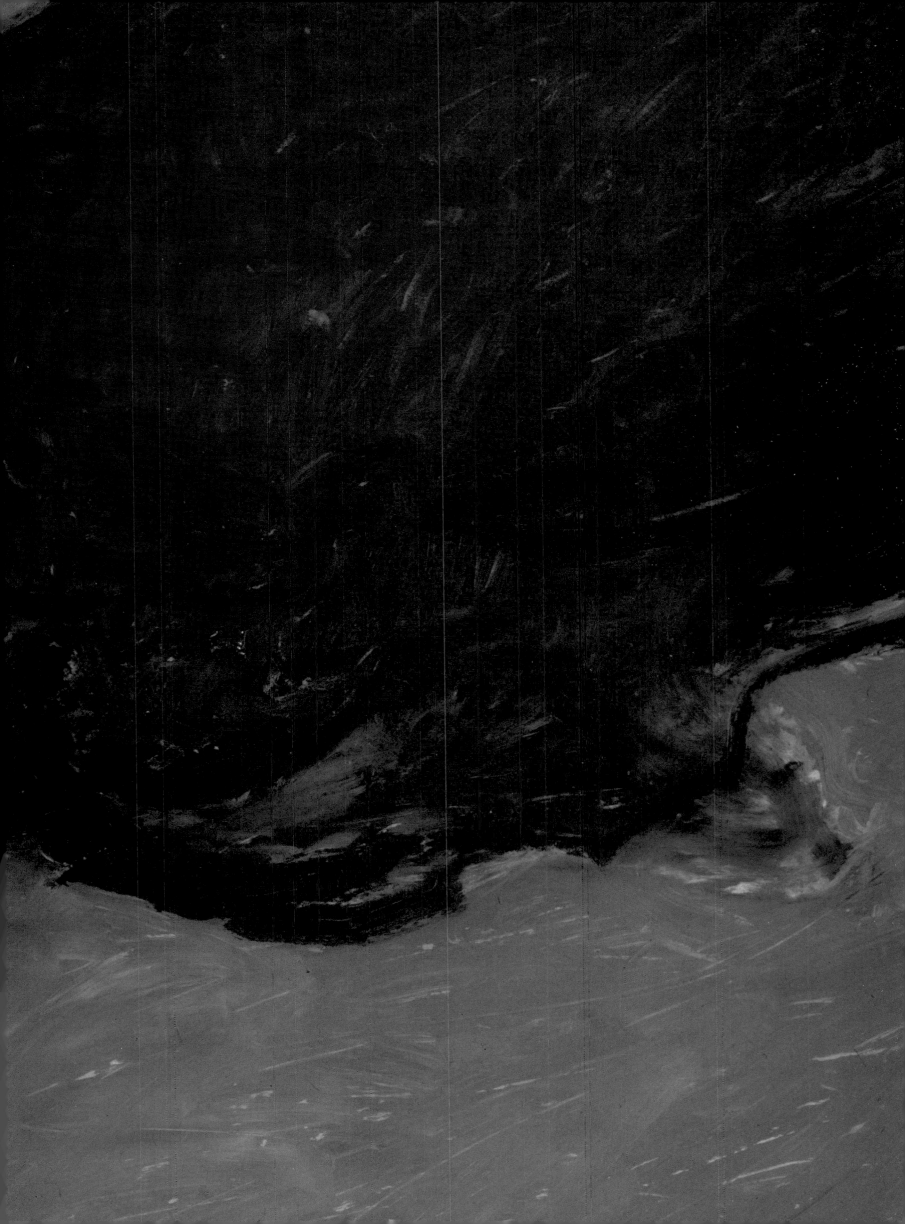

Modern Sleep I/Sommeil moderne I, 1989
Oil and pastel on paper, 35²/₅ × 23³/₅ inches, 90 × 60 cm
Kurt and Veronika Fliegerbauer, Germany

Modern Sleep II/Sommeil moderne II, 1989
Oil and pastel on paper, 35²⁄₅ × 23³⁄₅ inches, 90 × 60 cm
Kurt and Veronika Fliegenbauer, Germany

Antonin Artaud, 1990
Mixed media on canvas, 65⅘ × 51½ inches, 167 × 131 cm
Pfalzgalerie Museum, Kaiserslautern

162

Antonin Artaud, 1989
Oil and pastel on paper, 35⅖ × 23⅗ inches, 90 × 60 cm
Private Collection, Germany

The Death of Pinocchio/Der Tod des Pinocchio/La Mort de Pinocchio, 1988
Oil and pastel on paper, 19²/₃ × 24²/₅ inches, 49 × 62 cm
Wolfgang Schulz, Essen

God in Panic/Gott in Panik/Dieu pris de panic, 1989
Oil and pastel on paper, 35²⁄₅ × 23³⁄₅ inches, 90 × 60 cm

Courtesy Klaus Kiefer Gallery, Essen

Burnt Angel/Verbrannter Engel/Ange brûlé, 1989
Oil and pastel on paper, 35²⁄₅ × 23³⁄₅ inches, 90 × 60 cm
Private Collection, Germany

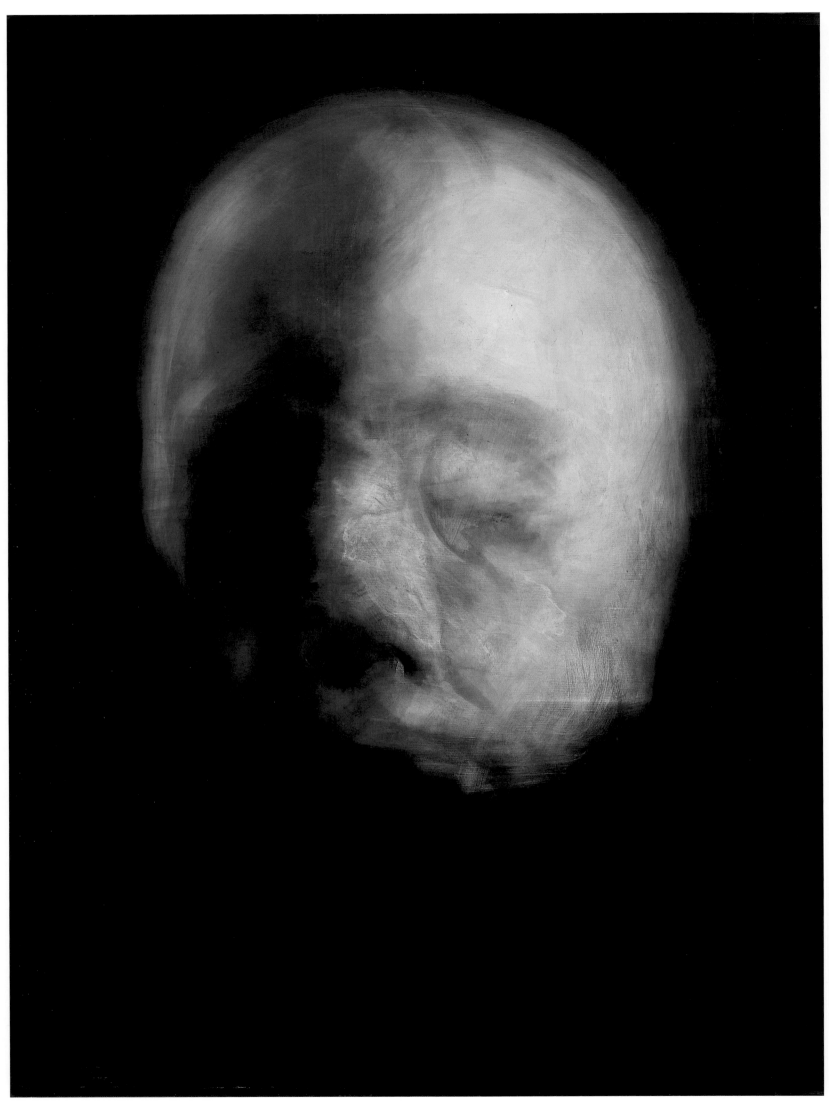

Ice-Man/Eismensch/Homme de glace, 1991
Mixed media on canvas, 76 × 59 inches, 192 × 150 cm
Kurt and Veronika Fliegerbauer, Germany

170

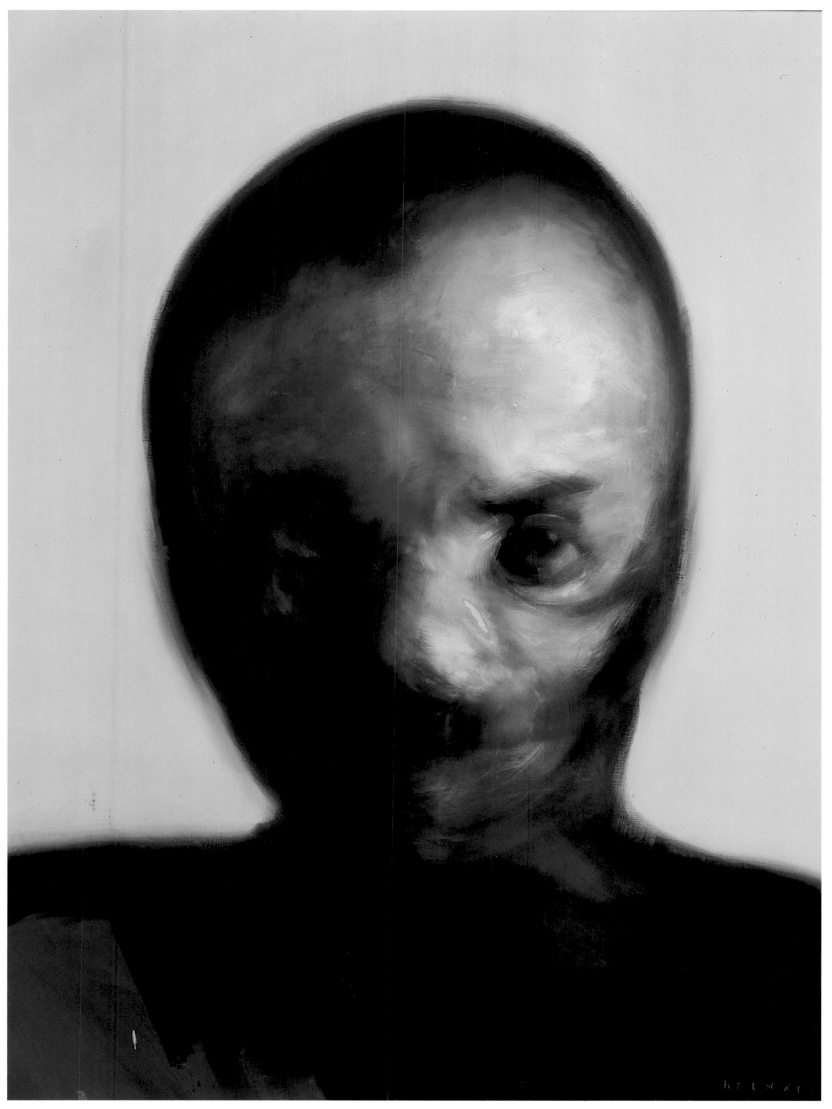

Fire-Man/Feuermensch/Homme de feu, 1991
Mixed media on canvas, 76 × 59 inches, 192 × 150 cm

Kurt and Veronika Fliegerbauer, Germany

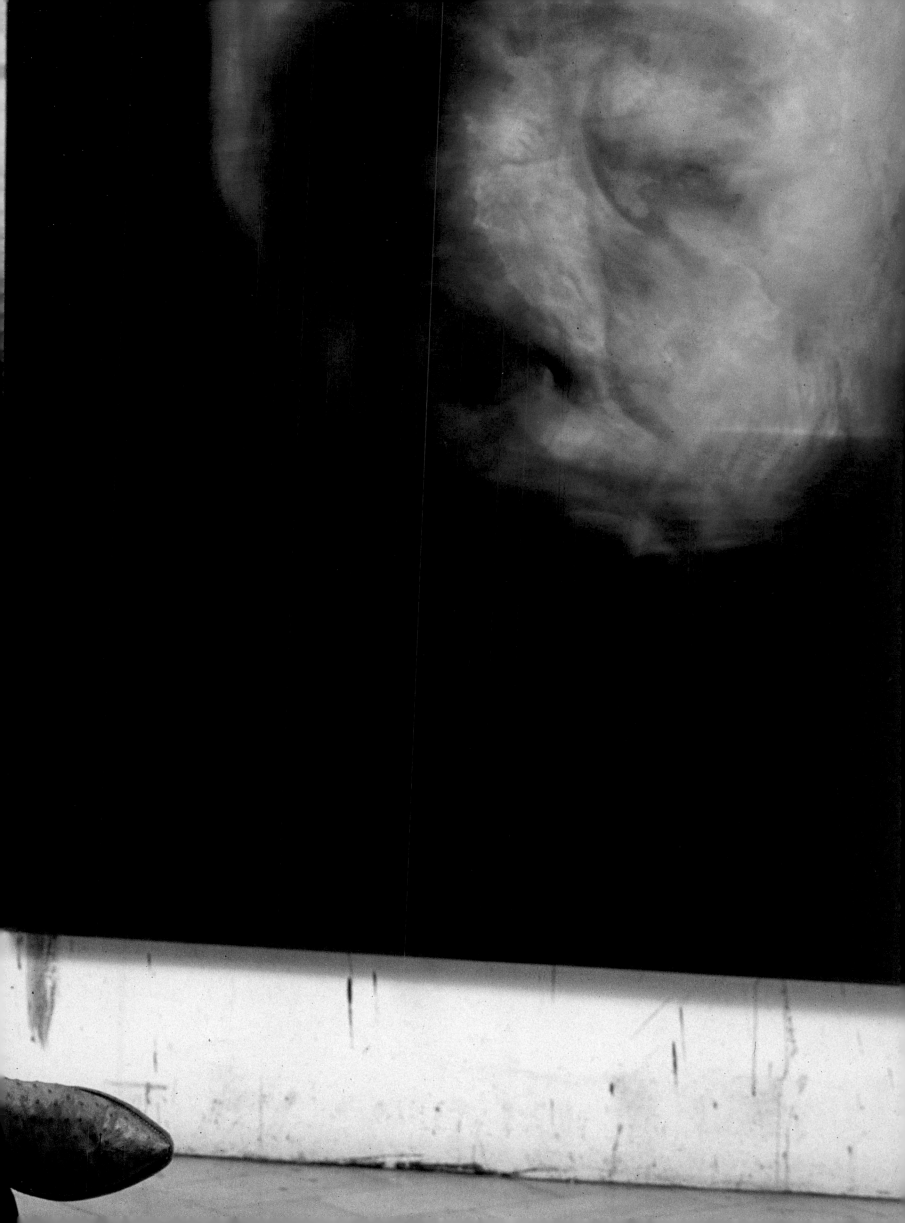

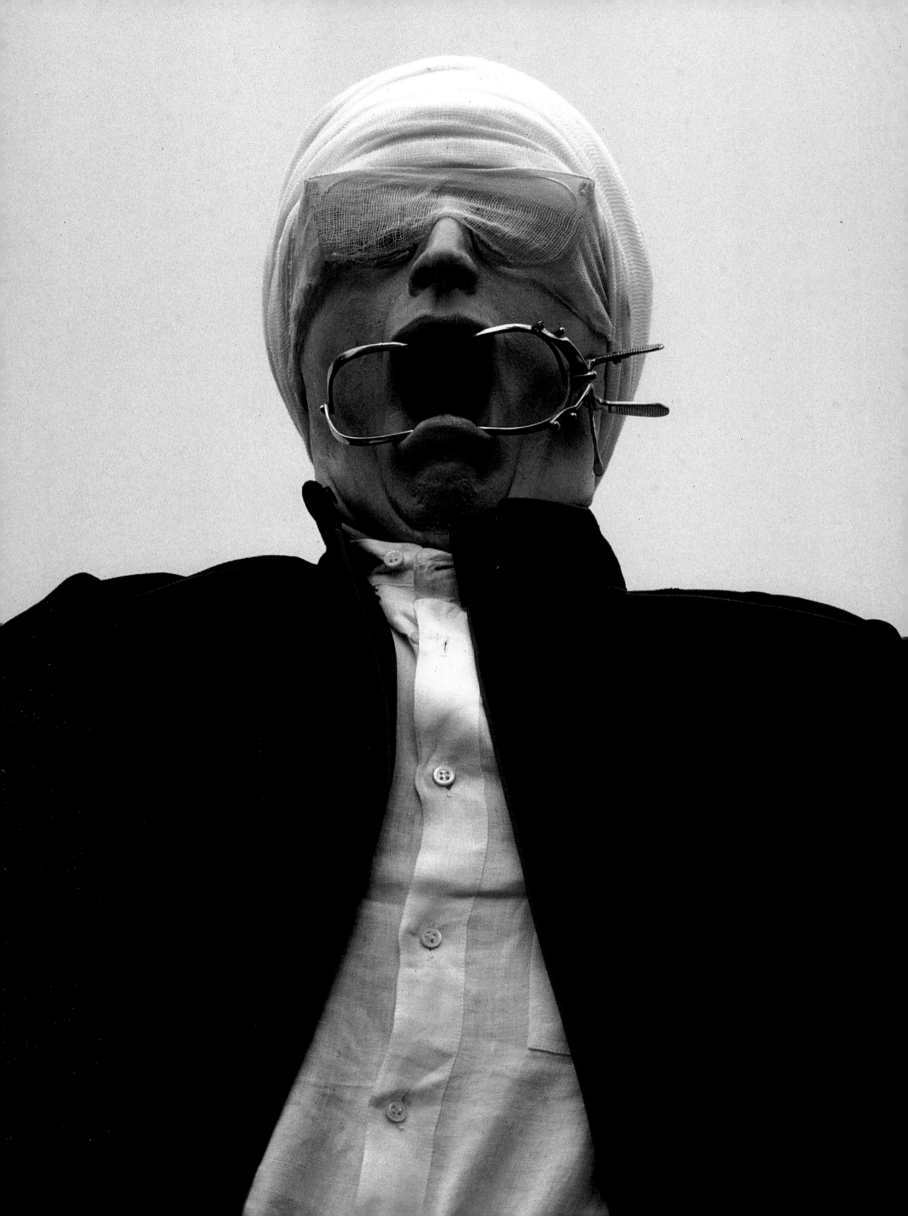

The Subversive Power of Art
Die Subversive Kraft der Kunst
Le Pouvoir Subversif de l'Art

Gottfried Helnwein –

A Concept Artist before the Turn of the Millennium

Ein Konzeptkünstler vor der Jahrtausendwende

Un Artiste Conceptuel à l'Orée du Siècle Nouveau

Klaus Honnef

In the light of a cultural criticism which believes that the world is on its way to a reality of total manipulation and simulation, promoted with all the force of an agenda by powerful media systems, the task falling to art is of central importance. It embodies, as it were, the human factor. Given the barrage of simulated and virtual images also to be found in art, the claim to show the world "as it is", an aspiration already pursued by emperor Frederick II of Staufen in his famous bird book, and equally important for seventeenth century Dutch painters and for empirical sociology two centuries later, seems fairly presumptuous. But art will only fulfil its task – should it still be willing to set itself any – if it is able to break the power of the systems and to lift the spell which their agendas are casting over people, causing their reactions to move in a perpetual cycle of virtual behavior, as analyzed by the media philosopher Vilém Flusser.[1, 2] Art must do without the means of physical violence, and the means of rhetoric are fuelling the imagery of the mass media. But artists are not left helpless. For they command the dangerous weapon of subversion. Handled with intelligence, it turns into the stone used by David, capable of bringing down

Im Lichte jener kulturkritischen Anschauung, die die Welt auf dem Wege zu einer Realität totaler Manipulation und Simulation sieht, befördert durch mächtige Medien-Apparate mit einem programmierenden Effekt, fällt der Kunst eine zentrale Aufgabe zu. Sie verkörpert gleichsam den verbleibenden menschlichen Faktor. Dem Anspruch, die Welt zu zeigen, »wie sie ist«, wollte schon der Stauferkaiser Friedrich II. in seinem berühmten Vogelbuch gerecht werden, ebenso wie die niederländischen Maler des 17. Jahrhunderts und die empirische Soziologie zwei Jahrhunderte später, und er erscheint unter dem Ansturm simulierter und virtueller Bilder auch in der Kunst ziemlich vermessen. Doch ihre Aufgabe – so sie sich noch eine zumuten will – erfüllt die Kunst nur, wenn es ihr gelingt, die Macht der Apparate zu brechen und den Bann aufzuheben, den ihre Programme auf die Menschen ausüben mit der Konsequenz, daß sich deren Reaktionen beständig im Kreislauf virtuellen Verhaltens bewegen, wie es der Medienphilosoph Vilém Flusser analysierte[1,2]. Die Kunst muß ohne physische Gewalt auskommen und die Rhetorik befeuert die Bilderwelt der Massenmedien. Chancenlos sind die Künstler aber dennoch nicht, denn ihnen steht die gefährliche Waffe der Subversion

D'après les critiques culturelles qui nous imaginent en chemin vers un monde où la manipulation et la simulation seront totales et développés d'après de rigoureux programmes par de puissants systèmes médiatiques, une tâche cruciale incombe à l'art. Il incarne, pour ainsi dire, le facteur humain. Or le désir de montrer le monde « tel qu'il est », qui se manifestait déjà chez Frédéric II, empereur de la dynastie des Staufer dans son célèbre livre sur les oiseaux, puis chez les peintres hollandais du 17e siècle et enfin dans la sociologie empirique, deux siècles plus tard, est plutôt impertinent, compte tenu de l'afflux d'images simulées et virtuelles que l'on trouve aussi en art. S'il s'assigne néanmoins une mission, l'art ne l'accomplira que s'il réussit à anéantir le pouvoir des systèmes et à rompre le sort que leurs programmes ont jeté sur les hommes, programmes qui, selon l'analyse du philosophe Vilém Flusser, les conduisent à se déplacer dans un cycle perpétuel de comportements virtuels[1,2]. L'art doit se passer de la violence physique et la rhétorique alimente les images des médias. Les artistes ne sont pas désarmés pour autant, puisqu'ils possèdent une arme dangereuse, la subversion. Maniée avec intelligence, elle devient la fronde de David qui provoque la

the Goliath of the world of systems. It was not by accident that in the second half of the twentieth century Joseph Beuys and Andy Warhol became key figures of art, forming a bridge between a gradually fading modernity and the emerging, as yet formless continent of the new. Beuys' universal world view, his missionary zeal, which did not shrink from the risks of life, the openness of his artistic works and his use of very simple materials were bound to challenge a world of systems with its one-dimensional models of explanation. Yet his artistic concept was motivated less by philosophy than by pragmatism. For he not only embraced traditional artistic techniques and disciplines like painting, sculpture and graphics, but included the whole spectrum of creative activity, no matter where it originated. There lived on in his œuvre the idea of an artistic concept where a work of art cannot be pressed into specific criteria, categories or forms. Beuys confronted the superficial utilitarianism of a vision guided by systems with the image of a richly interwoven and intertwined world. Warhol, on the other hand, played the systems game quite deliberately. Rather than undermining them, ·he forced their mechanisms to breaking point. True to this principle, he reversed the status of appearance and reality in his work. Even the horrific attempt on his life by a radical feminist turned into a spectacular – albeit involuntary – staging for him and his "factory". Is it sheer coincidence that Gottfried Helnwein, the Austrian artist, created a portrait of both the German and the American? Coincidence, that he captured Warhol as a disturbing spectre on photograph, but painted Beuys? And that he then photographed the painted portrait of Beuys in the hands of Arno Breker, Adolf Hitler's favourite sculptor? There are weighty reasons for considering Helnwein the legitimate heir to Beuys and Warhol.

On the one hand, his artistic practice participates in ritual, employing ritual

zur Verfügung. Intelligent gehandhabt, wird sie zum Stein Davids, der den Goliath der Apparate-Welt zu Fall bringen kann. Nicht von ungefähr avancierten Beuys und Warhol zu den Schlüsselgestalten der Kunst in der zweiten Hälfte des 20. Jahrhunderts, jener Kunst, die eine Brücke schlägt zwischen der allmählich verblassenden Moderne und dem noch konturlosen heraufdämmernden Kontinent des Neuen. Die universelle Weltsicht des Deutschen, sein missionarischer Eifer, der kein Lebensrisiko scheute, die Offenheit seiner künstlerischen Arbeiten sowie der Gebrauch einfachster Materialien mußte eine Welt der Apparate mit ihren eindimensionalen Erklärungsmodellen zwangsläufig herausfordern. Dabei war sein Kunstbegriff weniger philosophisch als pragmatisch motiviert, denn er umfaßte nicht nur die traditionellen künstlerischen Techniken und Disziplinen wie Malerei, Skulptur und Grafik, sondern schloß sämtliche schöpferischen Tätigkeiten ein, welcher Provenienz auch immer. In seinem Werk lebte die Idee einer künstlerischen Auffassung fort, wonach sich ein Kunstwerk nicht auf bestimmte Kriterien, Kategorien und Erscheinungsformen festlegen läßt. Den oberflächlichen Utilitarismus einer apparategesteuerten Vision konfrontierte Beuys mit der Imagination einer vielfältig verwobenen und verflochtenen Welt. Demgegenüber spielte Warhol das Spiel der Apparate ganz bewußt. Anstatt sie zu unterminieren, forcierte er ihr Getriebe bis zur Schmerzgrenze. Konsequent vertauschte er in seinem Werk den Status von Schein und Sein. Selbst der gräßliche Anschlag auf sein Leben durch eine radikale Feministin geriet ihm und seiner »Factory« zur spektakulären – wenn auch unfreiwilligen – Inszenierung. Ist es purer Zufall, daß der Österreicher Helnwein von dem Deutschen und dem Amerikaner ein Porträt entworfen hat? Zufall, daß er Warhol als erschreckendes Schattengespenst fotografisch fixiert und Beuys gemalt hat? Darüber hinaus das gemalte Porträt von Beuys wieder fotografiert hat, in den Händen von Arno

chute de ce Goliath qu'est l'univers des systèmes. Ce n'est pas un hasard si Joseph Beuys et Andy Warhol sont devenus les figures-clés de l'art de la seconde moitié du 20e siècle, de cet art qui tend une passerelle entre les modernes qui perdent peu à peu leur éclat, et un nouveau continent aux contours encore flous qui pointe à l'horizon. La vision universelle de Beuys, son ardeur de missionnaire, lui qui ne craignait pas de risquer sa vie, la franchise de son œuvre artistique, ainsi que sa prédilection pour les matériaux simples faisaient obligatoirement figure de défi à l'égard de systèmes dont les modèles explicatifs se réduisent à une seule dimension. Toutefois, sa conception artistique était moins motivée par la philosophie que par le pragmatisme, car elle faisait appel non seulement aux techniques et disciplines artistiques traditionnelles telles que la peinture, la sculpture et le dessin, mais englobait aussi toutes les activités créatives, quelles que soient leurs origines. Dans son œuvre perdurait l'idée d'une conception artistique qui refusait qu'une œuvre d'art ne se définisse en fonction de critères, catégories et apparences donnés. Beuys opposait l'utilitarisme superficiel d'une vision influencée par les systèmes au concept d'un univers fait de réseaux et d'imbrications multiples. A l'inverse, Warhol jouaient consciemment le jeu du système. Au lieu de le saper, il en forçait les rouages jusqu'au point de rupture. Selon ce principe, il inversa le statut de l'apparence et de la réalité dans son œuvre. Même l'horrible attentat à sa vie d'une féministe fanatique devint pour lui – bien qu'involontairement – et pour sa « Factory » une mise en scène spectaculaire. Est-ce un pur hasard si Gottfried Helnwein, l'Autrichien, a fait un portrait de ces deux hommes, de l'Allemand et de l'Américain ? Est-ce un hasard s'il a photographié Warhol sous les traits d'un fantôme inquiétant et s'il a peint Beuys ? Et si de surcroît, il a photographié le portrait peint de Beuys dans les mains d'Arno Breker, le sculpteur

patterns, charging its batteries on it, as it were; this is true in the early works with their conceptual echoes of Viennese Actionism no less than in the almost manic concentration on a few thematic challenges taken up time and again. On the other hand, the artist plays with the entire range of artistic possibilities at his disposal with great virtuosity, using the modern palette they provide, from carefully honed pastels to the ubiquitous magazine title, from the stage set with its powerful effect of spatial arrangements to the installation of photographic images, and it would hardly come as a surprise if one day he were also to turn to the cinema, the royal road of contemporary art. He is fascinated by film anyway, and a connoisseur. But in a time when artistic self-perception is still proclaiming the vanity of all artistic endeavors, Helnwein employs the available instruments not just for his aesthetic goals – he employs them in a very specific way. Beuys, too, was no modern shaman, nor was Warhol a mere media mogul. Helnwein uses these instruments in the spirit of subversion. He undermines the overwhelming magic of the world of images by building some sort of disturbance factor into the reciprocal process between a particular medium of artistic expression and the expectation which is, as it were, programmed by that medium. The disturbance factor consists in an imperceptible shift in the use of the medium's repertoire. His famous title pages for magazines like *Profil*, *Stern* and *Time* do not consist of photographic masters as it might seem at a cursory glance, but of painted images which have been photographically reproduced for printing and are superior to the quality of photographic masters in their optical brilliance. On the other hand, these subtly operating pastels and the peculiar characteristics of their contents cut across the familiar relationship between the work of art and the viewer and break up the conventional automatism of perception

Breker, Adolf Hitlers liebstem Bildhauer? Es spricht viel dafür, daß Helnwein der legitime Erbe von Beuys und Warhol ist.

Einerseits partizipiert seine künstlerische Praxis am Ritual und lädt sich gleichsam daran auf; man findet diese Phänomene in den frühen Werken mit ihren gedanklichen Anklängen an den Wiener Aktionismus sowie der beinahe manischen Konzentration auf wenige, immer wieder aufgegriffene thematische Herausforderungen. Andererseits spielt der Künstler virtuos mit dem gesamten, verfügbaren Instrumentarium künstlerischer Möglichkeiten, nutzt ihre moderne Palette vom penibel ausgefeilten Pastell über den massenhaft verbreiteten Illustrierten-Titel, das Bühnenbild mit seiner raumgestaltenden Wirkungskraft bis zur Installation mit fotografischen Bildern. Es wäre also keineswegs verwunderlich, wenn er sich auch dem Film zuwenden würde, dem Königsweg der zeitgenössischen Kunst. Fasziniert ist er ohnehin vom Film, ein Kenner obendrein. Doch Helnwein nutzt das vorhandene Instrumentarium nicht nur für seine ästhetischen Zwecke in einer Zeit, wo das künstlerische Selbstverständnis nach wie vor die Zwecklosigkeit aller künstlerischen Bemühungen proklamiert, sondern im Geiste der Subversion. Auch Beuys war weder ein moderner Schamane noch Warhol ein bloßer Medien-Mogul. Helnwein unterläuft die überwältigende Magie der Bilderwelt, indem er den reziproken Prozeß zwischen dem jeweiligen Medium einer künstlerischen Äußerung und der Erwartungshaltung, die das jeweilige Medium gewissermaßen programmiert, eine Art Störfaktor einbaut. Der Störfaktor besteht in einer unmerklichen Verschiebung im Umgang mit dem Medienrepertoire. Seine berühmten Titelblätter für Magazine wie *Profil*, *Stern* und *Time* bestehen nicht, wie es bei flüchtigem Hinsehen scheint, aus fotografischen, sondern aus gemalten und für den Druck fotografisch reproduzierten Vorlagen, welche an optischer Brillanz die fotografische Qualität fotografischer Vorlagen über-

favori d'Hitler? Il semble que certaines raisons autorisent à voir en Helnwein l'héritier légitime de Beuys et de Warhol.

D'une part, sa pratique artistique participe du rituel, elle fait appel à des schémas rituels, en tire en quelque sorte son énergie. On retrouve ce phénomène dans ses premières œuvres, dans lesquelles on retrouve certains concepts rappelant l'actionnisme viennois, ainsi qu'une concentration presque obsessionnelle sur quelques défis thématiques qu'il relève de temps à autre. D'autre part, l'artiste jongle avec virtuosité, tirant parti de l'ensemble des possibilités et des outils dont dispose l'art. Il a recours à la palette moderne qu'il lui fournit, des pastels exécutés avec une minutie besogneuse aux titres omniprésents, des illustrés, de la scénographie et l'effet puissant que procure l'aménagement spatial, à l'utilisation d'images photographiques ; nous ne serions d'ailleurs pas surpris si un jour, il se tournait vers le cinéma, la voie royale de l'art contemporain. De toute façon, le cinéma le fascine et qui plus est, l'artiste est un connaisseur en la matière. Pourtant, Helnwein n'emploie pas les outils existants à des seules fins esthétiques, à une époque où l'art, comme dans le passé, prône la futilité de toute démarche artistique – il les utilise d'une manière très spécifique. Beuys n'était pas non plus un chaman moderne, pas plus que Warhol n'était un simple nabab des médias. Helnwein utilise ces outils dans un esprit subversif. Il ébranle la formidable magie du monde des images en créant une sorte de facteur perturbateur dans le mécanisme de réciprocité entre un véhicule particulier de l'expression artistique et l'attente, d'une certaine manière programmée par ce véhicule. Ce facteur perturbateur consiste à passer de façon imperceptible d'un répertoire de véhicule à l'autre. Ses célèbres couvertures pour des revues comme, par exemple, *Profil*, *Stern* et *Time* ne sont pas, comme un coup d'œil rapide pourrait le faire croire, des photographies, mais des peintures photogra-

Self-Portrait/Selbstporträt/Autoportrait, 1970
Photograph

178

Self-Portrait/Selbstporträt/Autoportrait, 1970
Photograph

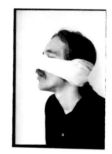

Self-Portrait/Selbstporträt/Autoportrait, 1972
Photograph

Self-Portrait/Selbstporträt/Autoportrait, 1972
Silver print, grattage, 15 × 10¼ inches, 38 × 26 cm

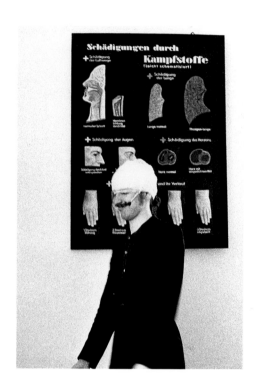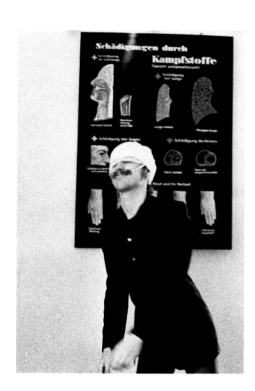

Poison Dance/Gifttanz/Danse de poison, 1972
Photograph

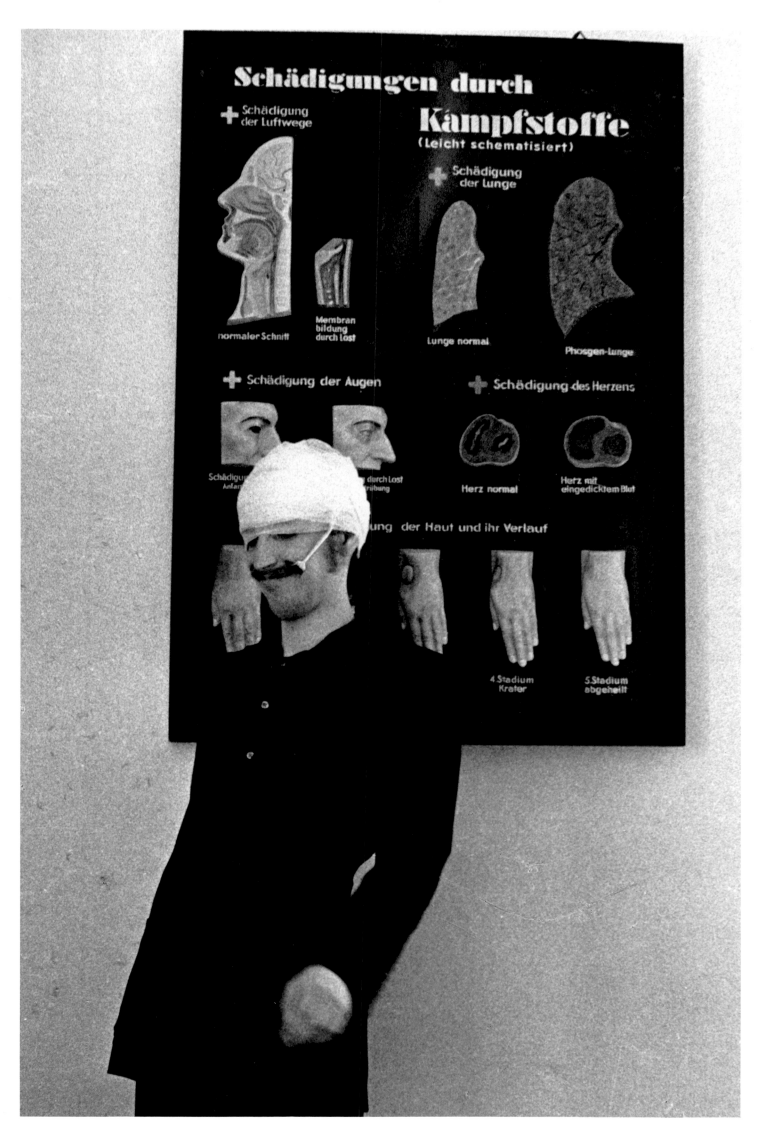

Poison Dance/Gifttanz/Danse de poison, 1972

Photograph

Aktion, Vienna, 1973

◁ *Aktion Always Prepared/Aktion Allzeit bereit/Action Toujours prêt*, Vienna, 1973

Aktion Café Alt Wien, Vienna, 1976

martyr."[5] Intent and coincidence complement each other in his endeavor "to sabotage, to smash, to destroy"[6], for on one occasion a wound resulted from his struggle with the technique of woodcutting or copperplate engraving, the tool had slipped and gone into his hand. But the crucial point was how he exploited the injury for his subversive aims, and therefore the real cause was unimportant. His first artistic action was taken in the same spirit. Tired of stupidly drawing from the nude, he decided in protest against the teaching to make a portrait of Adolf Hitler. The resonance caused by this aesthetic product was surprising. When his tutor saw it, he stormed from the classroom, returned with the school's entire professorial staff – "they looked like big white birds in their flowing coats"[7] – and the director of the institute held a long-winded exculpatory speech, to the amazement of Helnwein's fellow-students, who had not even seen his drawing. Its tenor: Whosoever recalls the accursed times of National Socialism is ruining the reputation of the Experimental Institute for Higher Graphic Education. There was general bewilderment, and the picture was confiscated. "This was the moment when I sensed for the first time: you can change something with aesthetics, you can get things moving in a very subtle way, you can get even the powerful and strong to slide and totter, anything actually if you know the weak points and tap at them ever so gently by aesthetic means"[8] – that is the insight the supposed miscreant distilled from this spectacular episode, presumably still more by intuition at the time. The artist had merely rearranged the coordinates of his teachers' expectation; a deranged result. Helnwein had thrown a stumbling block into the still waters of art, and suddenly there were ripples on its surface.

No doubt the young artist had chanced upon a potential of art which had been largely buried by the lengthy debate on the

Rebellion zu bekunden, schnitt er sich mit Rasierklingen die Hände auf. Obwohl die Gesellschaft nicht zögert, ein Verhalten gegen ihre Normen gewaltsam, bisweilen auch brutal zu unterdrücken, reagiert sie – dies hatte er rasch erkannt – merkwürdig hilflos auf physische Verletzungen und Verwundungen; die seelischen sieht man eben nicht. Helnwein hatte an einen tabuisierten Bezirk gerührt. Statt bestraft zu werden, galt ihm aber jetzt jegliche Fürsorge. »... jemand der verwundet war, war eine Art Märtyrer«[5]. Absicht und Zufall ergänzen sich in seinem Bemühen »zu sabotieren, kaputt zu machen, zu zerstören«[6], denn gelegentlich war die Verletzung auch eine Folge seiner Auseinandersetzung mit der Technik des Holzschnitts oder Kupferstichs, der Stichel war ihm abgerutscht und in die Hand gefahren. Doch wie er die Verletzung für seine subversiven Intentionen einsetzte, war entscheidend, und deshalb spielte ihre wirkliche Ursache keine Rolle. Im gleichen Geist vollzog sich auch seine erste künstlerische Tat. Des stupiden Aktzeichnens müde, hatte er sich aus Protest gegen den Unterricht entschlossen, das Konterfei Hitlers anzufertigen. Die Resonanz auf dieses ästhetische Produkt war überraschend. Sein Lehrer stürmte, als er es erblickte, aus der Klasse, kehrte mit der gesamten Professorenschaft der Schule zurück – »wie große weiße Vögel sahen sie aus in ihren wallenden Arbeitsmänteln«[7], und der Direktor des Instituts hielt zum Erstaunen von Helnweins Kommilitonen, die seine Zeichnung gar nicht gesehen hatten, eine weitschweifige exkulpatorische Rede; deren Tenor war: Den Ruf der Höheren Graphischen Bundeslehr- und Versuchsanstalt ruiniere, wer an die unseligen Zeiten des Nationalsozialismus erinnere. Die Verblüffung war allgemein, und das Blatt wurde beschlagnahmt. »Das war für mich der Moment, wo ich das erste Mal das Gefühl bekommen habe, Du kannst mit Ästhetik etwas verändern, Du kannst auf eine ganz subtile Art und Weise Bewegung hineinbringen, Du kannst auch die Mächtigen und

quelle connerie, de manière à peu près réaliste. Alors seulement, j'ai été admis avec égards »[4]. Mais la routine et l'enseignement ne tardèrent pas à l'ennuyer. En guise de protestation contre une situation ressentie comme « insupportable », mais encore incapable d'exprimer son mécontentement par une rébellion ouverte, il s'entailla les mains avec une lame de rasoir. Bien que la société n'hésite pas à réprimer sévèrement, et même parfois avec brutalité tout comportement déviant de la norme, il constata très vite qu'elle réagissait avec une déconcertante impuissance aux blessures corporelles. Bien sûr, celles de l'âme ne se voient pas. Helnwein avait touché à une zone tabou. Au lieu d'être sanctionné, on prenait désormais soin de lui. « ...une personne blessée était une sorte de martyr »[5]. Intention et hasard se complétaient dans son effort pour « saboter, foutre en l'air, détruire »[6], puisque, une fois, sa blessure avait été la conséquence de sa lutte avec la technique de la gravure sur bois ou sur cuivre, le burin avait dérapé et lui était entré dans la main. Mais la cause réelle de la blessure ne joue aucun rôle car l'aspect décisif réside dans la manière dont il tira profit de cet incident à des fins subversives. Il réalisa son premier acte artistique dans le même esprit. Las des sempiternels dessins de nus, il décida d'esquisser un portrait d'Hitler en signe de protestation contre l'enseignement. L'écho de ce produit esthétique fut surprenant. En voyant le résultat, le professeur se précipita hors de la classe et y revint avec tout le corps enseignant de l'école. « Dans leurs grandes blouses blanches qui virevoltaient, ils ressemblaient à de grands oiseaux blancs »[7]. A la grande surprise d'Helnwein, le directeur de l'institut tint à l'adresse des camarades de classe, qui n'avaient pas vu le dessin, un réquisitoire interminable. Son contenu était en résumé : quiconque rappelle l'époque maudite du national-socialisme nuit à la réputation de l'Institut expérimental d'enseignement supérieur des arts graphiques. La stupéfaction

Self-Portrait with Cyril/Selbstporträt mit Cyril/Autoportrait avec Cyril, 1981
Silver print

SELF-PORTRAITS
SELBSTPORTRÄTS
AUTOPORTRAITS

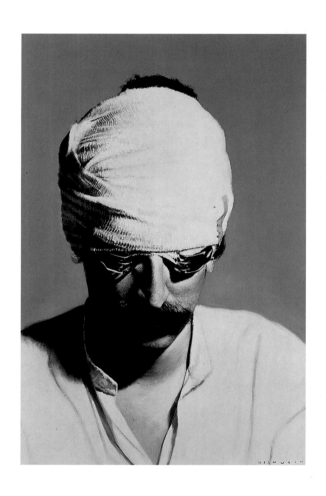

Self-Portrait 27/Selbstporträt 27/Autoportrait 27, 1990
Mixed media on canvas, 72 × 47⅗ inches, 183 × 121 cm
Courtesy Modernism Gallery, San Francisco

◁ *Self-Portrait 1/Selbstporträt 1/Autoportrait 1,* 1977
Watercolor on cardboard, 34⅗ × 24⅖ inches, 88 × 62 cm
Peter Grebner, Vienna

Self-Portrait 29/Selbstporträt 29/Autoportrait 29, 1990
Mixed media on canvas, 82⅗ × 55 inches, 210 × 140 cm
Private Collection, Germany

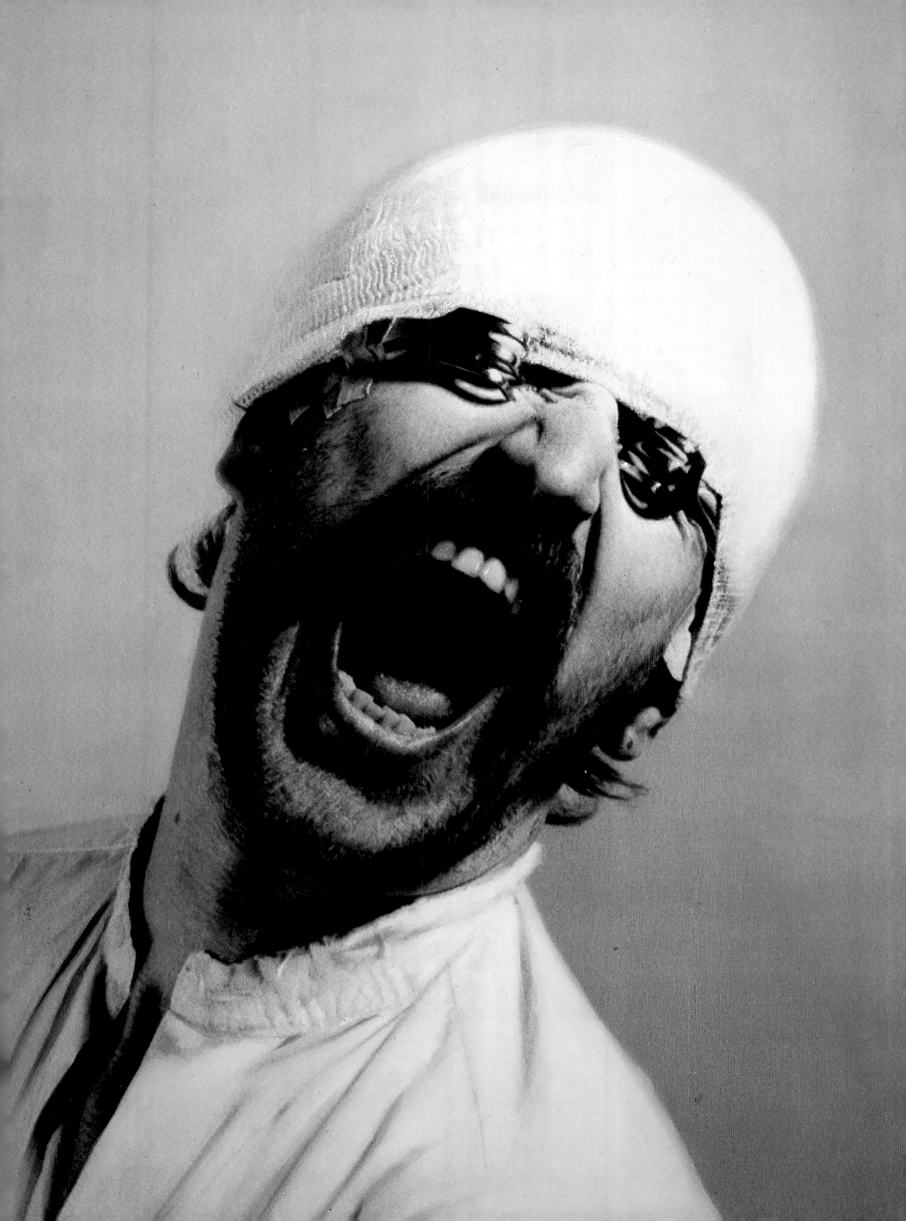

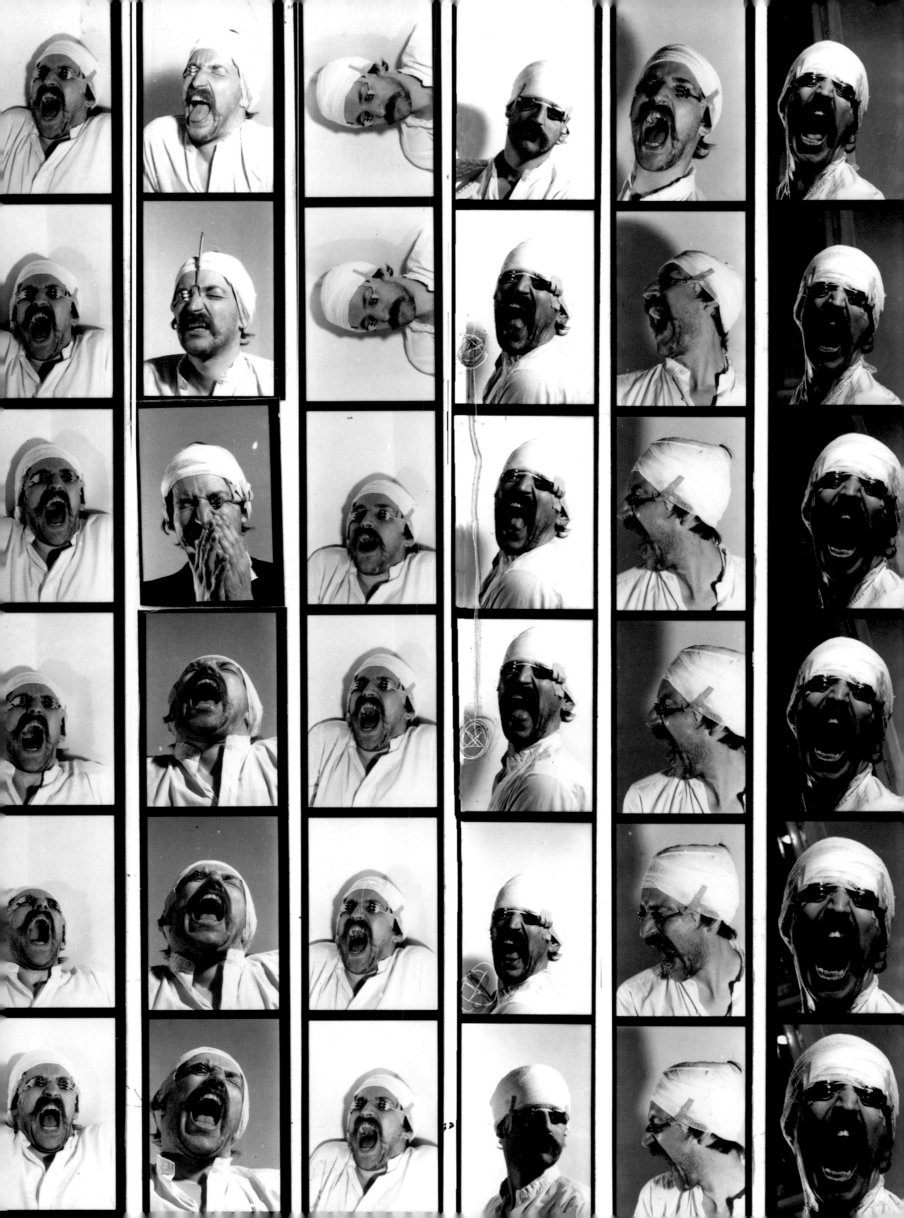

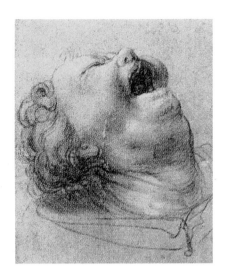
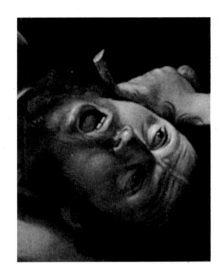

Matthias Grünewald
Crayon drawing, 1520

Caravaggio
Oil on canvas, 1598

Franz Xaver Messerschmidt
Tin, 18th century

autonomy of works of art: the ability to mobilize intense feelings and with the aid of this power to blast free, as it were, human insights and perceptions. In theoretical discussions, the possible potency of art was at best considered as a means to alter individual or collective awareness. There was distrust of feelings; the memory of the devastating consequences of the aestheticization of politics by the Nazis was still alive and was being repressed, and the most advanced version of contemporary art of the time appealed more to the intellect. Helnwein discovered that impassioned reactions were able to answer the intentions of the artistic author if they disclosed certain connections, illuminating them like the lightning in a cathartic thunderstorm. However, the connections might not necessarily produce intellectual progress in those addressed; instead, the viewers served as catalysts and became more or less involuntary actors in his artistic concept. Having graduated from the "Higher Graphic Education", he refined his artistic strategy at the Vienna Academy of Arts, where he found a sympathetic teacher in the painter Rudolf Hausner. Minor and major revolts were an everyday occurrence

Stärkeren – kannst eigentlich alles ins Rutschen und Wanken bringen, wenn Du die Schwachpunkte kennst und mit ästhetischen Mitteln dran tippst, ganz leicht«[8] – destillierte der vermeintliche Übeltäter, damals wohl eher noch intuitiv, als Erkenntnis aus diesem spektakulären Auftritt. Der Künstler hatte lediglich die Koordinaten der Erwartung seiner Lehrer verrückt; ein verrücktes Ergebnis. In das ruhige Gewässer der Kunst hatte Helnwein einen Stein des Anstoßes geworfen, und seine Oberfläche kräuselte sich plötzlich.

Keine Frage, der junge Künstler war auf ein Potential der Kunst gestoßen, das die langwährende Debatte um die Autonomie des Kunstwerks weitgehend verschüttet hatte: das Vermögen, heftige Gefühle zu mobilisieren und mit Hilfe dieser Kraft menschliche Einsichten und Erkenntnisse gewissermaßen freizusprengen. In der theoretischen Diskussion fand die mögliche Wirkungsmacht der Kunst allenfalls Berücksichtigung als Mittel, individuelles oder kollektives Bewußtsein zu verändern. Den Gefühlen mißtraute man, die Erinnerung an die verheerenden Folgen, mit denen die Nationalsozialisten die Politik ästhetisiert hatten, war noch wach und wurde verdrängt,

fut générale, et la feuille de papier confisquée. « Cela a été pour moi le moment où, pour la première fois, j'ai eu le sentiment de pouvoir changer quelque chose par l'esthétique ; je me suis dit, tu peux faire bouger les choses d'une manière très subtile, tu peux aussi tout ébranler, faire trébucher les plus puissants et les plus forts, c'est facile si tu connais leurs points faibles et si tu les touches avec des moyens esthétiques »[8]. Telles étaient à l'époque les conclusions encore intuitives que tirait le prétendu fautif de cette spectaculaire démonstration. L'artiste s'était contenté de réarranger les attentes de ses professeurs ; un résultat plutôt « dérangé ». Dans les eaux calmes de l'art, Helnwein avait lancé une pierre, et soudain, des rides se dessinèrent à la surface.

Il est indéniable que le jeune artiste s'était heurté à une potentialité de l'art que le perpétuel débat sur l'autonomie de l'œuvre avait considérablement étouffée. Il découvrait la possibilité de mobiliser des sentiments violents, puis, à l'aide de cette énergie, de libérer en quelque sorte les idées et opinions humaines, comme par une déflagration. Dans les débats théoriques, la puissance potentielle de l'art était tout au plus considérée comme un moyen de transfor-

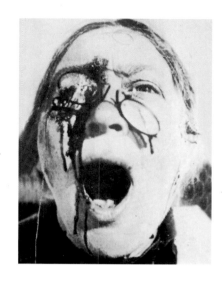

Edvard Munch
Oil, tempera, pastel, 1893

Sergej Eisenstein
Battleship Potemkin/Panzerkreuzer Potemkin/
Le Cuirassé Potemkine, 1925

Francis Bacon
Oil on canvas, 1951

in Austrian universities as well, and Gottfried Helnwein participated in many an action though few of them went beyond the usual student pranks.

What was more remarkable was that he began to get involved in one of the motif cycles which were later to preoccupy him time and again. Children keep recurring in his pictures, he has drawn and photographed them, painted them and used their giant-size images in his artistic stage sets and installations. Sometimes there are also people of different ages, but mostly children, and with them the idols of the media world, live manifestations perhaps of the universe of comics, which has continued to fascinate him since his encounter with the world of Donald Duck, and which is very close to the universe of children. Children and colorful comics meet in some of his early pictures, but occasionally there are only a few selected ingredients of the cosmos of comics, ones which have become an integral part of the children's world. A pastel like *Embarrassing* (1971, cf. p. 69), drawn with great intensity and sensitivity, shows a terribly injured little girl with a gaping gash from nose to jaw, the index finger of her left and the

und die damals avancierteste Version der zeitgenössischen Kunst gab sich eher kopflastig. Helnwein entdeckte, daß auch emotionsgeladene Reaktionen die Intentionen des künstlerischen Urhebers erfüllen konnten, wenn sie bestimmte Zusammenhänge aufdeckten, sie gleichsam wie die Blitze eines reinigenden Gewitters ausleuchteten, obwohl sie bei den Adressaten nicht unbedingt geistige Fortschritte zeitigten. Dafür dienten diese als Katalysatoren, wurden zu mehr oder minder unfreiwilligen Akteuren seines künstlerischen Konzepts. Nachdem er die »Graphische« mit Examen verlassen hatte, verfeinerte er seine künstlerische Strategie an der Wiener Kunstakademie, wo er bei dem Maler Rudolf Hausner auf einen verständnisvollen Lehrer stieß. Revolten kleineren oder größeren Ausmaßes waren auch an österreichischen Hochschulen an der Tagesordnung, und Helnwein nahm an mancher Aktion teil, von denen die wenigsten über die üblichen Studentenulks hinausgingen.

Er begann sich mit einem jener Motivkreise zu beschäftigen, die ihn auch später nicht in Ruhe ließen. Immer wieder tauchen Kinder in seinen Bildern auf, er hat sie gezeichnet und fotografiert, gemalt und als riesenhafte Formate in seinen künstlerischen

mer la conscience individuelle ou collective. On se méfiait des sentiments. Comme dans le passé, on refoulait le souvenir des conséquences catastrophiques de la manière dont le national-socialisme avait esthétisé la politique. Quant aux tendances les plus avancées de l'art contemporain du moment, elles étaient trop intellectuelles. Helnwein découvrit que des réactions chargées d'émotions pouvaient aussi correspondre aux intentions de l'auteur de l'œuvre si elles éclairaient certaines corrélations comme sous l'effet de l'éclair d'un orage purificateur, sans pour autant entraîner obligatoirement un progrès intellectuel chez ceux à qui elles s'adressaient. Au contraire, Helnwein se servait des spectateurs comme des catalyseurs, devenant ainsi plus ou moins volontairement les acteurs de son concept artistique. Après avoir quitté l'école des arts graphiques muni de son diplôme, il affina sa stratégie artistique à l'Académie des Beaux-Arts de Vienne, où il rencontra en la personne de Rudolf Hausner un maître très compréhensif. Dans les universités autrichiennes, la contestation de plus ou moins grande ampleur faisait aussi partie de la vie quotidienne ; et Gottfried Helnwein participa à maintes actions, bien que peu

 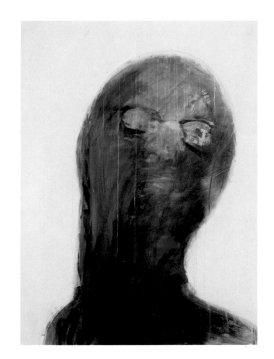 

Self-Portrait 6/Selbstporträt 6/Autoportrait 6, 1986
Acrylic on paper and aluminium, 83 × 59 inches, 210 × 150 cm
Private Collection, Switzerland

Self-Portrait 7/Selbstporträt 7/Autoportrait 7, 1986
Acrylic on paper and aluminium, 83 × 59 inches, 210 × 150 cm
Private Collection, Switzerland

Self-Portrait 12/Selbstporträt 12/Autoportrait 12, 1986
Oil and acrylic on canvas, 83 × 59 inches, 210 × 150 cm
Collection of the Artist

Self-Portrait 8/Selbstporträt 8/Autoportrait 8, 1986
Oil and acrylic on canvas, 83 × 59 inches, 210 × 150 cm
Private Collection, Vienna

Self-Portrait 9/Selbstporträt 9/Autoportrait 9, 1986
Oil and acrylic on canvas, 83 × 59 inches, 210 × 150 cm
Private Collection, Germany

Self-Portrait 15/Selbstporträt 15/Autoportrait 15, 1986
Oil and acrylic on canvas, 83 × 59 inches, 210 × 150 cm
Private Collection, Germany

Self-Portrait 17/Selbstporträt 17/Autoportrait 17, 1988
Oil and acrylic on canvas, 83 × 59 inches, 210 × 150 cm
Collection of the Artist

210

Self-Portrait 16/Selbstporträt 16/Autoportrait 16, 1988
Oil and acrylic on canvas, 83 × 59 inches, 210 × 150 cm
Collection of the Artist

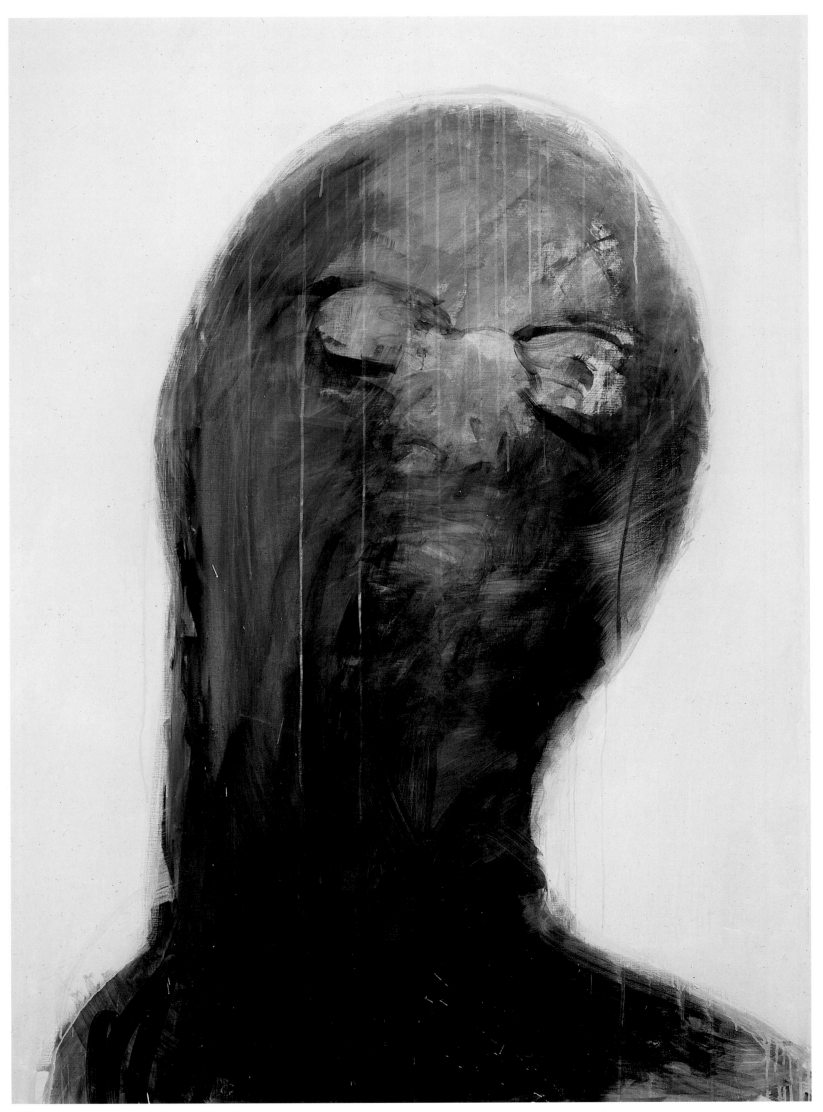

Self-Portrait 7/Selbstporträt 7/Autoportrait 7, 1986
Acrylic on paper and aluminium, 83 × 59 inches, 210 × 150 cm
Private Collection, Zürich

Self-Portrait 15/Selbstporträt 15/Autoportrait 15, 1987
Oil and acrylic on canvas, 83 × 59 inches, 210 × 150 cm
Private Collection, Germany

whole right hand in bandages, with a comic under her arm on the pink dress, and the open page of the comic is about a botched-up love story. The subtle, exceptionally delicate painting technique of this pastel, masterly executed by the artist, creates an almost screaming tension between itself and the disfigured model of the picture. Her round eyes are staring into the void, scared and without comprehending, her face is distorted by a terrible grin, the result of her horrific injury.

While the artist had sorely disturbed the expectations of his professors at the Experimental Institute for Higher Graphic Education, prompting a kaleidoscope of conflicting reactions and, through these reactions, a glimpse of some vaguely outlined model for the reception of artistic works, he developed an analogous model in his pastel *Embarrassing* and in further pictures full of injured children, and occasionally adults; however, this was unlike the Hitler picture, which was solely restricted to the context of art. Subjects like those of ill-treated and bandaged children are nothing special in daily news shows on television, they are almost part and parcel of the medium. By portraying the maimed children and their bandaged heads and limbs in the subtle and delicate pastel technique, Helnwein caused the shock which the electronic pictures, their effect weakened by perpetual repetition, now only create subliminally, and brought horror back to art, making it visual once more. Thus he laid open the cynicism of a society which no longer sees "how things are", but whose seeing has long been blocked by pictures about things. And it is altogether revealing how the art world reacted to such images – with disgust, of course, though not, as one might at first assume, because of the cruel nature of the chosen topic or the artistically flawless realization, but hiding behind the argument that pictures marked by such "realism" had long been overtaken by the history of art and simply failed the

Bühnenbildern und Installationen eingesetzt. Bisweilen auch Menschen verschiedenen Alters, aber namentlich Kinder und die Idole der Medienwelt, vielleicht die lebendigen Manifestationen des Universums der Comics, das ihn seit seiner Bekanntschaft mit der Welt von Donald Duck stets gefesselt hat, und dem Universum der Kinder sehr nahe ist. Kinder und die bunten Comic-Hefte begegnen sich auf einigen seiner frühen Bilder, und mitunter sind es auch nur ein paar ausgesuchte Bestandteile des Kosmos der Comics, die sich wie selbstverständlich in der Welt der Kinder eingenistet haben. Ein eindringlich, überaus sensibel gezeichnetes Pastell wie *Peinlich* (1971, vgl. S. 69) zeigt ein gräßlich verletztes kleines Mädchen mit klaffender Schnittwunde von der Nase bis zum Unterkiefer, den Zeigefinger der linken und die rechte Hand vollständig verbunden, mit einem Comic unter dem Arm. Die aufgeschlagene Seite des Bilderheftes auf seinem rosa Kleidchen handelt von einer verkorksten Liebesgeschichte. Die subtile, außergewöhnlich delikate Maltechnik des Pastelles, vom Künstler virtuos gehandhabt, reißt ein geradezu schreiendes Spannungsverhältnis zum entstellten Modell des Bildes auf. Die runden Augen starren verschreckt und ohne Begreifen ins Leere, das Gesicht ist verzerrt von einem furchtbaren Grinsen, das Resultat der grauenhaften Verletzung ist.

Hatte der Künstler mit seinem Hitlerbild an der Höheren Graphischen Bundeslehr- und Versuchsanstalt die Erwartungen seiner Professoren empfindlich gestört und einen Fächer von widersprüchlichen Reaktionen entfaltet, die so etwas wie ein Modell der Rezeption von künstlerischen Werken umrißhaft aufscheinen lassen, entwickelte er mit dem Pastell *Peinlich* und weiteren Bildern verletzter Kinder und gelegentlich auch Erwachsener ein analoges Modell, freilich allein auf den Kontext der Kunst beschränkt. Sujets wie die von dem malträtierten und bandagierten Kindern sind in den täglichen Nachrichten des Fernsehens

d'entre elles ne dépassât le genre de la farce estudiantine.

Il faut toutefois noter qu'il commença à s'intéresser à des thèmes qui le préoccuperont souvent par la suite. Des enfants apparaissaient de plus en plus fréquemment dans ses travaux ; il les dessinait, photographiait, peignait, et les reproduisait sur des formats gigantesques dans ses scénographies et expositions artistiques. De temps en temps, on rencontrait aussi des êtres d'âges différents, mais la plupart du temps des enfants accompagnés des idoles du monde des médias, peut-être les incarnations de l'univers de la bande dessinée qui n'a cessé de le passionner depuis qu'il avait découvert Donald Duck si proche des enfants. Ces mêmes enfants et les albums des bandes dessinées colorés se retrouvent sur quelques œuvres de jeunesse ; mais parfois, on y retrouve aussi seulement quelques composantes bien choisies du microcosme de la bande dessinée, celle-ci étant devenue partie intégrante du monde des enfants. *Gênant* (1971, voir p. 69), un pastel poignant, dessiné avec une grande sensibilité, montrait une fillette horriblement mutilée avec une plaie béante qui allait du nez à la mâchoire inférieure, son index gauche et sa main droite étaient entièrement couverts de pansements, mais sous le bras, elle tenait une bande dessinée ouverte sur sa robe rose, une page racontant une histoire d'amour ratée. La technique subtile et exceptionnellement délicate de ce pastel admirablement réalisé par l'artiste, généraient une tension presque insoutenable entre la technique et le modèle défiguré que l'on voyait sur l'image. Ses yeux ronds et terrifiés fixaient le vide sans comprendre, son visage était déformé par un sourire atroce, résultat de cette horrible blessure. Si, avec le portrait d'Hitler de l'Institut expérimental d'enseignement supérieur des arts graphiques, l'artiste avait manifestement déjoué les attentes de ses professeurs et déclenché tout un éventail de réactions contradictoires, réactions qui, même ébauchées, font apparaître quelque chose qui

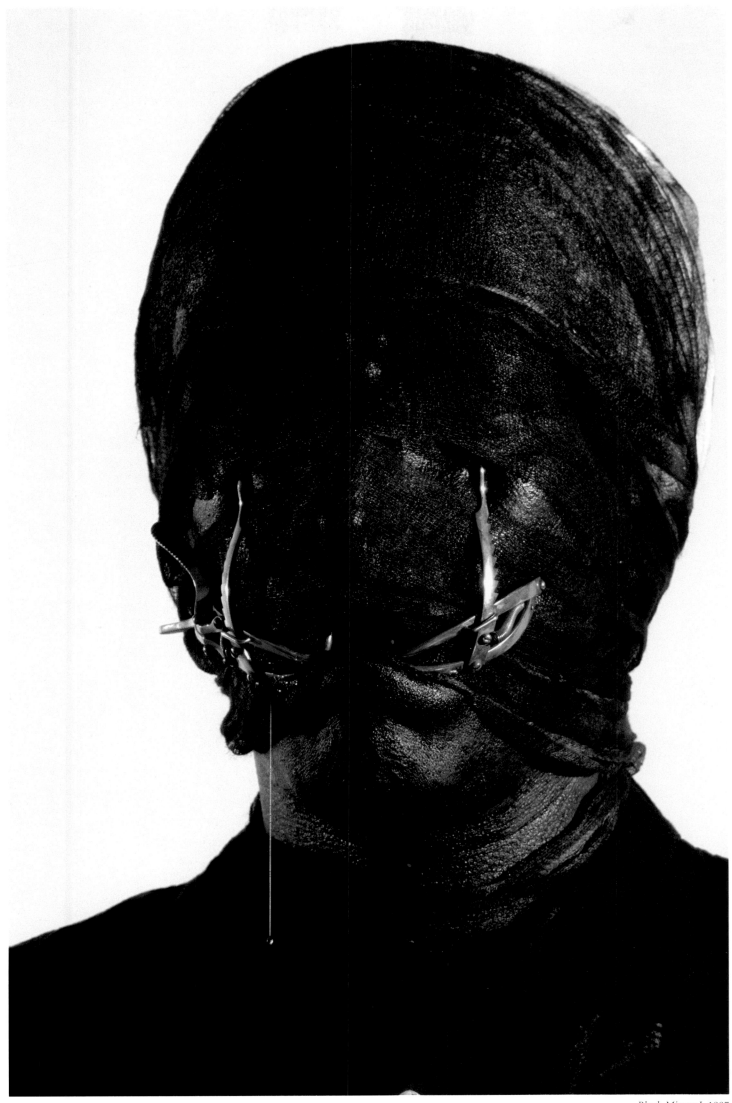

Black Mirror I, 1987
Photograph
Los Angeles County Museum of Art

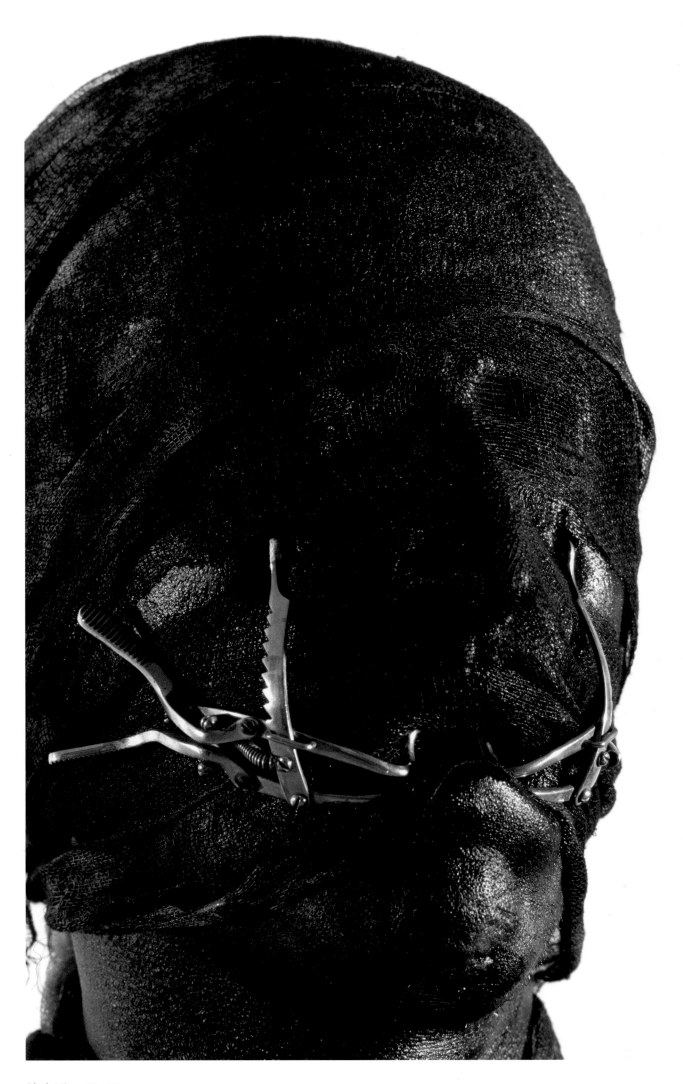

Black Mirror II, 1987
Photograph

216

Black Mirror III, 1986
Photograph

Black Mirror IV, 1986
Photograph

218

Black Mirror V, 1986
Photograph

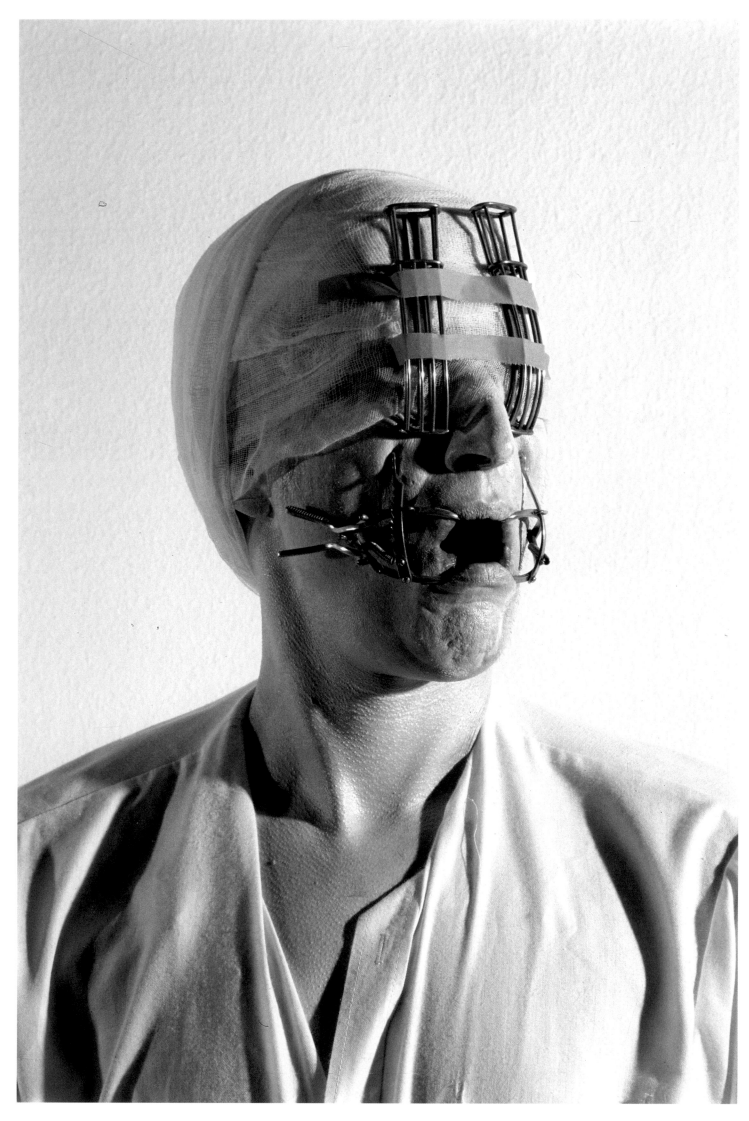

The Last Days of Pompei I/Die letzten Tage von Pompeji I/Les Derniers jours de Pompéii I, 1987
Photograph

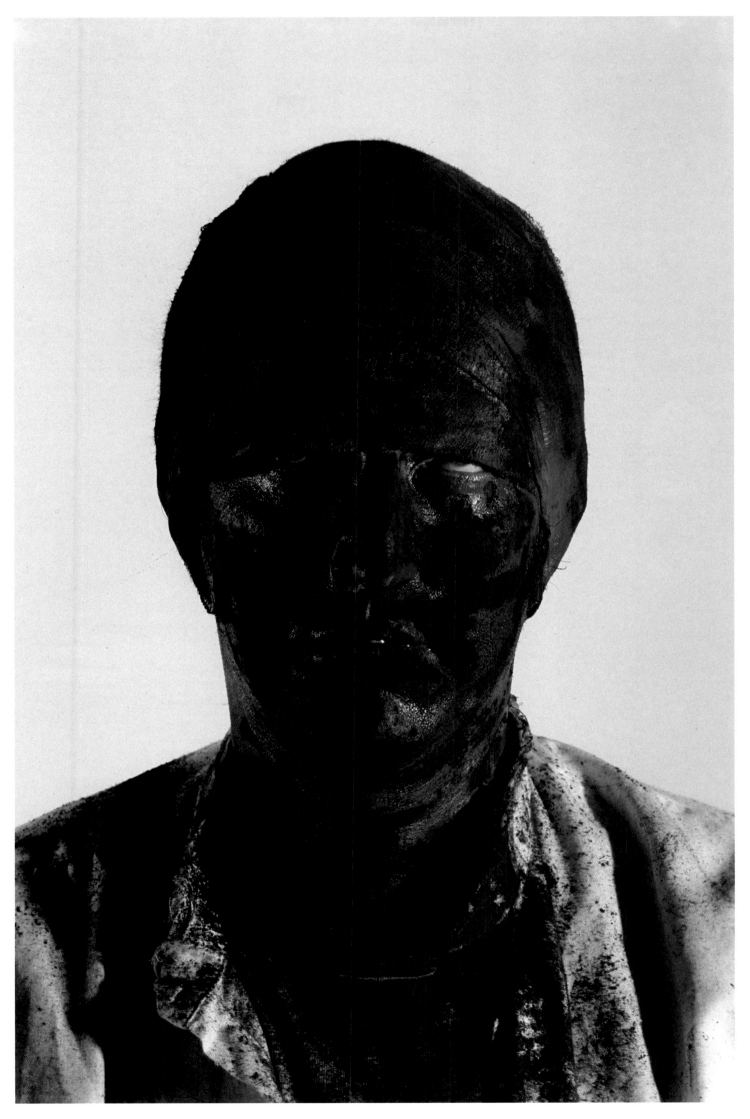

Lucky Devil/Glückspilz/Veinard, 1987
Photograph

Untitled/Ohne Titel/Sans titre, 1987
Photograph

222

Untitled/Ohne Titel/Sans titre, 1987
Photograph

Self-Portrait/Selbstporträt/Autoportrait, 1987
Polaroid, 28 × 20 inches, 70 × 52 cm   224

HELNWEIN 87

Self-Portrait/Selbstporträt/Autoportrait, 1987
Polaroid, 28 × 20 inches, 70 × 52 cm
Los Angeles County Museum of Art

Self-Portrait/Selbstporträt/Autoportrait, 1987
Polaroid, 28 × 20 inches, 70 × 52 cm

226

HELNWEIN 87

Self-Portrait/Selbstporträt/Autoportrait, 1987

227

Polaroid, 28 × 20 inches, 70 × 52 cm

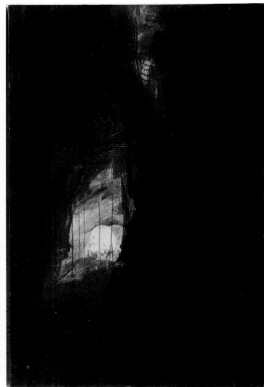

Self-Portrait 18 (triptych)/*Selbstporträt 18* (Triptychon)/*Autoportrait 18* (triptyque), 1989
Oil and acrylic on photograph, each painting 47¼ × 31½ inches, 120 × 80 cm
Collection of the Artist

◁ *Self-Portraits/Selbstporträts/Autoportraits,* 1970–1987
Photo-collage, 22⅖ × 35 inches, 57 × 89 cm   230

The Silent Glow of the Avant-Garde I (triptych)/*Das stille Leuchten der Avantgarde I* (Triptychon)/
L'Eclat discret de l'avant-garde I (triptyque), 1986
Photograph, oil and acrylic, 47⅕ × 133⅘ inches, 120 × 340 cm
Dillard Denson, Little Rock, Arkansas

God of Sub-Humans (triptych)/*Gott der Untermenschen* (Triptychon)/*Dieu des sous-hommes* (triptyque), 1986
Photograph, oil and acrylic on canvas, 82 × 233⁴/₅ inches, 210 × 594 cm
Leopold Hoesch Museum, Düren

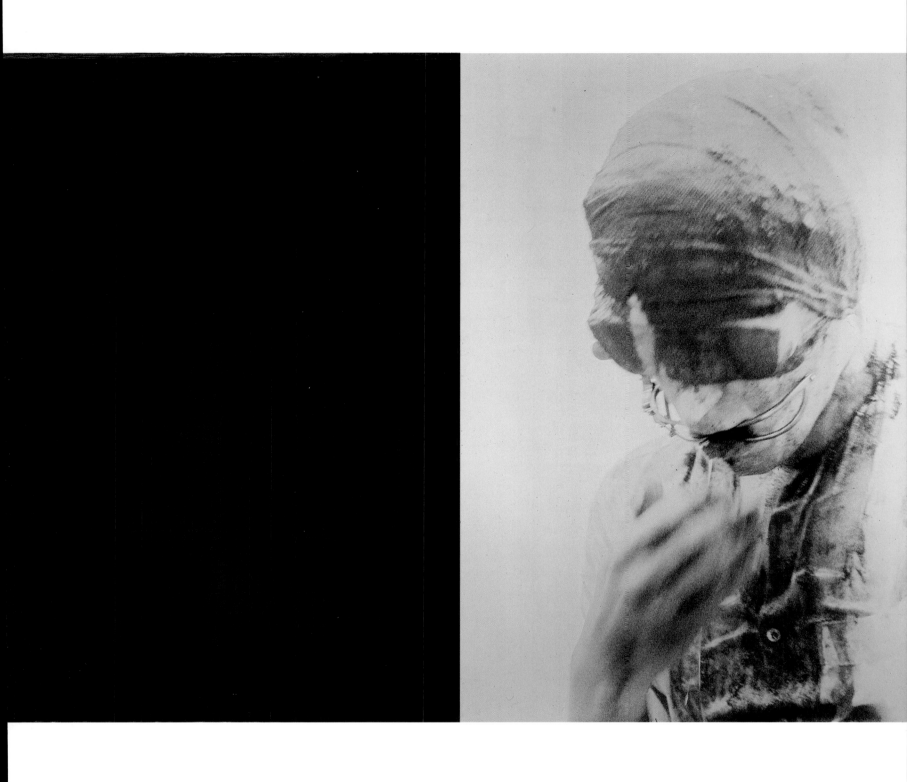

A Tear on a Journey (diptych)/*Eine Träne auf Reisen* (Diptychon)/
Une larme en voyage (diptyque), 1986
Photograph   240

The Evidence (triptych)/*Der Beweis* (Triptychon)/*La Preuve* (triptyque), 1986
Photograph, oil and acrylic on canvas, 82⅗ × 250 inches, 210 × 610 cm
Niederösterreichisches Landesmuseum, Vienna   242

Breaking of Vessels/Br ch der Gefäße/Rupture des artères, 1987

Photograph

God as Baron I/Gott als Baron I/Dieu baron I, 1987
Photograph

God as Baron II/Gott als Baron II/Dieu baron II, 1987
Photograph

244

Untitled/Ohne Titel/Sans titre, 1987

Photograph

though, in the sense of Concept Art, where theory says the idea of the autonomous work of art has been entirely fulfilled, but in connection with artistic practice, as an artist who, instead of producing trenchant trademarks, remains critical in the face of his social environment and its convictions, flexible in dealing with the existing media and their possibilities and dangers.

It was only consistent that the artist took his next steps in the streets of Vienna. He created apparently spontaneous "actions", having them photographed or operating the camera himself, and he chose children as protagonists, the models of his watercolors. He provided them with bandages clipped together by surgical instruments. "The central theme of my art was children. And I found children, adults as well at times, with whom I staged actions in the street. For instance, I would wind bandages round a child, tie him up, affix surgical clips, and lay him on the floor. I always discussed it with the children beforehand, explaining what I intended to do. To them it was a game."[10] The stagings were meant to place an unexpected lock into the calm river of everyday life, and he intended to provoke a reaction from chance passers-by. But people did not necessarily react, though this certainly did not devalue the result of the actions; taking no notice of an incident is also a form of reaction, and a revealing one at that. Although Helnwein and his actions were becoming increasingly noticed in Austria's capital, the direct encounter of his art with an institution of the mass media at first ended in disaster. Following the massive protest by the employees at the House of the Press, his exhibition in the gallery there was closed after three days, and the pictures were taken down. His response was astonished, but relaxed: "I wanted to spark off emotions, I wanted to learn something about others, I didn't really care what. I had no particular expectations. In this sense, protest and outrage were just as good as praise or any other reaction."[11]

seiner ungebrochenen Abneigung gegen eine Kunst um ihrer selbst willen andererseits. Bert Brecht und Walter Benjamin lieferten die entsprechenden Anregungen für die ästhetischen Theoretiker; Walt Disney und die Rockmusik mit ihrer gewaltigen Reichweite die Impulse für den künstlerischen Praktiker Helnwein. Kunst müsse wie Rockmusik sein, behauptete er damals, und er habe mehr von Disney als von Leonardo da Vinci gelernt. Intuitiv erfaßte der Künstler, daß die Kunst in einem grundsätzlichen Wandlungsprozeß begriffen war, der weder ihre materielle Beschaffenheit noch ihren Geist unangetastet ließ. Das Aufkommen der Massenmedien hatte diesen Prozeß eingeleitet und dank der kontinuierlichen Ausweitung ihrer Einflußsphäre hatte sich ihre Macht auf das Bewußtsein der Menschen in unvorstellbarem Ausmaß vertieft. Darum mußte dem jungen Kunstadepten das sektiererische Gehabe der zeitgenössischen Künstler als untrügliches Indiz für den Ausklang einer Epoche der Kunst erscheinen und nicht, wie die Avantgarde stolz verkündet hat, als ein Anfang. Marcel Duchamp als Erbe und Vollstrecker einer künstlerischen Tradition, die mit der Renaissance begonnen hat, nicht aber als der Begründer eines neuen künstlerischen Kapitels[9]. Träfe das zu, hätte man der Avantgarde einen falschen Namen zugemessen, sie wäre tatsächlich eine Nachhut. Die Konsequenzen wären unübersehbar – sowohl für die Kunst und ihre Geschichte als auch für ihr Verhältnis zu Politik und Gesellschaft. Vor diesem Hintergrund leuchtet ein, daß Gottfried Helnwein sich als Konzept-Künstler versteht. Im gegenteiligen Sinne der Concept Art zwar, in deren Theorie sich die Vorstellung vom autonomen Kunstwerk gänzlich erfüllt hat, aber in bezug auf die künstlerische Praxis als ein Künstler, der statt prägnante Markenzeichen zu produzieren eine ästhetische Haltung kultiviert, die sich kritisch angesichts ihrer gesellschaftlichen Umwelt und deren Überzeugungen verhält, flexibel im Umgang mit den zu handelnden

populaires et pas seulement dans les cercles élitistes de l'art. Cette optimisme était dû à la situation historique de ces années agitées par la contestation et à l'assurance des jeunes intellectuels de gauche qui savaient que les « masses populaires » étaient prêtes à risquer une révolution sociale, et il était également dû à la répugnance intacte de Helnwein à l'égard de l'art pour l'art. Les idées de Bert Brecht et de Walter Benjamin servaient de référence aux théoriciens de l'esthétique, tandis que Walt Disney et la musique rock avaient une portée telle qu'ils inspiraient le praticien artistique qu'était Helnwein. L'art devrait être comme le rock, déclarait-il à l'époque, et il ajoutait avoir davantage appris de Disney que de Léonard de Vinci. Intuitivement, l'artiste comprenait que l'art était pris dans un processus de transformation fondamental qui ne le laisserait pas indemne ni dans sa matérialité ni son esprit. C'est l'avènement des mass media qui avait déclenché ce processus et aussi l'accroissement continu de ces sphères d'influence, leur pouvoir sur la conscience des hommes agissait en profondeur et avec une ampleur inimaginable. C'est pourquoi, l'attitude sectaire des artistes contemporains devait aux yeux du jeune peintre faire figure d'indice infaillible du déclin d'une période de l'art, et non, comme le proclamait fièrement l'avant-garde, de son nouveau départ : Marcel Duchamp, héritier et exécutant testamentaire d'une tradition artistique née avec la Renaissance, mais pas fondateur d'un nouveau chapitre de l'histoire de l'art[9]. Dans ce cas, on attribuait à l'avant-garde un nom erroné, car dans ces conditions elle devait être en fait l'arrière-garde. Les conséquences seraient imprévisibles – autant pour l'art et son histoire que pour son rapport avec la politique et la société. Sur cette toile de fond, il semble évident que Helnwein se considère comme un artiste conceptuel. Certes, dans un sens qui s'oppose aux théories de l'art conceptuel entièrement imprégnées de l'idée de l'œuvre d'art autonome, mais concernant sa pra-

Let it Bleed, 1987
Photograph

Ikarus I/Icare I, 1987
Photograph

248

The Miracle/Das Wunder/Le Miracle, 1987

Photograph

Last Supper II/Abendmahl II/Dernier repas II, 1987
Photograph
Museum Ludwig, Cologne   256

Untitled/Ohne Titel/Sans titre, 1987
Polaroid, 27½ × 20½ inches, 70 × 52 cm

The Evidence for the Existence of God/Der Gottesbeweis/
La Preuve de l'existence de Dieu, 1987
Photograph

Untitled/Ohne Titel/Sans titre, 1987
Polaroid, 27½ × 20½ inches, 70 × 52 cm

WORKS
ARBEITEN
TRAVAUX
1988–1998

Ali (detail), 1991
Mixed media on canvas, 65 × 44 inches, 166 × 113 cm
Private Collection, Germany

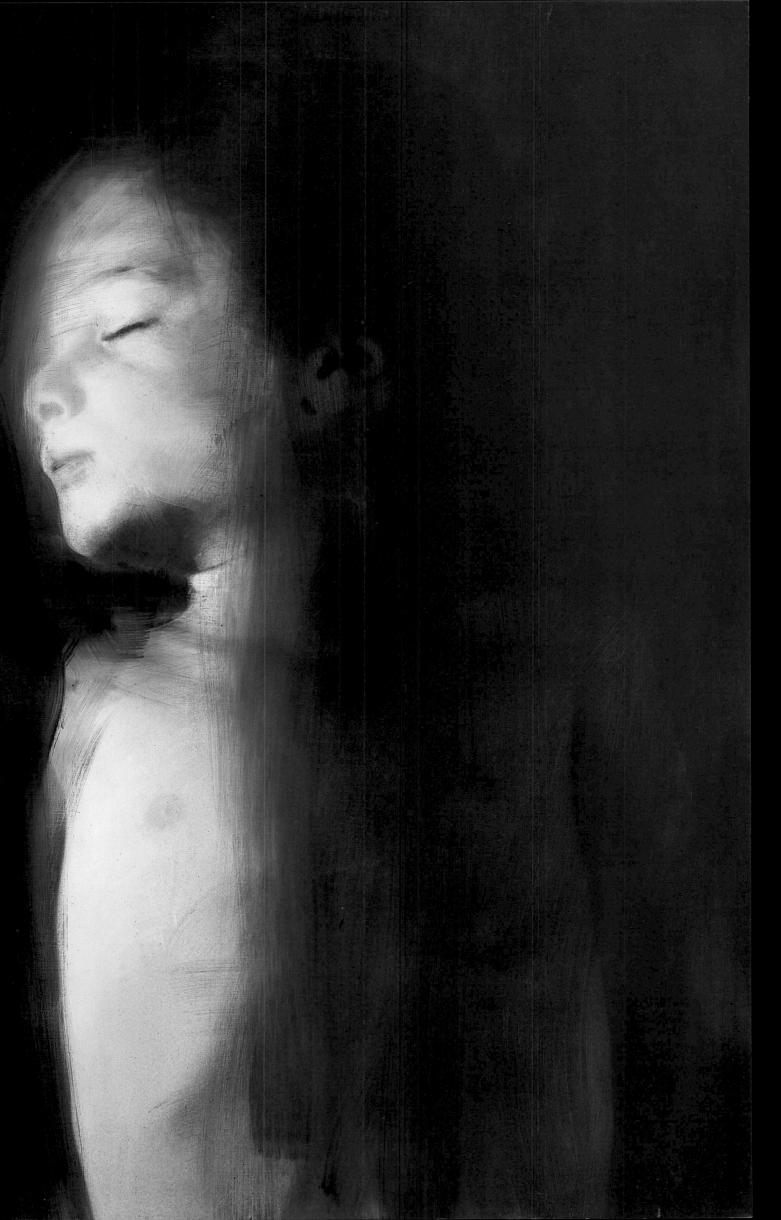

A number of years later, constantly varied self-portraits also harked back to the injury motif. A key picture is a watercolor from 1977 – the young artist with a bandaged head, his eyes behind the bars of spectacles made from two bent forks, dressed in a blazer and open-necked shirt and without a tie, turned to the viewer in three-quarter face, before a hued blue background which fades into a greyish white at the top and bottom of the picture, a somewhat elongated bust accurately positioned on the sheet in the golden section. Above his bandaged head, the picture extends by another half. The precise and sensitive execution presents a strangely ambivalent contrast to the apparently stoically borne injury. The longer one looks at the picture, the more it makes one's flesh creep. With stunning subtlety, Helnwein blends apparently incongruous elements. It is an image of shrill sensitivity. He had produced photographic self-portraits before; one of them shows him with his mouth wrenched open by two table forks, folding down his lower lip with a carving fork, thereby contriving a ghastly grin: *Self-Portrait with Smiling Aid* (1972, cf. p. 25). His hair and his forehead down to the eyebrows are swathed in gauze. In *Aktion Café Alt Wien* (Aktion Café Old Vienna, 1976, cf. p. 190) the muffled artist is sitting at a table next to an elderly man reading the newspaper, before him the usual café fare, gazing at the other's newspaper. In Delmer Daves's film noir "Dark Passage" (1947), Humphrey Bogart walks about in similar masquerade after having undergone a facial operation in order to escape his pursuers.

Subsequently, the artist has constantly modified the genre of the self-portrait in photographic and painted variants; the most famous was the screaming *Self-Portrait* (1990) in oil, acrylic and ink-jet on canvas, a graphic paradigm of the tormented human creature, which also exists as a photograph; a variant was a second version with cracking glass, the

Medien samt ihren Möglichkeiten und Gefährdungen.

So war es nur konsequent, daß der Künstler seine nächsten Schritte auf den Straßen Wiens absolvierte. Er realisierte spontan erscheinende »Aktionen«, ließ sie fotografieren oder bediente selber die Kamera, und als Protagonisten wählte er Kinder aus, die Modelle seiner Aquarelle. Er versah sie mit Bandagen, die mit chirurgischen Instrumenten verklammert waren. »Das Zentralthema meiner Kunst waren Kinder. Und ich fand Kinder, auch Erwachsene manchmal, mit denen ich auf der Straße Aktionen inszenierte. Ich habe zum Beispiel ein Kind bandagiert, verschnürt, mit chirurgischen Klammern versehen, auf den Boden gelegt. Ich sprach mit den Kindern vorher immer darüber, erklärte ihnen, was ich vorhabe. Es war eine Art Spiel für sie.«[10] Hinter den Inszenierungen verbarg sich die Idee, in den ruhigen Fluß des Alltags ein unvorhersehbares Wehr zu plazieren, und seine Absicht, eine Reaktion bei den Passanten zu provozieren. Aber nicht zwangsläufig reagierten die Menschen, wodurch das Ergebnis der Aktionen beileibe nicht geschmälert wurde, auch das Ignorieren eines Vorfalls ist eine Reaktion, eine entlarvende zumal. Obwohl Helnwein mit seinen Unternehmungen in Österreichs Hauptstadt steigende Aufmerksamkeit erfuhr, endete die unmittelbare Begegnung seiner Kunst mit einer Einrichtung der Massenmedien zunächst fatal. Auf massiven Protest der Beschäftigten im Pressehaus wurde seine Ausstellung in der dortigen Galerie nach drei Tagen Laufzeit geschlossen und abgehängt. Er quittierte es mit Erstaunen, aber gelassen: »Ich wollte Emotionen damit auslösen, ich wollte von anderen etwas erfahren, was, war mir eigentlich egal. So gesehen, waren Protest und Empörung genausogut wie Lob oder irgendeine andere Reaktion«.[11]

Das Motiv der Verwundungen klang ebenfalls bei einer Reihe später unaufhörlich variierter Selbstporträts an. Ein Schlüsselbild ist ein Aquarell von 1977 – der junge

tique artistique, en tant qu'artiste qui, au lieu de produire des images de marque incisives, cultive une attitude esthétique et qui reste sévère à l'égard de son environnement social et de ses convictions. Il traite les médias ainsi que les possibilités et les dangers qu'ils représentent avec flexibilité.

Il est désormais logique que l'artiste franchisse le pas qui le conduit dans les rues de Vienne. Il met des actions spontanées en scène, les fait photographier ou prend lui-même l'appareil. Comme protagonistes, il choisit des enfants, les modèles de ses aquarelles. Il leur met des bandages fixés par des instruments chirurgicaux. « Le thème central de mon art était les enfants. J'ai trouvé des enfants, et parfois même des adultes, avec qui j'organisais des actions dans les rues. Par exemple, j'enveloppais un enfant de bandes, j'ajoutais des pinces chirurgicales, puis je l'allongeais ainsi ficelé sur le sol. J'en parlais toujours avec eux avant ; je leur expliquais ce que j'allais faire. Pour eux c'était une sorte de jeu. »[10] L'idée sous-jacente à ces mises en scène était de placer un obstacle imprévu dans le cours tranquille du quotidien. Elles visaient à provoquer une réaction chez les passants. Mais les gens ne réagissaient pas forcément, ce qui ne réduisait en rien le résultat de l'action, car même ignorer un événement est une réaction ; qui plus est, c'est une réaction qui démasque la personne. Bien qu'Helnwein et ses entreprises aient attiré de plus en plus souvent l'attention dans la capitale autrichienne, la confrontation directe entre son art et une institution des mass média finit au début en catastrophe. Son exposition à la galerie de la maison de la presse fut fermée au bout de trois jours, et ses tableaux furent décrochés à la suite des protestations massives des employés. Il la quitta étonné mais serein : « Je voulais par là susciter des émotions, je voulais apprendre quelque chose des autres, n'importe quoi. Je n'avais aucune attente particulière. Vu sous cet angle, les protestations et l'indignation étaient tout aussi positives

Untitled/Ohne Titel/Sans titre, 1994
Mixed media on canvas, 60¼ × 38 inches, 153 × 97 cm
Courtesy Modernism Gallery, San Francisco

master for a record cover of the hardrock group Scorpions (1982) which has since become a cult image. A series of pictures in the eighties more or less obliterated the motif in several stages. Each was marked by a particular stylistic approach, adding up to a kind of express history of art from expressive painting to expressionist, abstract and tachist painting, ending with the serious monochrome which merely preserves the self-portrait as a barely perceptible shadow. This is another facet which reflects both the typical and the Janus-faced quality of his artistic activity: The continuous dissolution of a person's physiognomic identity is an expression of the acute and at the same time unfathomable threat to mankind from the excesses of modern civilization; the artist, however, is able to free himself through this reduction in content and form from a motif or medium whose immense success not only gains a life of its own, but also threatens his artistic integrity.

The artist categorically denies there is any autobiographical character in his self-portraits; they are no more auto-biographical than the works for which his own children were later to pose. "The reason why I took up the subject of self-portraits and why I have put myself on stage was to function as a kind of representative. There is nothing autobiographical, no therapy, and it says nothing about me personally. I am not talking about myself, I just use myself because I am always available as a model: What I am talking about is simply … a 'human being'".[12] If anything, it is the process of the "obliter-ation" of a motif which might be said to display autobiographical characteristics – or just a psychologically motivated reflex in the face of everyday horror and dread. Had not the late poet Heiner Müller asked: "How can an affable man like Helnwein bear to make his – excellent – painting the mirror of horrors?"[13] In a novel by his Austrian compatriot Thomas Bernhard

Künstler mit verbundenem Kopf, die Augen durch eine Brille aus zwei gebogenen Gabeln vergittert, im Sakko und offenen Hemd ohne Krawatte, den Betrachtern in Dreiviertelansicht zugekehrt, vor tonigem blauem Hintergrund, der am oberen und unteren Bildrand ins Weißgraue übergeht, akkurat als etwas verlängerte Büste und im goldenen Schnitt auf das Blatt postiert. Über seinem bandagierten Kopf verlängert sich die Bildfläche noch einmal um die Hälfte. Die genaue und feinfühlige Ausführung steht in merkwürdig ambivalentem Kontrast zu der in augenscheinlich stoischer Geduld ertragenen Verletzung. Je länger man das Bild anschaut, desto stärker die Gefahr, sich eine Gänsehaut zu holen. Mit verblüffender Subtilität vereint Helnwein vermeintlich Unvereinbares. Ein Bild von schriller Innerlichkeit. Zuvor hatte er schon fotografische Selbstbildnisse angefertigt. Eines zeigt ihn, wie er mit einer Tranchiergabel die Unterlippe seines von zwei Eßgabeln aufgerissenen Mundes herunterklappt, und so ein schauriges Grinsen bewerkstelligt: *Selbstbildnis mit Schmunzelhilfe* (1972, vgl. S. 25). Die Stirn und das Haupthaar sind mit Mull umwickelt. In der *Aktion Café Alt Wien* (1976, vgl. S. 190) sitzt der vermummte Künstler neben einem zeitunglesenden älteren Mann an einem Tisch, das übliche Cafégedeck vor sich, und blickt auf dessen Zeitung. In Delmer Daves' Film noir »Dark Passage« (1947) sieht man Humphrey Bogart in ähnlicher Maskerade, nachdem er sich einer Gesichtsoperation unterzogen hat, um seinen Verfolgern zu entgehen.

In der folgenden Zeit hat der Künstler die Gattung des Selbstporträts unentwegt abgewandelt, in fotografischen und gemalten Varianten. Am berühmtesten wurde das *Selbstporträt* (1990) mit Schrei in Öl, Acryl und Ink-Jet auf Leinwand, ein anschauliches Paradigma der geschundenen menschlichen Kreatur, das auch als Fotografie existiert. Eine Spielart davon war eine zweite Version mit zerspringendem Glas, Vorlage für ein Plattencover der Hardrock-Gruppe Scor-

que les éloges ou n'importe quelle autre réaction. »[11]

Le thème de la blessure sera de nouveau évoqué quelques années plus tard dans une série de nombreuses variations sur l'auto-portrait. L'œuvre clé en est une aquarelle de 1977 avec le jeune artiste, la tête bandée et les yeux emprisonnés derrière des lunettes faites de deux fourchettes tordues ; il porte une veste et une chemise ouverte sans cravate, il se présente au spectateur avec un profil de trois quarts sur un fond d'un bleu ardoise qui vire au gris blanchâtre en haut et en bas du tableau, un buste quelque peu allongé et campé sur le papier en respectant le nombre d'or. Au-dessus de la tête bandée, la surface picturale s'étend encore d'une moitié. L'exécution précise et consciente contraste d'une manière étrange et ambiguë avec la blessure qu'il porte avec un apparent stoïcisme. Plus on s'attarde sur cette œuvre, plus on en a la chair de poule. Avec une subtilité stupéfiante, Helnwein associe des éléments que l'on présume inassociables. Un tableau d'une sensibilité aiguë. Dans le passé, il avait déjà réalisé des autoportraits photographiques, l'un d'eux, *Autoportrait avec prothèse à sourire* (1972, voir p. 25), le montrait la bouche largement ouverte par des fourchettes, la lèvre inférieure rabattue par une fourchette à découper provoquant ainsi une grimace épouvantable. Ses cheveux et son front étaient couverts de gaze jusqu'aux sourcils. Lors de l'*Action Café Alt Wien* (1976, voir p. 190), l'artiste, couvert de bandes comme une momie, est assis à une table à côté d'un homme d'un certain âge qui lit le journal, il a devant lui ce que l'on sert communément dans un café, et regarde le journal de l'autre. Dans le film noir de Delmer Daves « Dark Passage » (1947), Humphrey Bogart se promène dans un accoutrement semblable après avoir subi une opération du visage pour échapper à ses poursuivants.

Par la suite, l'artiste n'a cessé de décliner le genre de l'autoportrait dans des variantes photographiques et peintes, dont la plus

Night III/Nacht III/Nuit III, 1990
Mixed media on canvas, 47¼ × 63⅘ inches, 120 × 162 cm
Private Collection, Germany

entitled "Obliteration", the first-person narrator erases both his cultural and – in effigy, as it were – his biographical origin through his writing. Though the author has remained in Austria, Helnwein, like the fictitious author in the novel, has fled for months, and then periodically, to the USA and Germany, restlessly alternating between town and country: no sooner established than ready to depart again. In the end, he also set up an aesthetic distance to the central theme of injuries in his work with a breathtaking set of photographic works, technically and electronically heavily treated, set behind glass and virtually entombed in a heavy lead frame. This happened with a daring artistic act. With the aid of computer technology and multiple reproductions he endowed the documentary photographs of horribly maimed faces with an alluring aesthetic gloss and a bewitching transparency of colors. Conjuring up true beauty in death alone, for all those pictured have died a violent death, he denounces as cynical and deeply inhuman the naturalistic exploitation of violence by the mass media. Simply leaving the authentic expression of the photographic masters would just have exposed the dead to voyeuristic curiosity. The artist uses his deliberately aestheticized images to undermine the "automatic programming" (Flusser) by the systems, and uses their own methods to wrest the pictures from that program, giving them new informative power by appealing to the imagination and vision of the viewers, challenging people with suggestive force and thus restoring to them a measure of freedom within the universe of photographic and electronic images.

No doubt it was partly due to chance that Helnwein's second attempt at establishing himself within the bastions of the media was more successful than the previous one. His former school-friend Bernhard Paul, newly installed as art director with the Austrian news magazine *Profil,* invited him

pions (1982), inzwischen ein Kultbild. In den 80er Jahren löschte er das Motiv in der Serie von Bildern gleichsam aus. Über mehrere Etappen vollzog sich dieser Vorgang, jeder markiert durch einen bestimmten stilistischen Ansatz, und deren Summe addiert sich zu einer Kunstgeschichte im Express, von der expressiven über die expressionistische zur abstrakten und tachistischen Malerei, schließlich die ernste Monochromie, die das Selbstbildnis im kaum noch wahrnehmbaren Schatten aufbewahrt. Auch darin spiegelt sich eine ebensowohl typische wie doppelgesichtige Qualität seiner künstlerischen Tätigkeit: In der kontinuierlichen Auflösung der physiognomischen Identität eines Menschen drückt sich die gleichermaßen akute wie unfaßliche Bedrohung der Menschheit durch die Auswüchse der modernen Zivilisation aus; dennoch befreit sich der Künstler mit Hilfe dieser inhaltlichen und formalen Reduktion von einem Motiv oder einem Medium, dessen immenser Erfolg sie ihrem Urheber gegenüber nicht nur verselbständigen, sondern auch zugleich seine künstlerische Integrität bedrohte.

Kategorisch dementiert der Künstler den autobiographischen Charakter seiner Selbstbildnisse, sie sind ebenso wenig autobiographisch wie die Arbeiten, für die nachher seine eigenen Kinder posierten. »Der Grund, warum ich zum Thema Selbstbildnis kam, warum ich von Anfang an Selbstinszenierungen gemacht habe, war eine Art Stellvertreter-Funktion. Das ist nichts Autobiographisches, keine Therapie und teilt nichts von mir persönlich mit. Damit meine ich überhaupt nicht mich, sondern ich nehme mich, weil ich als Modell jederzeit verfügbar bin: Was ich meine, ist einfach … ›einen Menschen‹«[12]. Wenn überhaupt, ist es der Prozeß der »Auslöschung« eines Motivs, das noch am ehesten autobiographische Züge aufweist oder nur einen psychologisch motivierten Reflex im Angesicht des alltäglichen Horrors und Schreckens. Hatte sich nicht der verstorbene Dichter Heiner Müller gefragt: »Wie hält ein freundlicher Mensch

célèbre, l'aigu autoportrait de 1990 à l'huile, acrylique et jet d'encre sur toile, paradigme évident des tourments de l'être humain, existe également sous forme de photographie. Une version comportant du verre se brisant en mille morceaux, qui a servi de modèle pour la pochette d'un album du groupe de hardrock les Scorpions (1982), fait depuis figure d'image-culte. Une série d'œuvres réalisée dans les années 80 en casse en quelque sorte le motif en plusieurs motifs. Chacune est marquée par une démarche stylistique particulière, y ajoutant une sorte de survol de l'histoire de l'art qui part de la peinture expressive, transite par l'expressionnisme, puis par l'abstrait et le tachisme, pour arriver à une monochromie sage qui permet de conserver à l'autoportrait son caractère d'ombre à peine perceptible. Ceci est une autre facette de l'œuvre qui reflète un trait caractéristique typique, mais aussi l'aspect double de l'activité artistique d'Helnwein. La menace pénétrante et inexplicable qui pèse sur l'humanité à cause des débordements de la civilisation moderne s'exprime dans la dissolution permanente de la physionomie d'un homme ; pourtant, l'artiste se libère par la réduction formelle et thématique d'un sujet ou d'un médium, dont l'immense succès lui donne non seulement une vie propre, mais il met aussi son intégrité artistique en péril.

Helnwein nie catégoriquement le caractère autobiographique de ses autoportraits ; ils sont aussi peu autobiographiques que les travaux pour lesquels ses propres enfants poseront par la suite. « La raison qui m'a amené à aborder le thème de l'autoportrait, à me mettre en scène, à pour but de jouer un rôle suppléance. Ceci n'est en rien autobiographique, ce n'est pas une thérapie et ne dit rien sur ma personne. Je ne veux absolument pas parler de moi, mais c'est moi que je prends parce que je suis toujours un modèle disponible ; ce que je veux transmettre est simple … un ‹ être humain ›. »[12] Si traits autobiographiques il y a, ceux-ci apparaissent plutôt dans le processus de

Blue Baron I!/Blauer Baron II/Baron bleu II, 1990
Mixe- media on canvas, 49⅗ × 51½ inches, 126 × 131 cm
Kurt and Veronika Fliegerbauer, Germany

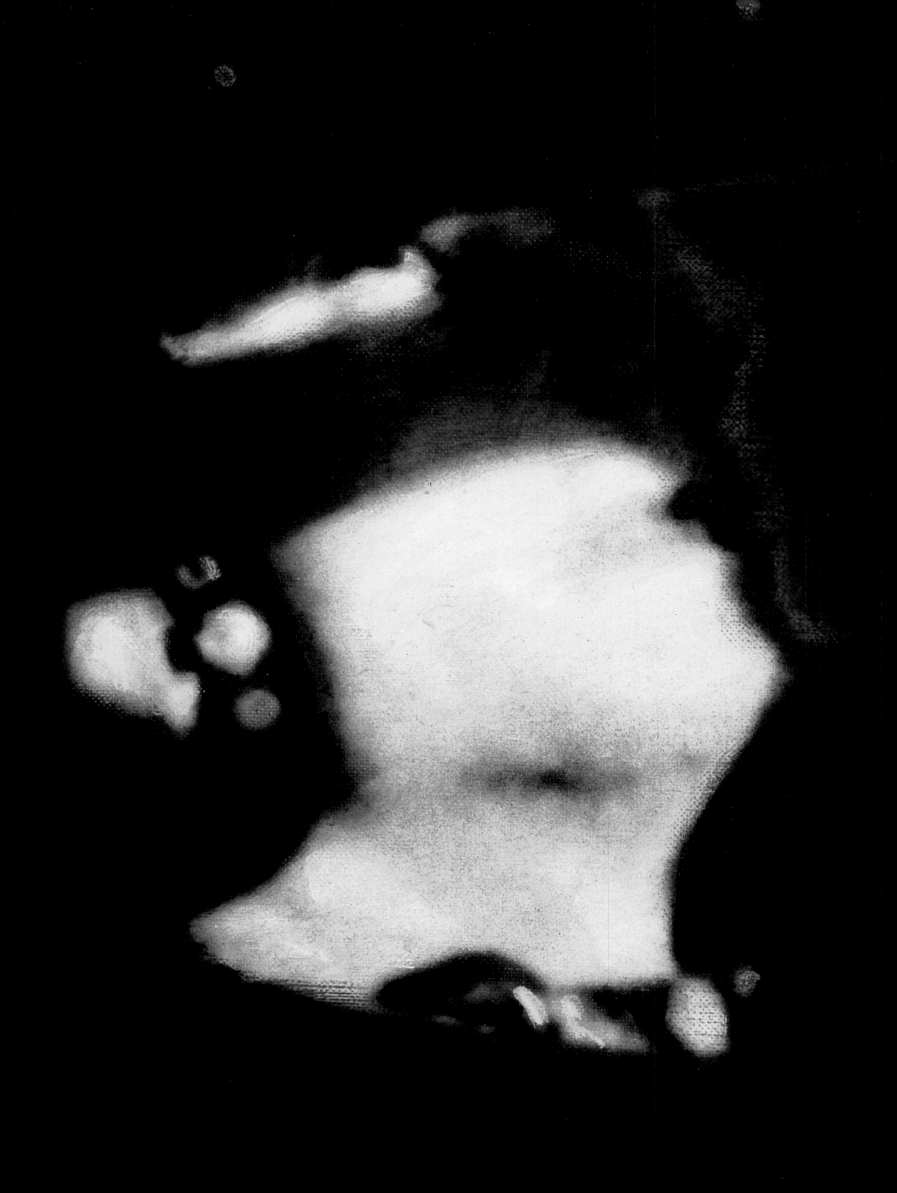

Before the Crash I (Joseph Beuys)/Vor dem Absturz I (Joseph Beuys)/Avant la chute I (Joseph Beuys), 1988
Mixed media on canvas, 39²/₃ × 27½ inches, 100 × 70 cm
Private Collection, Germany

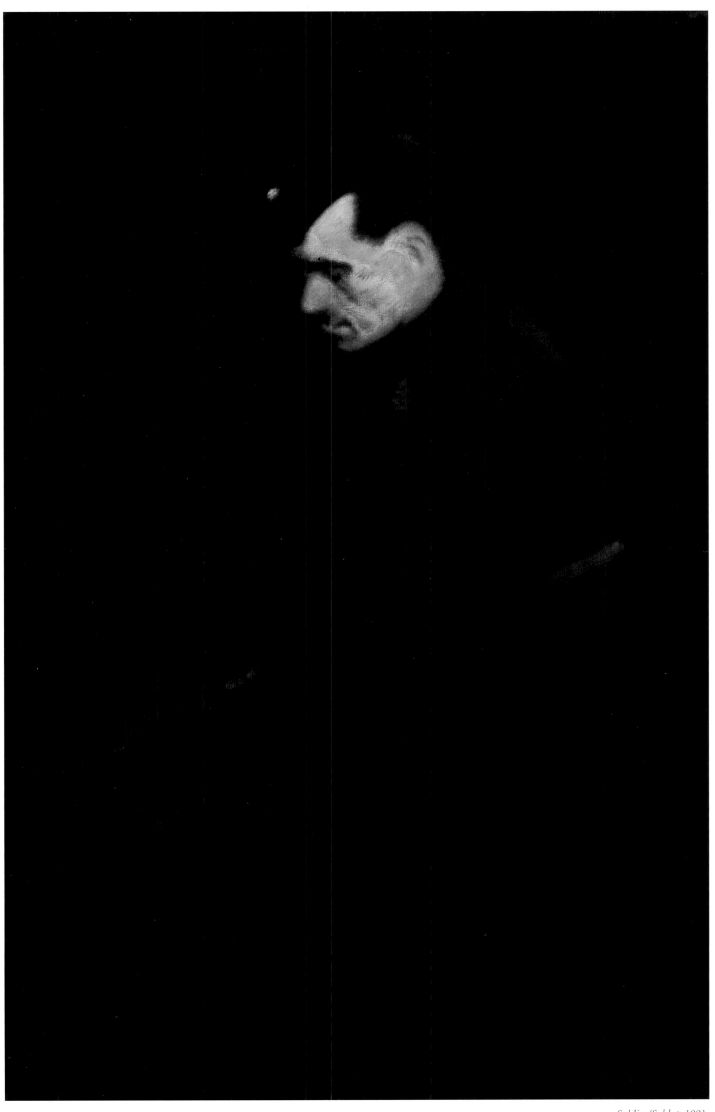

Soldier/Soldat, 1991
Mixed media or canvas, 55 × 36⅗ inches, 140 × 93 cm
Thomas Lundstrom, San Francisco

Late Regret/Späte Reue/Repentir tardif, 1997
Mixed media on canvas, 63 × 86⅗ inches, 160 × 220 cm

Courtesy Modernism Gallery, San Francisco

stigmatized but surviving martyr of his profession, did the rest. The artist had lived up to his motto of employing art "like a weapon, like a scalpel so that it touches the viewer."[16]

It is understandable that such artistic intentions are forestalled by the well-oiled system of art dissemination. Whilst its interest consists in selling or preserving works of art, which is inseparably tied to their quality as an object, Gottfried Helnwein's focus of aesthetic endeavors is not the artistic object, the work of art, but human perception. In this sense, the subversive use of pictorial media in his complex œuvre, whose effectiveness he really puts to the test, often even against their "technical" spirit, is an essential aesthetic principle. He drives the effects of the various techniques, drawing, water-color, painting and photography, beyond the limits of their (at least hitherto) exploited possibilities. With the striking result that his watercolors have the bright transparency of slides, together with the delicateness of watercolors; his naturalistic-realistic paintings have the brilliance of slide projections; and finally, his photographs have the structural variety of abstract landscapes. In drawing, painting and photography, his art constantly moves between the poles of over-definition and dissolution, each motif being the subject of a process of transformation within this movement. In a set of triptychs, the artist has made this process explicit, for instance in *God of Sub-Humans* (1986, cf. p. 238) and *The Silent Glow of the Avant-Garde,* an enlarged copy of Caspar David Friedrich's painting *Frustrated Hope* in cool-frosty blue, framed by two self-portrait busts of the artist apparently covered in blood, an ambiguous ironic reference to his position in the controversial history of art. In the sensational series of photographic portraits entitled *Faces* (cf. p. 364–374), a collection of images of pop idols from Mick Jagger to Keith Richards and Andy Warhol, of literary

Sicher war es auch eine Portion Zufall, daß Helnweins zweiter Versuch, sich in den Bastionen der Medien zu etablieren, glücklicher als der vorherige verlief. Sein ehemaliger Schulfreund Bernhard Paul, als Art-Director des österreichischen Nachrichtenmagazins *Profil* frisch bestellt, forderte ihn 1973 auf, einen »Innenteil« für eine Story über »Selbstmord in Österreich« über zwei Seiten zu gestalten. Die Bedingung des Künstlers: kein Text. Obwohl der Redaktion die eingereichte Zeichnung mißfiel, gelang es Paul, sie ohne ihr Placet zu veröffentlichen. Die Resonanz übertraf in jeglicher Hinsicht sämtliche Erwartungen. Des Künstlers einst geäußerter Wunsch: »Ich will auf allen Zeitschriften-Covers der Welt sein«[14] – wurde bald Wirklichkeit. Die deutschen Nachrichtenmagazine *Der Spiegel* und *Stern,* das amerikanische *Time Magazine, L'Espresso* aus Italien, die Szene-Zeitschrift *Rolling Stone,* auch das deutsche *Zeit Magazin* engagierten den brillanten Zeichner. Für diverse Inszenierungen des genialen Theatermachers Peter Zadek konzipierte er durchschlagende Plakate, und jedes von ihnen entfachte eine Fülle heftiger Diskussionen. Seine einprägsame Bildsprache, die seinen Ruf wie ein Lauffeuer um die Welt trug, entwickelte sich, ohne daß der Künstler es wollte, zu einem Markenzeichen, und auf dem Höhepunkt des Erfolgs brach er deshalb in radikaler Konsequenz seine publizistisch-künstlerische Tätigkeit ab. Er hatte den Kunstmarkt nachdrücklich irritiert und dennoch als Künstler eine öffentliche Wirkung erreicht, wie unter seinen Zeitgenossen allenfalls noch Andy Warhol. Seine Methode war die gezielte Subversion. »Die allgemeine Vorstellung des Kunstmarkts ist, daß zum Beispiel ein Druckverfahren umso wertvoller ist, je antiquierter und elitärer es ist (Radierung, Lithographie etc.) und je geringer die Auflage. Ich war jedoch der Meinung, je ordinärer das Druckverfahren (z. B. Offsetdruck) und je größer die Auflage, desto höher der künstlerische Wert«[15]. Helnwein, der künstlerische Anar-

l'imagination et au pouvoir visionnaire du spectateur, les défiant d'une force subjective et leur restituant une part de liberté dans l'univers des images photographiques et électroniques.

Il ne fait aucun doute que c'est grâce au hasard que la tentative d'Helnwein pour s'établir dans les bastions des médias fut couronnée de plus de succès la seconde fois que la première. En 1973, Bernard Paul, son ancien camarade d'école, qui vient d'entrer dans l'équipe du magazine autrichien *Profil* comme directeur artistique, lui demande d'imaginer une sorte d'« intertitre » en double page pour un article sur le « suicide en Autriche ». L'artiste pose ses conditions : aucun texte. Bien que le dessin envoyé déplaise à la rédaction, Paul réussit à le publier sans son aval. L'écho dépasse toutes les attentes à tous égards. Le souhait jadis exprimé par l'artiste : « Je veux être sur toutes les couvertures de magazines du monde »[14] ne tarde pas à devenir réalité. Les hebdomadaires allemands *Der Spiegel* et *Stern,* le *Time Magazine* américain, *L'Espresso* en Italie, la revue branchée *Rolling Stone,* mais aussi le *Zeit Magazin* en Allemagne engagent ce dessinateur brillant. Pour diverses mises en scène du génial Peter Zadek, il conçoit des affiches faisant sensation et qui, à chaque fois, déclenchent de violentes polémiques. Sans le vouloir, les œuvres mémorables de l'artiste – qui permettent à sa notoriété de se répandre comme une traînée de poudre dans le monde entier – se transforment peu à peu en une image de marque, ce qui le pousse, au sommet de sa gloire, à mettre un terme avec une radicale détermination à ses activités artistiques dans le domaine de la presse. Il a profondément provoqué le marché de l'art mais a tout de même réussi, en tant qu'artiste, à toucher le public comme aucun autre de ses contemporains, à l'exception peut-être d'Andy Warhol. Sa méthode relevait de la subversion ciblée. « Le marché de l'art s'imagine en général qu'un procédé d'impression a d'autant plus de valeur – et d'autant moins

Entrance to Paradise/Eingang ins Paradies/Entrée au Paradis, 1990
Mixed media on canvas, 47¼ × 59 inches, 120 × 150 cm
Courtesy Modernism Gallery, San Francisco

Dresden/Dresde, 1993
Mixed media on canvas, 65¾ × 106¾ inches, 167 × 271 cm
Ludwig Museum for International Art, Chinese Museum of Art, Beijing   286

Ascension/Himmelfahrt, 1995
Mixed media on canvas, 83½ × 55½ inches, 212 × 141 cm
Margret Jhin Walsh, San Francisco

authors from William S. Burroughs to Charles Bukowski, of artists from Roy Lichtenstein to Roland Topor and Arno Breker, of politicians like Willy Brandt and the Nazi-hunter Simon Wiesenthal and of film directors from Billy Wilder to Leni Riefenstahl – in other words, images from a very personal cultural universe – the artist proves himself to be one of the eminent portrait artists at the close of the twentieth century. His images speak of something which the American writer William S. Burroughs addresses in a text for Helnwein on "the function of the artist", namely "the experience of surprised recognition…": They are able to "show the viewer what he knows, but does not know that he knows. Helnwein is a master of this surprised recognition."[17]

In the end, even the international art scene could no longer ignore the successful nonconformist from Austria; important exhibitions in renowned museums and galleries in Europe, America, and the whole western and eastern hemisphere testify to the status bestowed on his art. And the artist is now using the exhibition system with aplomb as a specific communication system in order to visualize his concepts. "I think that the diversity of aspects – realistic images, abstract series, watercolors, crayon drawings and photographs – is also important in my work; if one follows and compares all the things I have made down to the monochrome pictures, one realises that in the end, in spite of the different styles, media or materials there is a connection, there is the same statement in all of them."[18] Consequently, he plans his major exhibitions as carefully prepared installations. Gottfried Helnwein embodies a new type of artist, an artist who does not see himself as a specialist although his artistic work revolves exclusively around a very concrete conceptual world whose facets he makes visible in the multifaceted world of his multimedia images. The outer and inner world of his art are inextricably

chist aus Prinzip, hatte an den tönernen Mauern des falschen Scheins merkantiler Seriosität gerüttelt, und seine Gemälde von einheimischen Pop-Idolen wie Hans Krankl, der einst das illustre deutsche Fußballteam aus einer internationalen Meisterschaft herausgeschossen hatte, Peter Alexander, der die meisten Mütter zu Tränen gerührt hatte, und Niki Lauda, dreifacher Weltmeister in der Formel 1 des Automobilrennsports, unverbesserlicher Lästerer und ein stigmatisierter, aber überlebender Märtyrer seiner Profession, taten ein übriges. Der Künstler war seiner Devise gerecht geworden, die Kunst einzusetzen »wie eine Waffe, wie ein Skalpell, damit sie im Betrachter etwas berührt«[16].

Derlei künstlerische Intentionen unterbindet der eingefahrene Apparat der Vermittlung von Kunst aus verständlichen Gründen. Während dessen Interesse darin besteht, Kunstwerke zu verkaufen oder zu bewahren, was untrennbar mit ihrer Objekthaftigkeit verbunden ist, bildet nicht das künstlerische Objekt, das Kunstwerk, sondern die menschliche Wahrnehmung den Focus der ästhetischen Bestrebungen Helnweins. Insofern ist die subversive Verwendung der visuellen Medien seiner komplexen Œuvres, deren Wirkmacht er regelrecht testet, öfter auch gegen ihren »technischen« Geist, ein wesentliches ästhetisches Prinzip. Er treibt die Wirkungen der einzelnen Techniken, Zeichnung, Aquarell, Gemälde und Fotografie, über die Grenzen ihrer (wenigstens bis dahin) ausgeschöpften Möglichkeiten hinaus. Mit dem frappierenden Resultat, daß seine Aquarelle die leuchtende Transparenz von Diapositiven haben, verbunden mit der Duftigkeit der Wasserfarben; seine naturalistisch-realistischen Gemälde haben die Brillanz von Diaprojektionen und die Fotografien schließlich die strukturelle Vielgestaltigkeit von abstrakten Landschaften. Ständig bewegt sich seine Kunst in Zeichnung, Malerei und Fotografien zwischen den Polen von Überschärfe und Auflösung, jedes Motiv ist Gegenstand eines

de tirage – qu'il est artisanal et élitaire (gravure, lithographie etc.). J'étais toutefois d'avis que la valeur artistique était d'autant plus grande que la technique d'impression était banale (p. ex. l'offset), et que le tirage était important. »[15] Helnwein, l'anarchiste par principe, avait ébranlé les murailles d'argile des fausses apparences, du sérieux mercantile, et ses tableaux représentant des idoles nationales comme le footballeur Hans Krankl, qui jadis avait tiré le but qui avait éliminé l'illustre équipe d'Allemagne du Championnat du monde, le chanteur de variété Peter Alexander qui émouvait aux larmes la plupart des mères, ou Niki Lauda, coureur automobile de Formule 1, trois fois champion du monde, éternel insatisfait, martyr stigmatisé mais survivant de la profession, firent le reste. L'artiste agissait conformément à sa devise, utiliser l'art « comme une arme, comme un scalpel, pour émouvoir le spectateur. »[16]

Pour des raisons évidentes, le système bien huilé de propagation de l'art s'oppose à ce genre d'attitude artistique. Alors que son intérêt consiste à vendre des œuvres ou à les conserver, ce qui est indissociable de leur qualité d'objet, la motivation de la démarche esthétique d'Helnwein ne réside pas dans l'objet artistique, l'œuvre d'art, mais dans la perception humaine. Ainsi, l'utilisation subversive des moyens plastiques dans son œuvre complexe dont il teste véritablement l'efficacité, souvent même en allant contre leur esprit « technique », est un principe esthétique essentiel. Il force les langages de différentes techniques, le dessin, l'aquarelle, la peinture et la photographie au-delà des limites (au moins jusqu'ici) des possibilités. Résultat frappant, ses aquarelles possèdent la transparence lumineuse des diapositives associée à la délicatesse des aquarelles ; ses tableaux naturalistes et réalistes ont l'éclat de projections de diapositives, enfin, ses photographies présentent la diversité structurelle de paysages abstraits. Que ce soit en peignant, en dessinant ou en photographiant, son art évolue constam-

◁ *Untitled/Ohne Titel/Sans titre*, 1996
Mixed media on canvas, 86³/₅ × 118 inches, 220 × 300 cm
Holger Timm, Berlin

Duck III, 1989
Mixed media on canvas, 47½ × 69⅗ inches, 120 × 177 cm
Private Collection, Germany

Untitled (after Andrea Mantegna)/Ohne Titel (nach Andrea
Mantegna)/Sans titre (d'après Andrea Mantegna), 1993
Mixed media on canvas, 48⅘ × 34⅗ inches, 124 × 88 cm
Courtesy Modernism Gallery, San Francisco   298

Untitled (after Andrea Mantegna)/Ohne Titel (nach Andrea Mantegna)/Sans titre (d'après Andrea Mantegna), 1994
Mixed media on canvas, 55 × 42½ inches, 140 × 108 cm
Courtesy Modernism Gallery, San Francisco

interwoven, self and world correspond in a reciprocal relationship, and in an amazing, but enlightening way, his pictures put into perspective the belief of emperor Frederick II that the world confronts the self as a closed system: an apparently understandable philosophical error arising from the time. For even Descartes is now hardly more than an important historical figure. Not least thanks to the artists, modern tought has left them behind.

Bonn, March/April 1996

Notes

1 Vilém Flusser, *Für eine Philosophie der Fotografie,* Göttingen, 7th edition, 1997

2 op. cit., p. 48

3 *Malerei muss sein wie Rockmusik,* Gottfried Helnwein im Gespräch mit Andreas Mäckler, München 1992, p. 12

4 op. cit., p. 23

5 op. cit., p. 24

6 ibid.

7 op. cit., p. 26

8 op. cit., p. 27

9 The Belgian-french art-historian Thierry de Duve presented a similar view at the Association of International Critics of Art international congress in Macao in October 1995.

10 Helnwein/Mäckler op. cit., p. 47

11 op. cit., p. 50

12 *Helnwein quotes Helnwein* (text by Andreas Mäckler), Köln 1992, p. 36

13 Heiner Müller, in: Kat. *Gottfried Helnwein, Arbeiten auf Papier,* Essen, Ludwigsburg, Bremen 1989, p. 22

14 quoted from Helnwein, op. cit., p. 81

15 *Malerei muss sein wie Rockmusik,* op. cit., p. 51

16 in conversation with the author

17 William S. Burroughs, in: *Helnwein, Faces,* Schaffhausen 1992. The Text was originally written for the artist's self-portraits.

18 *Malerei muss sein wie Rockmusik,* op. cit., p. 117

Prozesses der Verwandlung innerhalb dieser Bewegung. In einer Werkgruppe von Triptychen hat der Künstler diesen Prozeß anschaulich gemacht, wie zum Beispiel in *Gott der Untermenschen* (1986, vgl. S. 238) und *Das stille Leuchten der Avantgarde,* eine vergrößerte Kopie von Caspar David Friedrichs Gemälde *Gescheiterte Hoffnung* in kühlkaltem Blau, eingerahmt von zwei Selbstporträts der Büsten des scheinbar blutüberströmten Künstlers, vieldeutiger ironischer Verweis auf seine Position in der widersprüchlichen Geschichte der Kunst. In der aufsehenerregenden Reihe fotografischer Porträts mit der Bezeichnung *Faces* (vgl. S. 364–374), eine Versammlung von Bildnissen der Popidole von Mick Jagger über Keith Richards bis Andy Warhol, der Literaten von William S. Burroughs bis Charles Bukowski, der Künstler von Roy Lichtenstein über Roland Topor bis zu Arno Breker, von Politikern wie Willy Brandt und dem Nazi-Jäger Simon Wiesenthal sowie den Filmregisseuren von Billy Wilder bis Leni Riefenstahl, also einem sehr persönlichen Universum der Kultur, erweist sich der Künstler als einer der herausragenden Porträtisten am Ausgang des 20. Jahrhunderts. Seine Bildnisse künden von dem, was der amerikanische Schriftsteller William S. Burroughs in einem Text für Helnwein über »die Funktion des Künstlers« apostrophiert, nämlich, »die Erfahrung eines überraschten Erkennens…«. Sie vermögen »dem Betrachter zu zeigen, was er weiß, von dem er aber nicht weiß, daß er es weiß. Helnwein ist ein Meister dieses überraschten Erkennens«[17].

Letztlich kam auch die internationale Kunstszene nicht an dem erfolgreichen künstlerischen Außenseiter aus Österreich vorbei; bedeutende Ausstellungen in renommierten Museen und Galerien Europas, Amerikas, der gesamten westlichen und östlichen Hemisphäre zeugen von dem Rang, den man seiner Kunst beimißt. Und souverän nutzt der Künstler inzwischen das Ausstellungswesen als ein spezifisches Vermittlungssystem, um seine Vorstellungen zu

ment entre la sur-définition et la dissolution. Chaque sujet fait l'objet d'un processus de métamorphose au sein de ce mouvement. L'artiste démontre ce processus dans un groupe de triptyques tels que *Dieu des sous-hommes* (1986, voir p. 238) et *L'Eclat discret de l'avant-garde,* une copie agrandie du tableau de Caspar David Friedrich *Gescheiterte Hoffnung* interprété dans un bleu froid, encadré de deux autoportraits représentant le buste de l'artiste et couvert de sang, allusion ironique et ambiguë à sa position controversée dans l'histoire de l'art. Dans une remarquable série de portraits photographiques appelée *Faces* (voir p. 364–374), il réunit des idoles de la scène pop comme Mick Jagger, Keith Richards et Andy Warhol, des écrivains comme William S. Burroughs et Charles Bukowski, des artistes allant de Roy Lichtenstein, à Arno Breker en passant par Roland Topor, et des hommes politiques comme Willy Brandt ou le traqueur de nazis Simon Wiesenthal, mais aussi des réalisateurs de cinéma dont Billy Wilder et Leni Riefenstahl. Cet univers culturel très personnel le révèle comme un des portraitistes majeurs en cette fin de 20e siècle. Ses portraits illustrent ce que, dans un texte écrit pour Helnwein, l'écrivain américain William S. Burroughs entend par « fonction de l'artiste », c'est-à-dire, « l'expérience de la surprise d'identifier… », puisqu'ils sont en mesure de « montrer au spectateur ce qu'il sait mais sans savoir qu'il le sait. Helnwein est un maître dans l'art de la surprise d'identifier. »[17]

Finalement, même les milieux de la scène internationale de l'art ne peuvent plus passer à côté de cet artiste autrichien marginal et talentueux ; d'importantes expositions dans des galeries et des musées européens et américains réputés ainsi que tout l'orient et l'occident témoignent de la place accordée à son art. Désormais, l'artiste se comporte de manière souveraine, il utilise les expositions comme une courroie de transmission qui lui sert à visualiser ses idées. « Je crois

Untitled (after Andrea Mantegna)/Ohne Titel (nach Andrea Mantegna)/Sans titre (d'après Andrea Mantegna), 1993
Colored pencil on paper, 33 × 22⅖ inches, 84 × 58 cm
Collection of the Artist

Annunciation/Die Verkündigung/Annonciation, 1993
Mixed media on canvas, 69¼ × 47⅗ inches, 176 × 121 cm
Private Collection, Germany

Madonna I/Madone I, 1996
Mixed media on canvas, 63 × 41¾ inches, 160 × 106 cm
Courtesy Modernism Gallery, San Francisco

Epiphany I (Adoration of the Magi)/Epiphanie I (Die Anbetung der Heiligen Drei Könige)/Epiphanie I (L'Adoration des rois Mages), 1996
Mixed media on canvas, 82¾ × 131 inches, 210 × 333 cm
Vicki and Kent Logan, San Francisco

Epiphany II (Adoration of the Shepherds)/Epiphanie II (Die Anbetung der Hirten)/Epiphanie II (L'Adoration des bergers), 1998
Mixed media on canvas, 82¾ × 122 inches, 210 × 310 cm
Fine Arts Museum of San Francisco

Epiphany III (Presentation at the Temple)/Epiphanie III (Darbringung im Tempel)/Epiphanie III (Présentation au temple), 1998 ▷
Mixed media on canvas, 82¾ × 122 inches, 210 × 310 cm
Courtesy Modernism Gallery, San Francisco

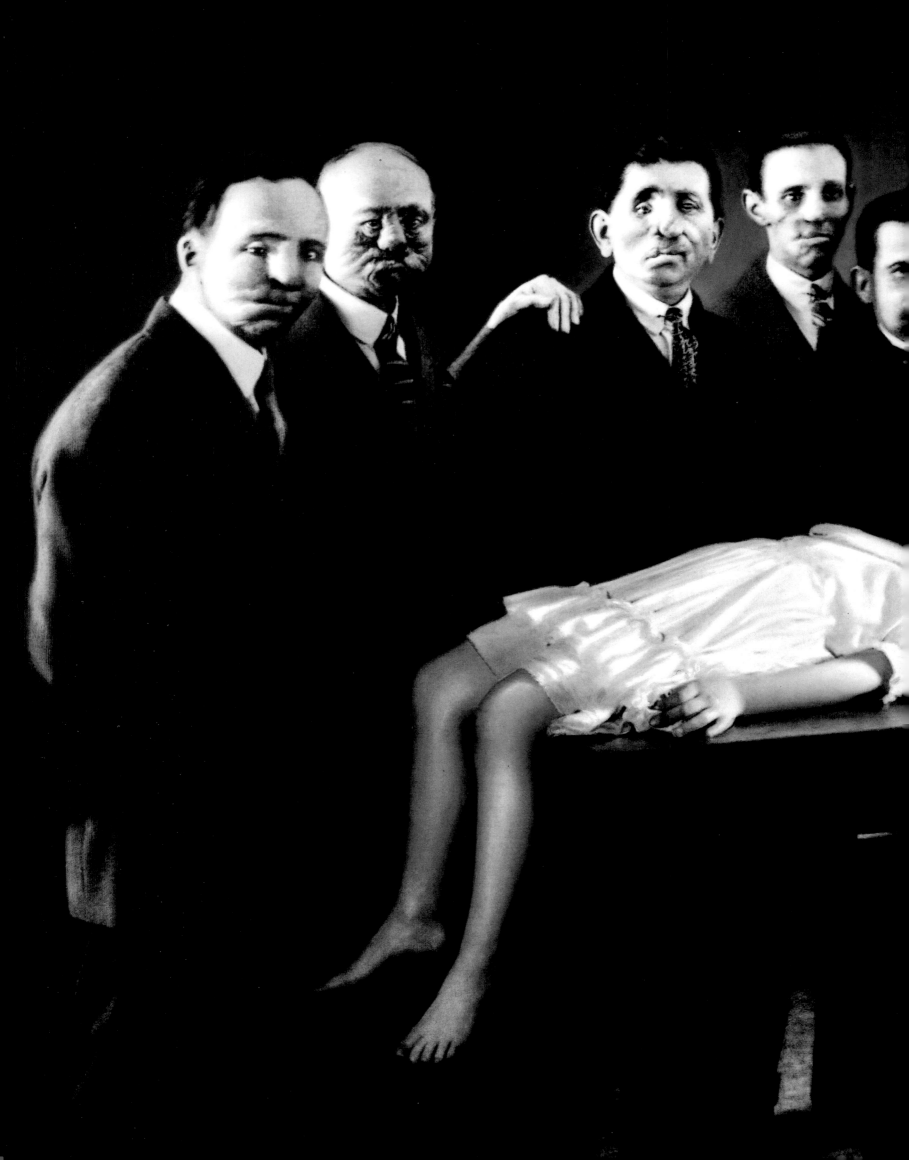

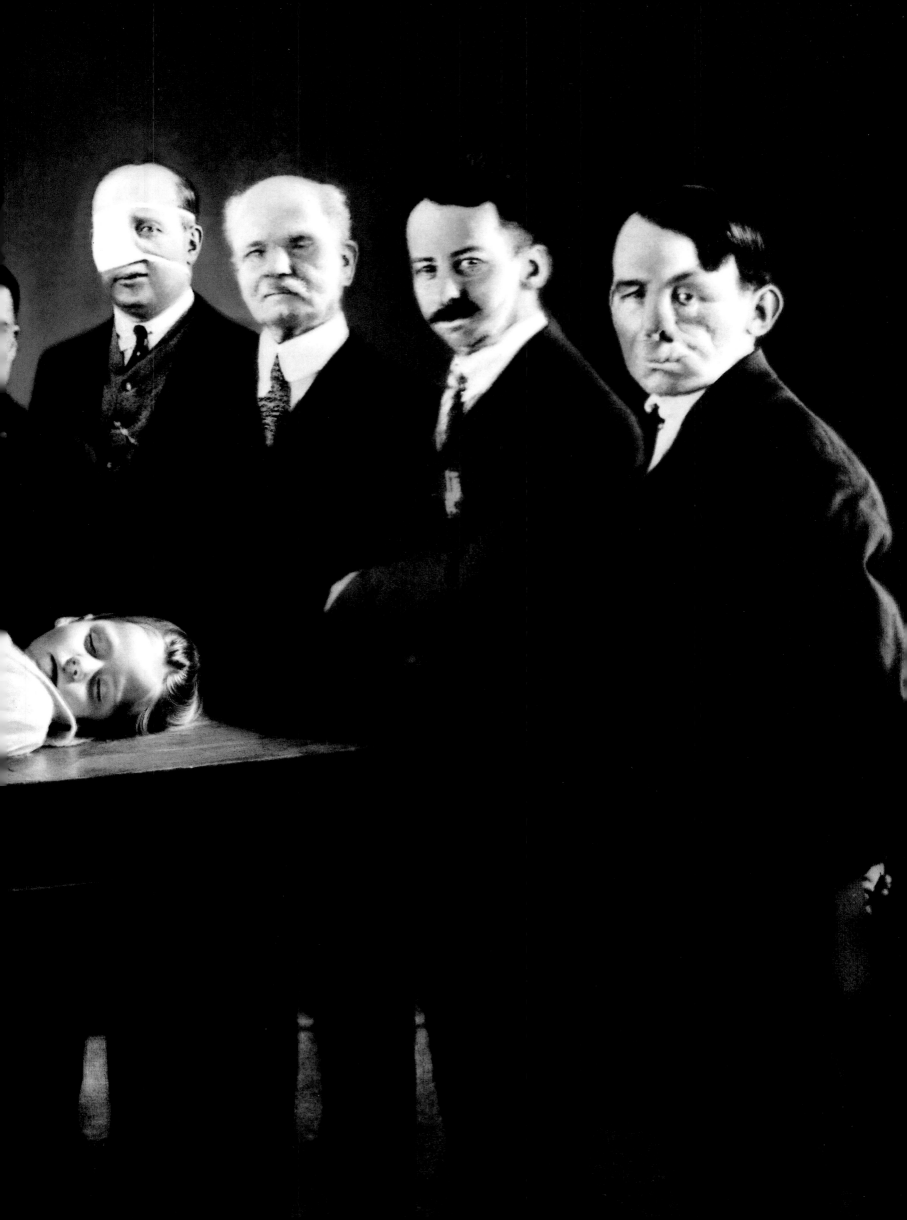

48 Portraits/48 Porträts, 1991
Mixed media on canvas, each painting 27½ × 21⅗ inches, 70 × 55 cm
Ludwig Forum for International Art, Aachen

visualisieren. »Wichtig an meinen Arbeiten ist, glaube ich, auch die Verschiedenheit der Aspekte: die realistischen Bilder, die abstrakten Serien, die Pastelle, die Farbstift-Zeichnungen und die Fotografien – wenn man all die Dinge, die ich gemacht habe, bis zu den monochromen Bildern hin verfolgt und vergleicht, merkt man, daß am Ende überall trotz anderem Stil, anderem Medium oder Material, eine Verbindung vorhanden, daß dieselbe Aussage da ist«[18]. Infolgedessen sind seine großen Ausstellungen auch sorgfältig vorbereitete Installationen. In Gottfried Helnwein verkörpert sich ein Künstler neuen Typs, der sich nicht als Spezialist begreift, obwohl seine künstlerische Arbeit ausschließlich um eine ganz konkrete Vorstellungswelt kreist, deren Facetten er in der vielfältig gebrochenen Welt seiner multi-medialen Bilder zur Erscheinung bringt. Außen- und Innenwelt seiner Kunst sind unablösbar miteinander verwoben, Ich und Welt korrespondieren in reziprokem Verhältnis, und in einer verblüffenden aber erhellenden Wendung relativieren seine Bilder Kaiser Friedrichs II. Überzeugung, daß die Welt als abgeschlossene Einheit dem Ich gegenübertritt: augenscheinlich ein aus der Zeit verständlicher philosophischer Irrtum. Denn auch Descartes ist kaum mehr noch als eine bedeutende historische Figur. Die Erkenntnisse der Menschen, nicht zuletzt dank der Künstler, sind darüber hinweggegangen.

Bonn, im März/April 1996

que l'important dans mes travaux est aussi leur diversité : les tableaux réalistes, les séries abstraites, les aquarelles, les dessins aux crayons de couleur et les photographies. Quand on suit tout ce que j'ai fait avant d'en arriver aux monochromes et que l'on compare, on remarque qu'il existe quand même un lien entre eux malgré la différence de styles, de média ou de matériau, et qu'ils véhiculent le même message. »[18] Il conçoit donc ses grandes expositions comme des installations soigneusement préparées. Un artiste d'un nouveau genre s'incarne en la personne de Gottfried Helnwein, un artiste qui n'entend pas être un spécialiste, bien que son travail tourne exclusivement autour d'un imaginaire très concret dont il dévoile les aspects dans le monde aux multiples faces de ses œuvres multimedias. Dans son art, un monde extérieur et intérieur s'imbriquent l'un dans l'autre de façon indissociable ; le moi et le monde se répondent dans une relation de réciprocité, et d'une manière étrange mais révélatrice, ses tableaux relativisent la conviction de l'empereur Frédéric II qui croyait que le monde était une entité achevée confrontée au moi : visiblement une erreur philosophique compréhensible compte tenu de l'époque. Car au fond, même Descartes n'est plus guère aujourd'hui qu'un important personnage historique. Or ce sont finalement les artistes qui ont permis aux hommes d'acquérir une connaissance qui va au-delà des apparences.

Bonn, mars/avril 1996

Selektion (Ninth November Night)/Selektion (Neunter November Nacht)/Sélection (La Nuit du neuf novembre), 1988
Scanachrome on vinyl, each picture 146 × 98 inches, 370 × 250 cm
100-meter-long installation between the Museum Ludwig and the Cathedral of Cologne. The pictures of this installation were destroyed one night by strangers with knife cuts

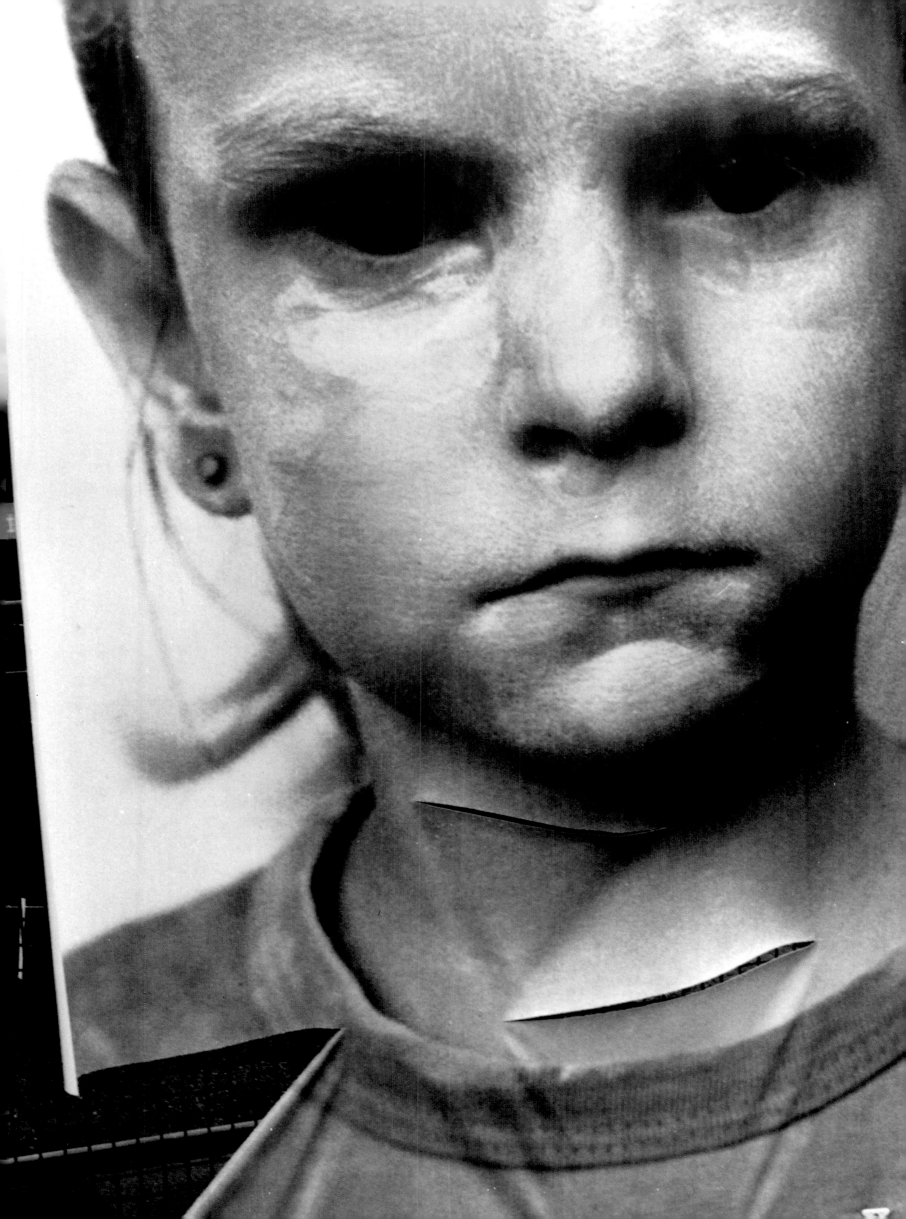

Untitled/Ohne Titel/Sans titre, 1994
Mixed media on canvas, 82⅗ × 59 inches, 210 × 150 cm
Vicki and Kent Logan, San Francisco

Head of a Child/Kindskopf/Tête d'enfant, 1991
Installation at the Minoriten Church in Krems/Stein, Niederösterreichisches Landesmuseum, Austria
Mixed media on canvas, 236 × 157½ inches, 600 × 400 cm
Ludwig Museum in the Russian Museum, St. Petersburg

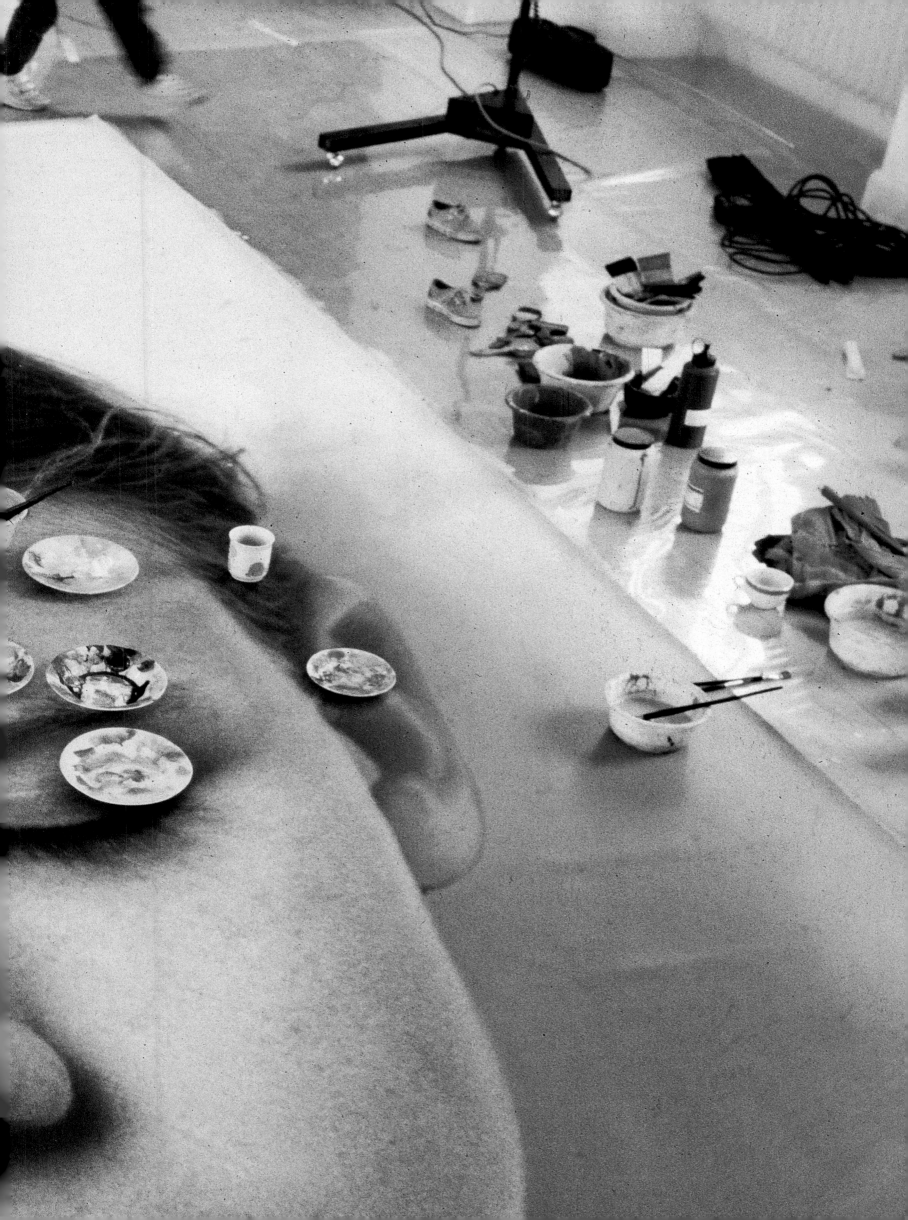

Poem 1/Poème 1, 1996
Photograph, acrylic glass and iron, 24 × 18 inches, 60 × 45 cm

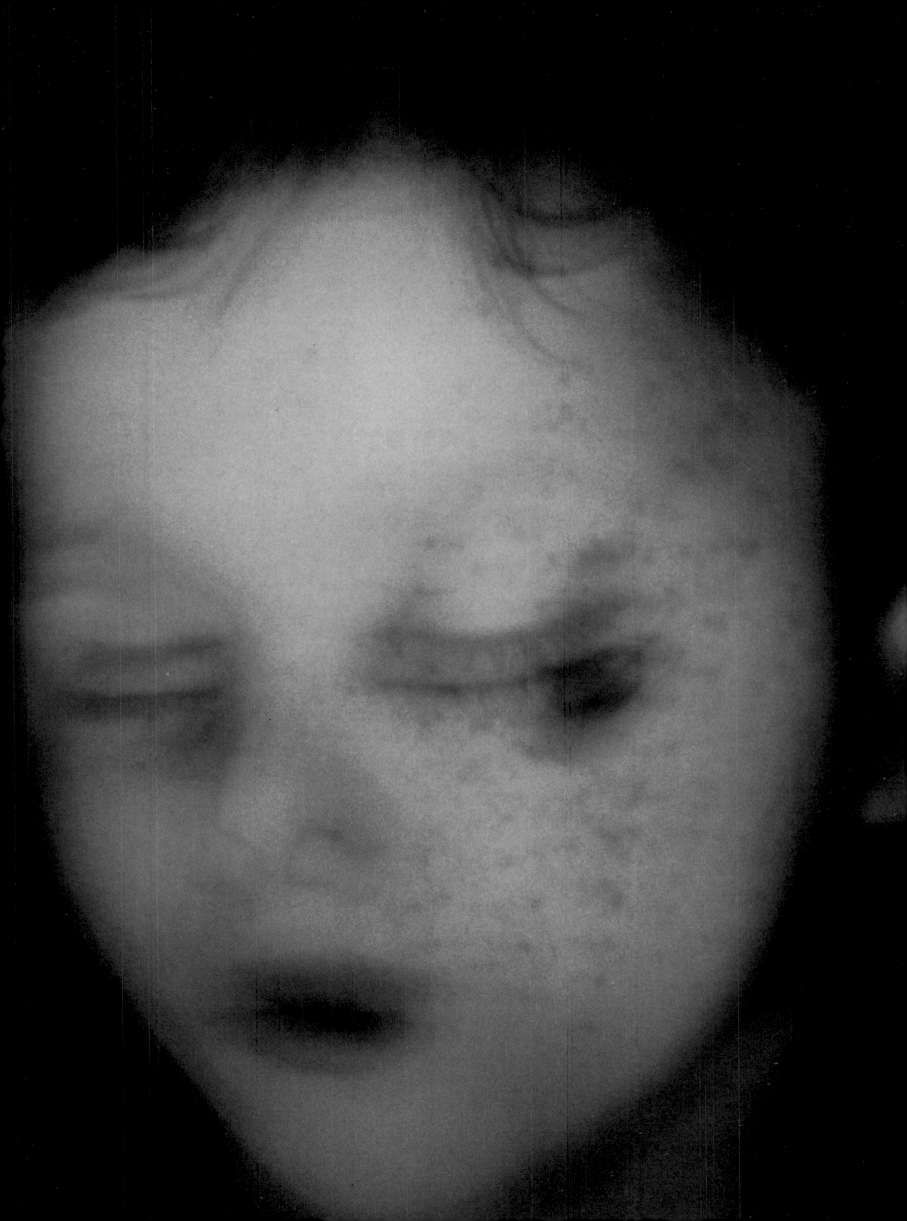

Poem 2/Poème 2, 1997
Photograph, acrylic glass and iron, 24 × 18 inches, 60 × 45 cm

Poem 3/Poème 3, 1977
Photograph, acrylic glass and iron, 24 × 18 inches, 60 × 45 cm

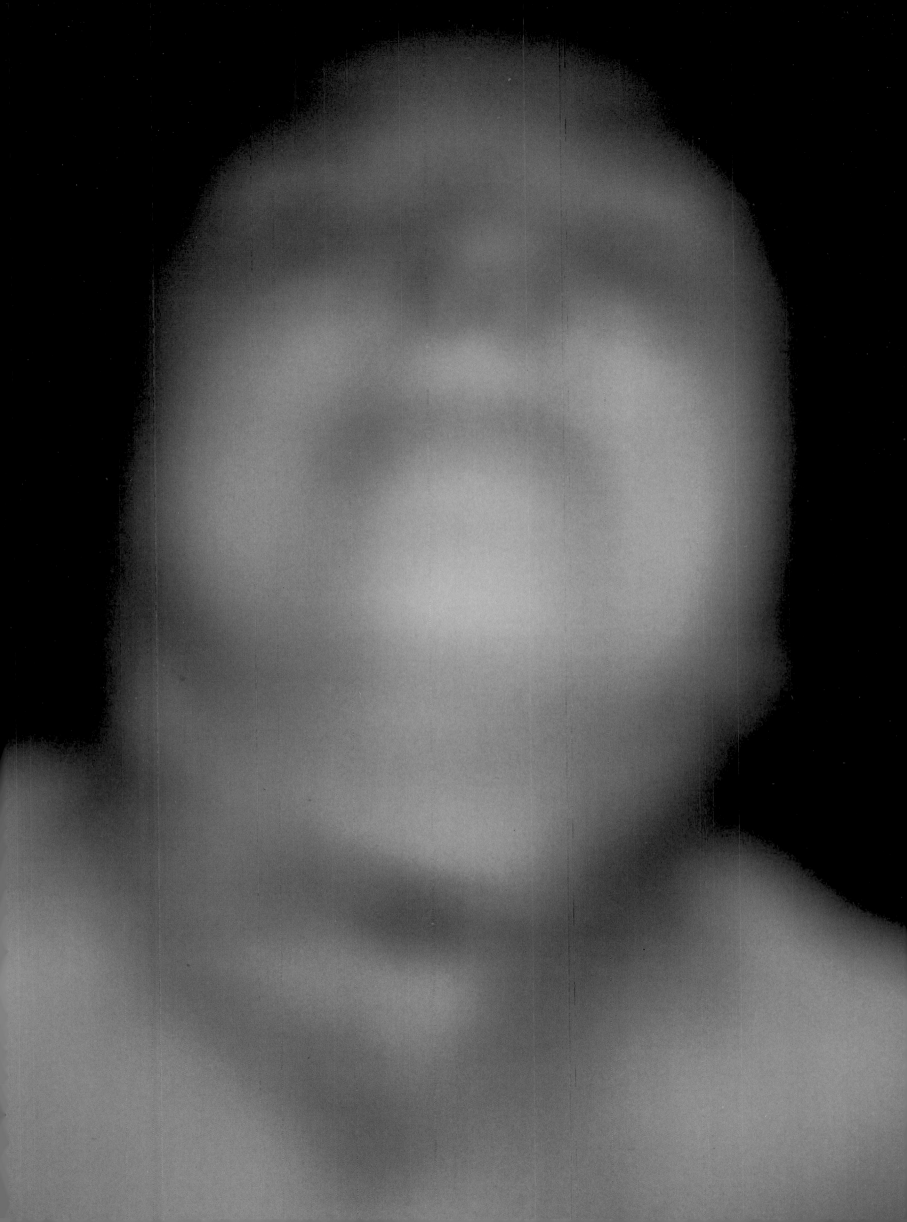

Poem 4/Poème 4, 1996
Photograph, acrylic glass and iron, 24 × 18 inches, 60 × 45 cm

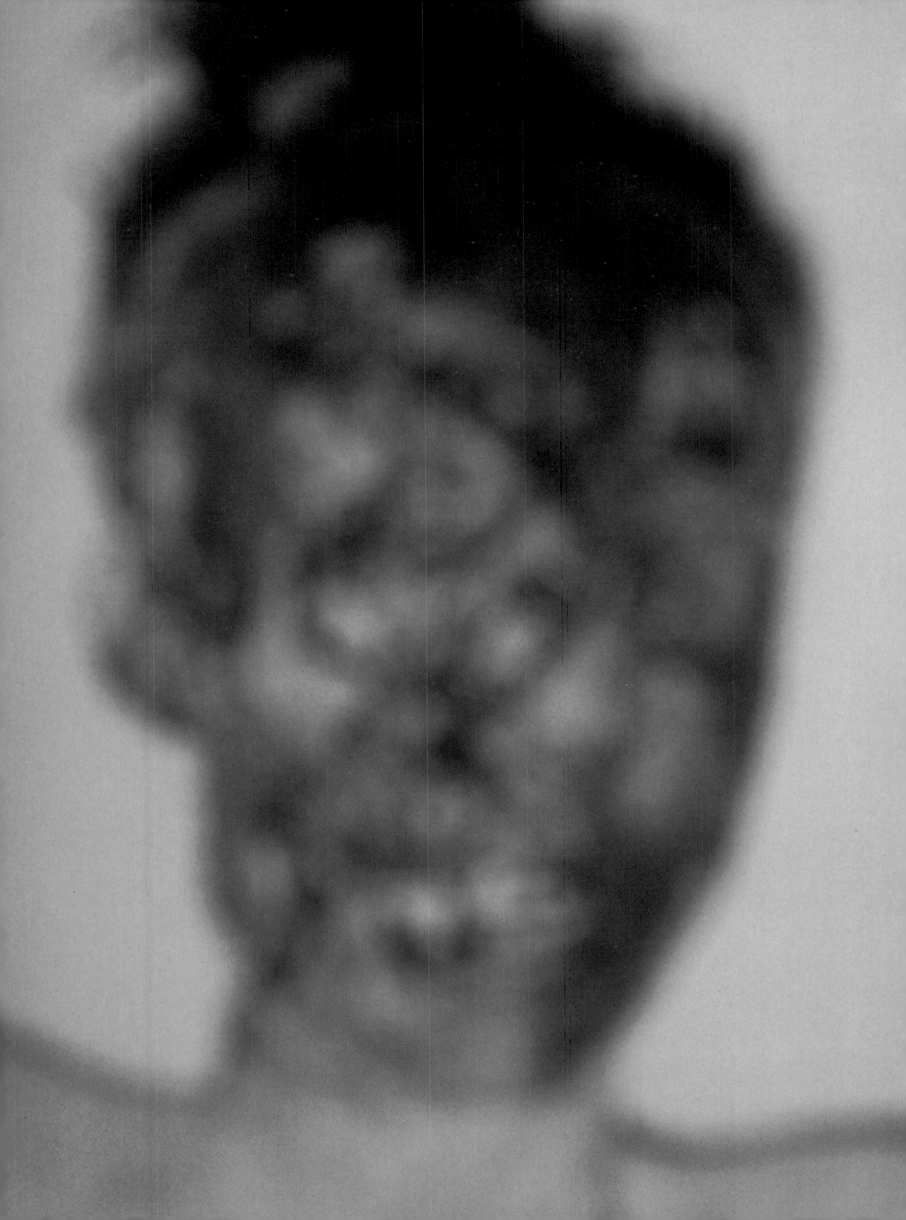

Poem 5/Poème 5, 1997
Photograph, acrylic glass and iron, 24 × 18 inches, 60 × 45 cm

Poem 6/Poème 6, 1996
Photograph, acrylic glass and iron, 24 × 18 inches, 60 × 45 cm

Poem 7/Poème 7, 1997
Photograph, acrylic glass and iron, 24 × 18 inches, 60 × 45 cm

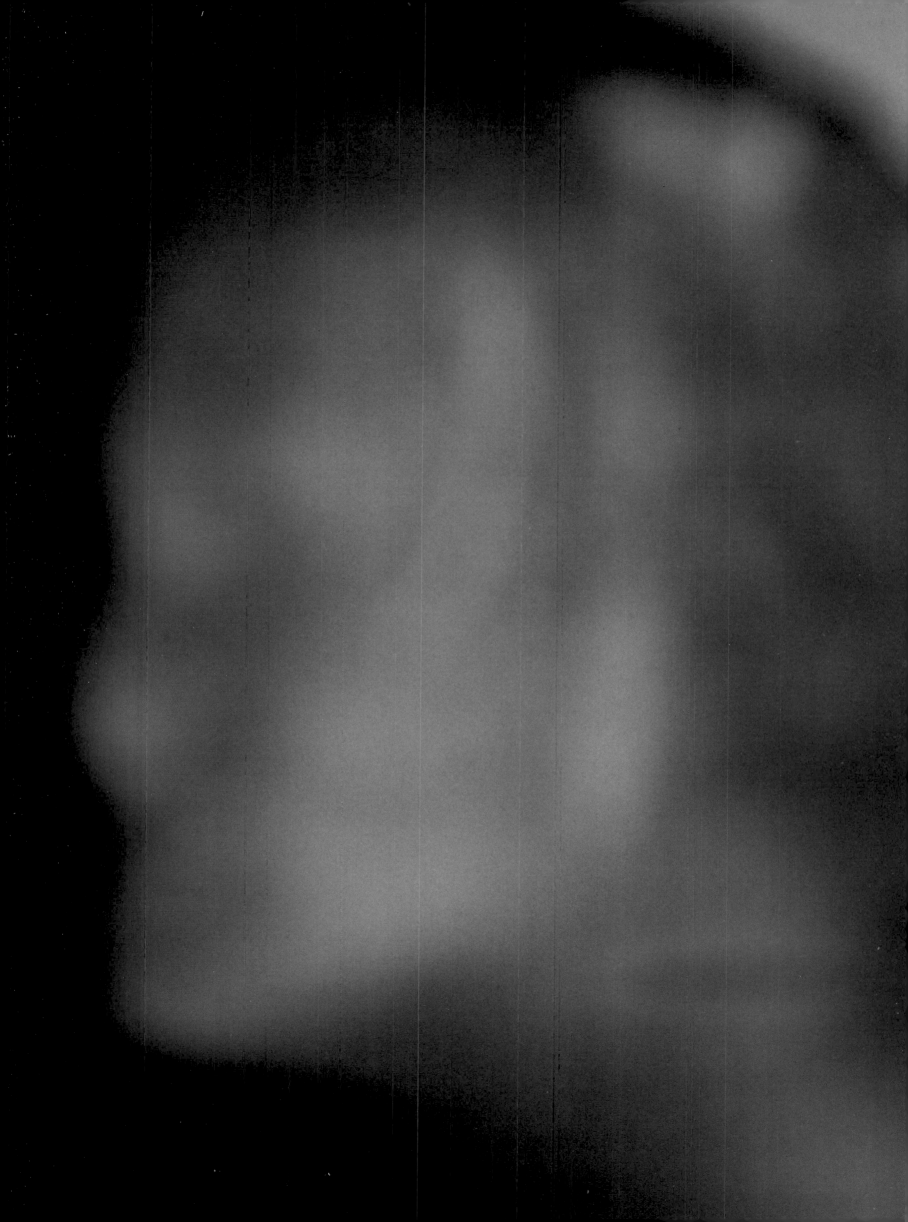

Poem 8/Poème 8, 1996
Photograph, acrylic glass and iron, 24 × 18 inches, 60 × 45 cm

Poem 9/Poème 9, 1996
Photograph, acrylic glass and iron, 24 × 18 inches, 60 × 45 cm

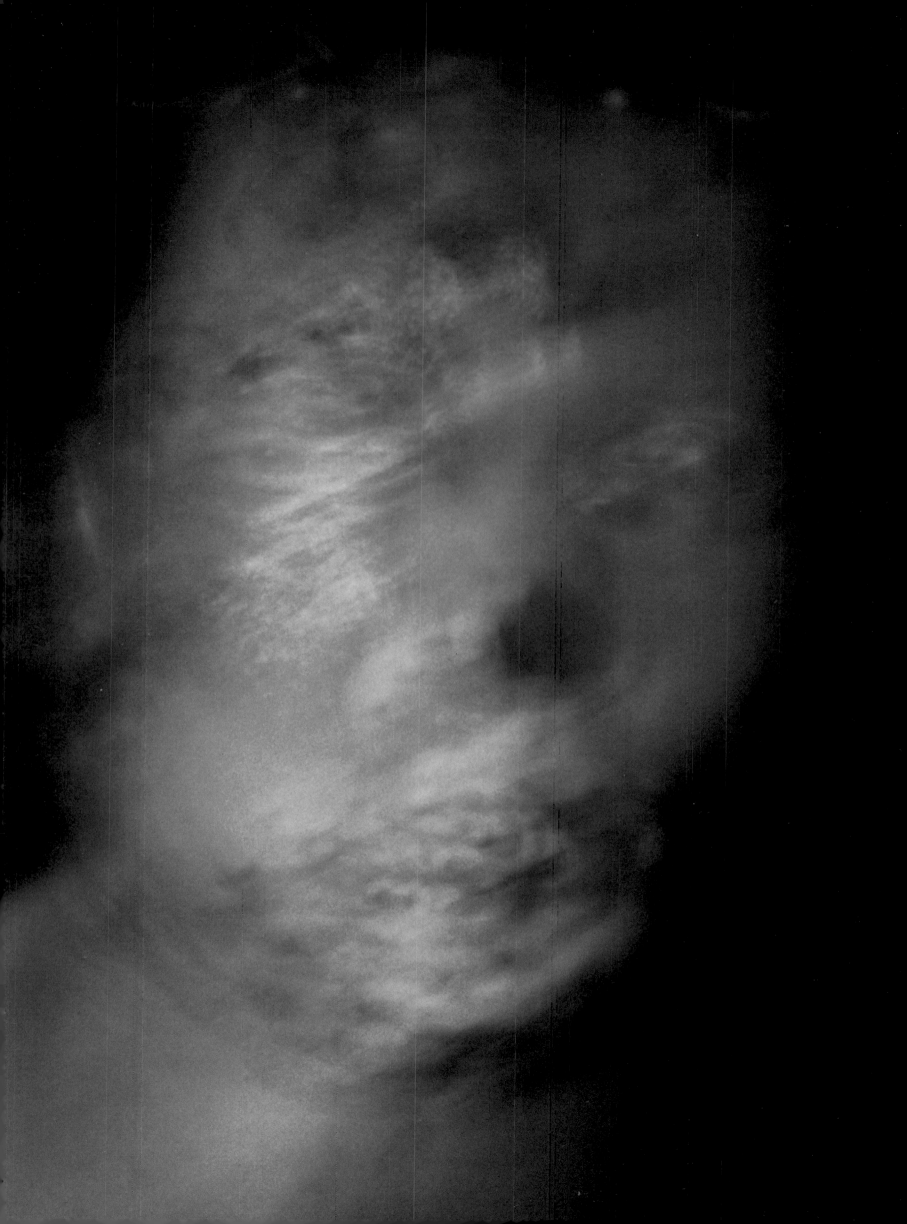

Poem 10/Poème 10, 1997
Photograph, acrylic glass and iron, 24×18 inches, 60×45 cm

Poems/Poèmes, Installation 1997
Collection Gruber, Cologne

Fire (Mishima)/Feuer (Mishima)/Feu (Mishima), 1996
Mixed media, 39½ × 31 inches, 100 × 79 cm
Courtesy Modernism Gallery, San Francisco   356

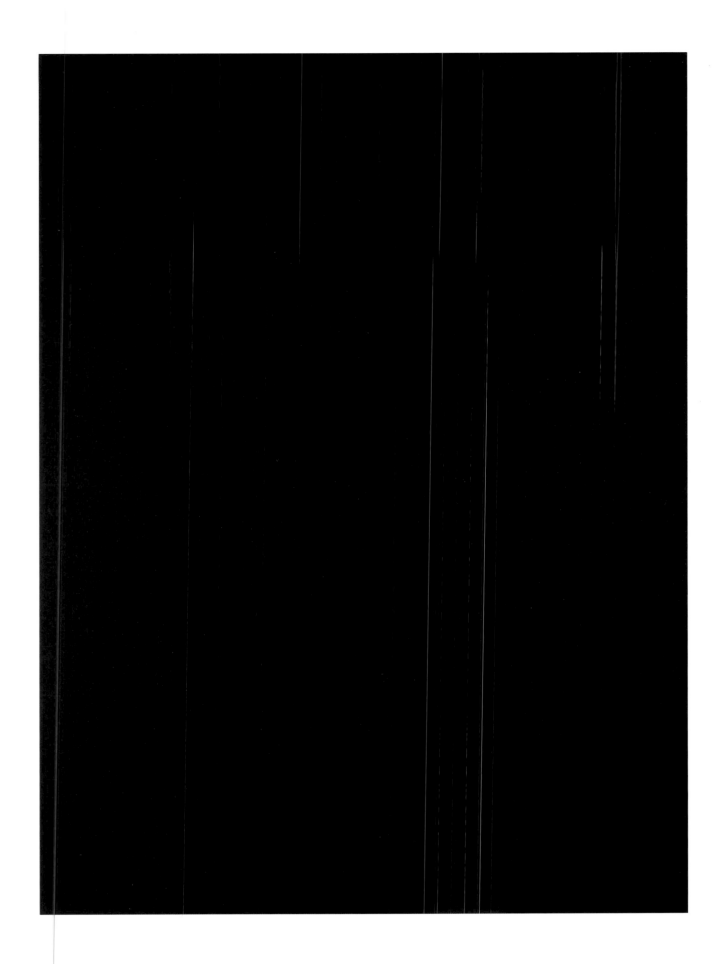

Fire (Mayakovski)/Feuer (Majakowski)/Feu (Maïakovski), 1994
Mixed media, 39½ × 31 inches, 100 × 79 cm
Courtesy Modernism Gallery, San Francisco

357

Charles Bukowski, 1991
Silver print, 39 × 26 inches, 99 × 66 cm
San Francisco Museum of Modern Art

Michael Jackson, 1988
Silver print, 39 × 26 inches, 99 × 66 cm
Museum Ludwig, Cologne

Keith Richards, 1990
Silver print, 39 × 26 inches, 99 × 66 cm
Rheinisches Landesmuseum, Bonn

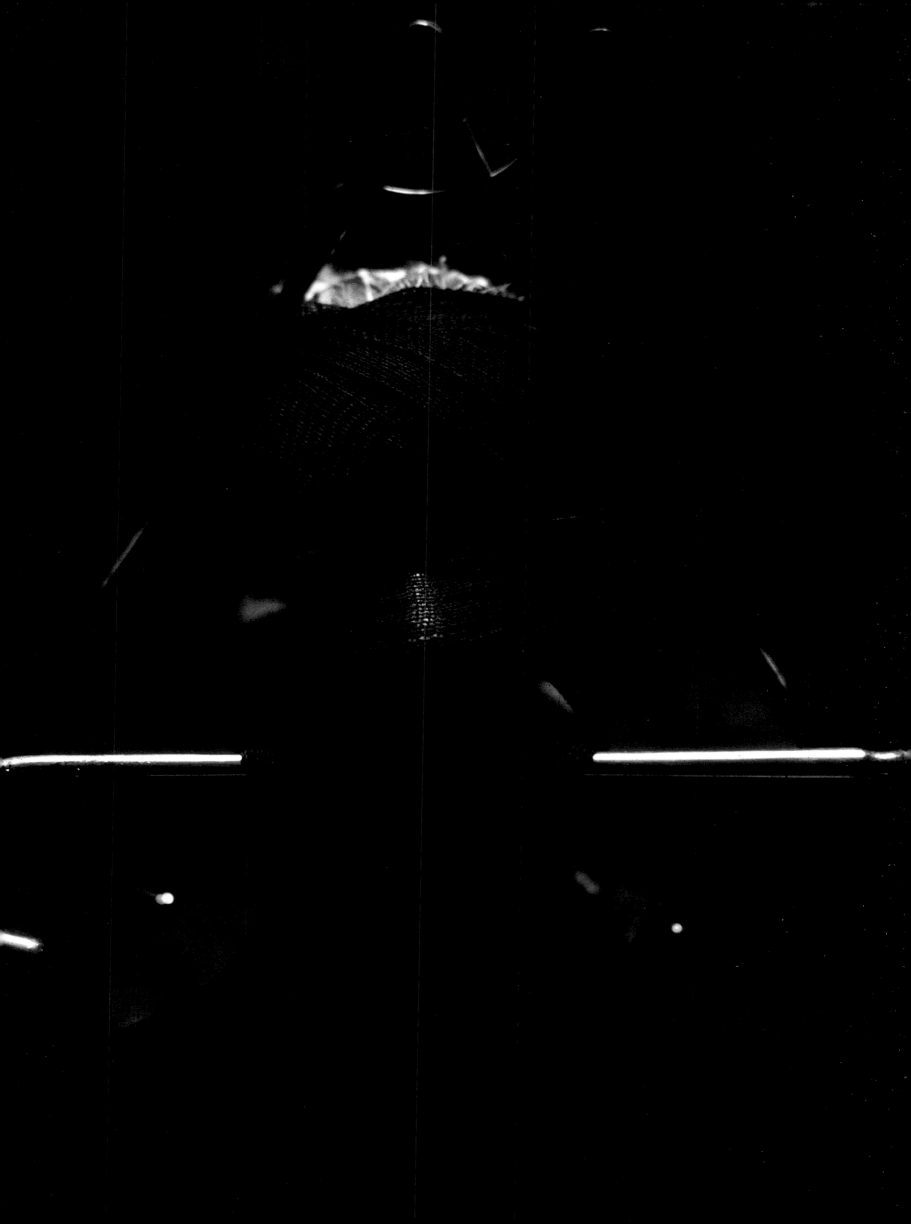

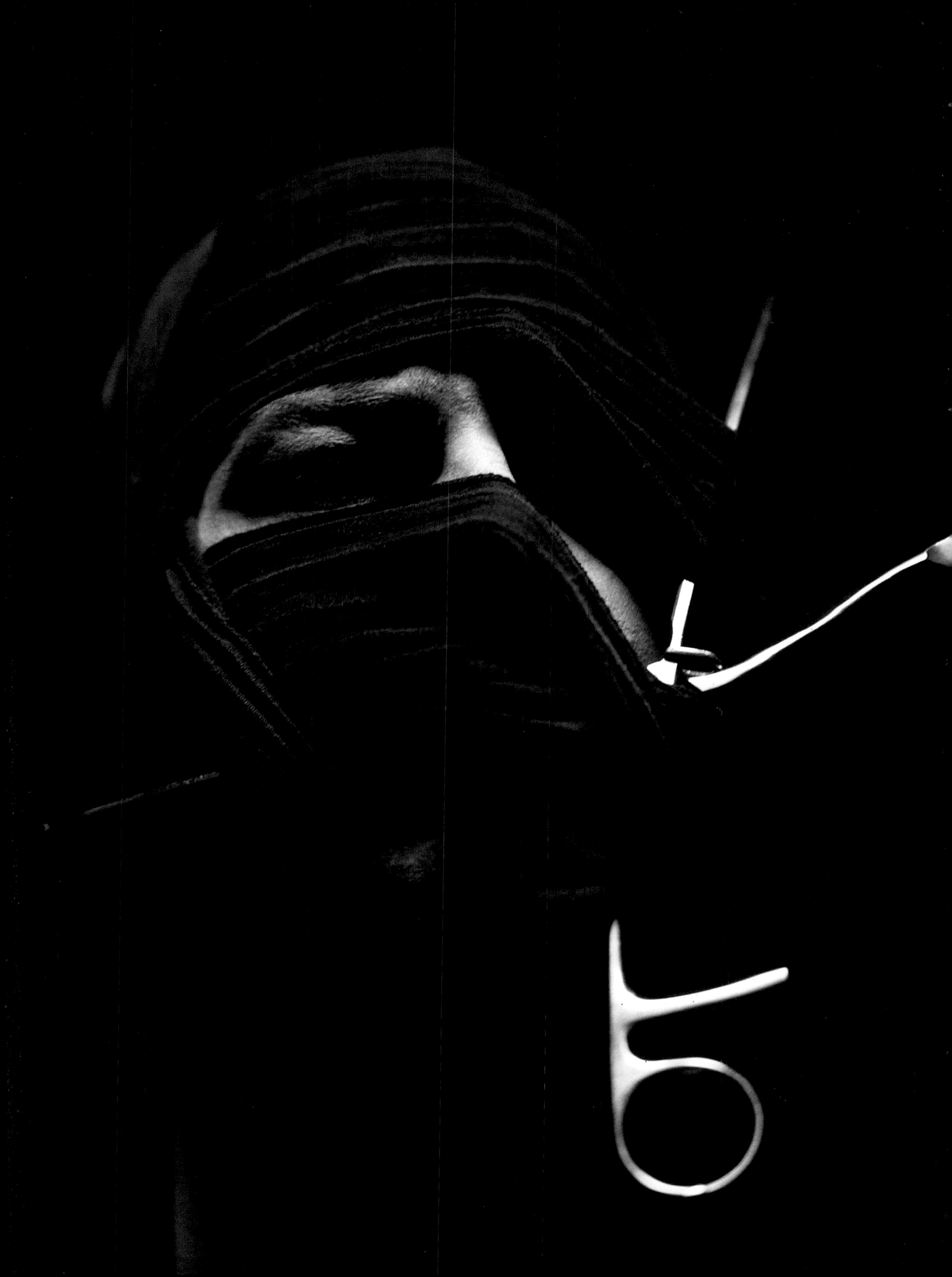

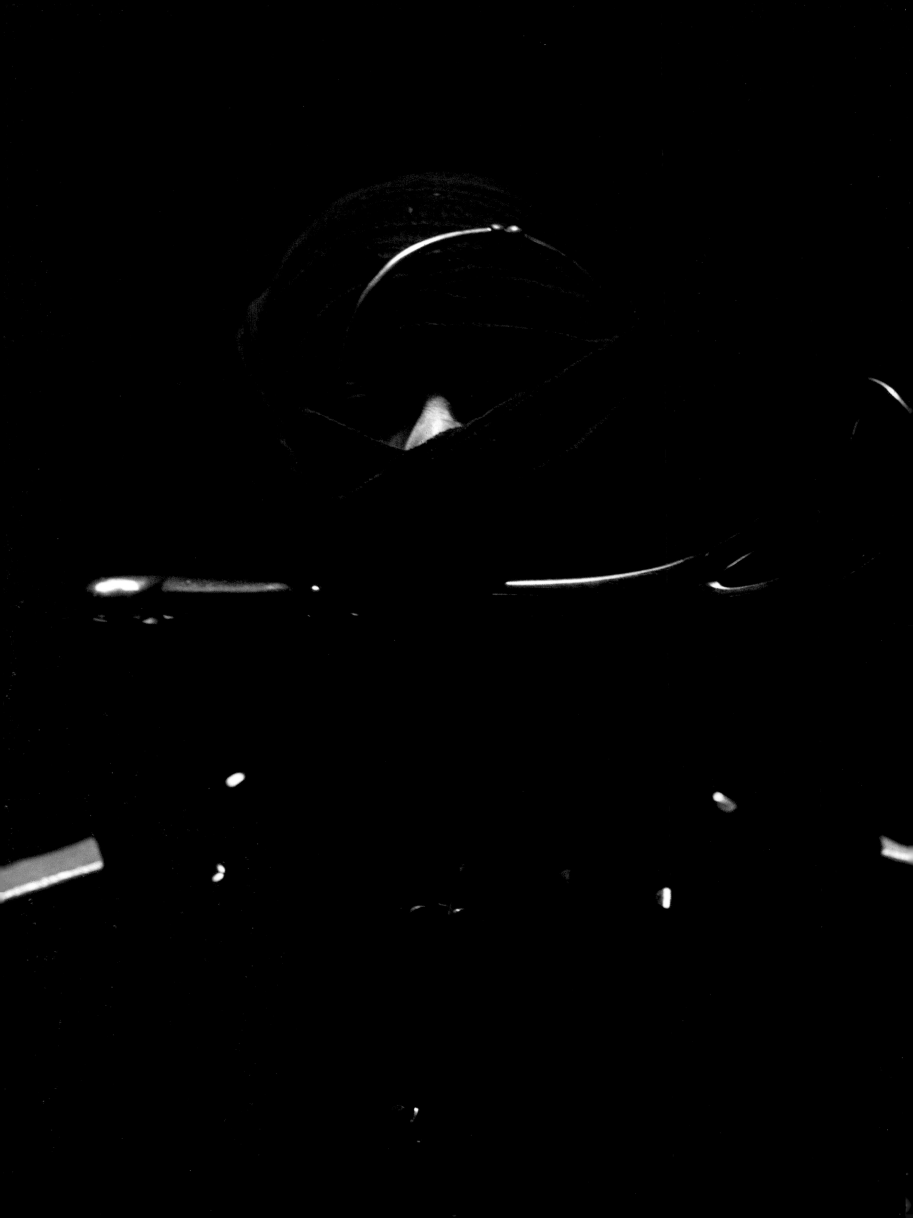

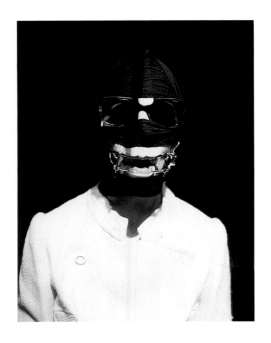

Scene from "Macbeth"/Szene aus »Macbeth«/
Scène de « Macbeth », Volksbühne Berlin, 1995

Scenes from "Macbeth"/Szenen aus »Macbeth«/
Scènes de « Macbeth », Theater der Stadt Heidelberg, 1988

One of the Witches in "Macbeth"/Eine der Hexen in »Macbeth«/
Une des sorcières de « Macbeth », Volksbühne Berlin, 1995

"Lady Macbeth", Volksbühne Berlin, 1995

Scene from "Macbeth"/Szene aus »Macbeth«/
Scène de « Macbeth », Theater der Stadt Heidelberg, 1988   394

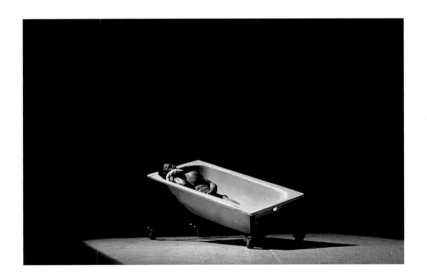

Scenes from "Macbeth"/Szenen aus »Macbeth«/Scènes de « Macbeth », Theater der Stadt Heidelberg, 1988

Stage scenery and costumes for "The Persecution and Assassination of Jean Paul Marat, ▷
performed by the Charenton's hospice theater group, directed by the Marquis of Sade"/
Bühnenbild und Kostüme zu »Die Verfolgung und Ermordung Jean Paul Marats, dargestellt
durch die Schauspielgruppe des Hospizes zu Charenton unter Anleitung des Herrn de Sade«/
Scénographie et costumes pour « L'Arrestation et l'assassinat de Jean Paul Marat, interprétée
par la troupe de l'hospice de Charenton dirigée par le Marquis de Sade », by Peter Weiss
Staatstheater Stuttgart, 1990, directed by/Regie/Mise en scène Hans Kresnik.

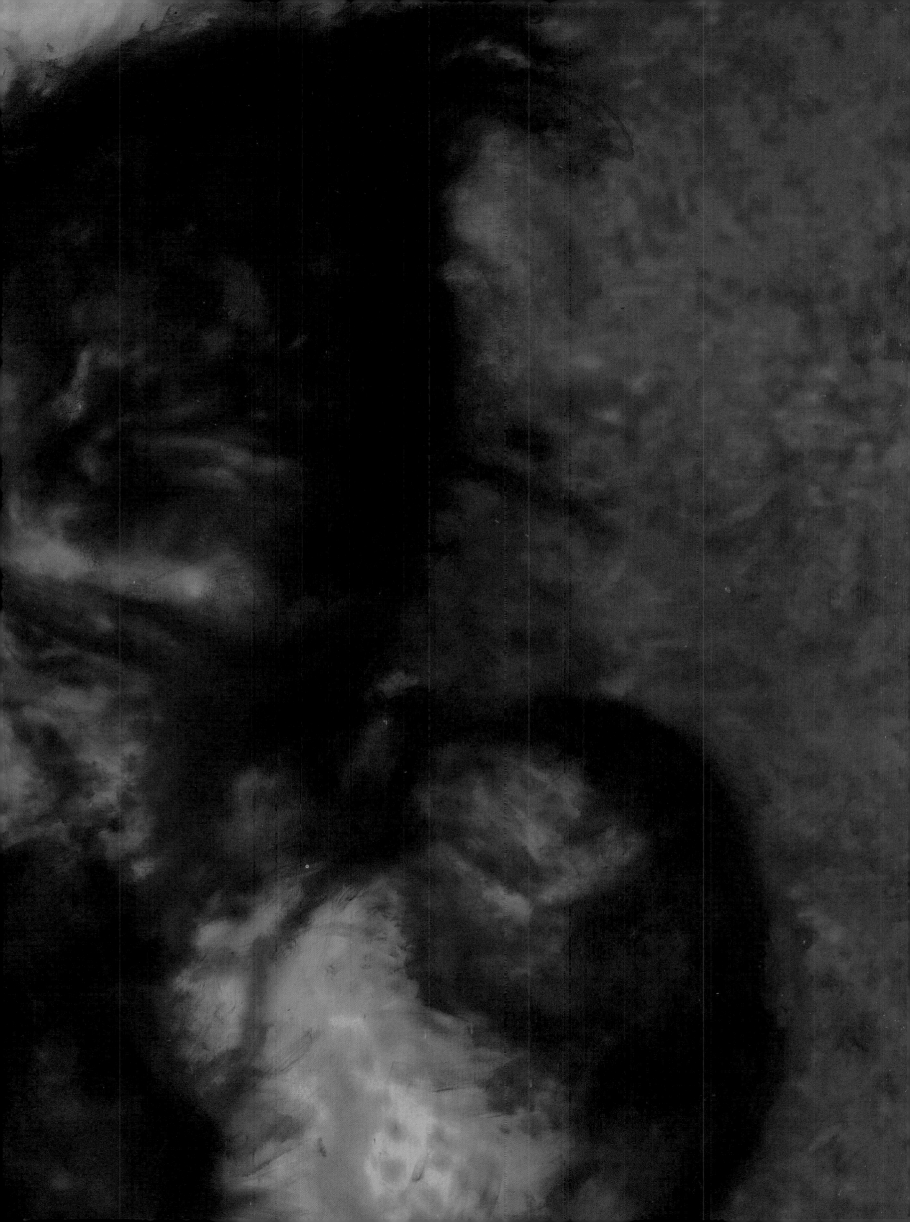

◁ "Pasolini", 1996
Oil and acrylic on canvas, 82⅗ × 122 inches, 210 × 310 cm
Design for the theater play "Pasolini"/Entwurf für das Theaterstück »Pasolini«/Maquette pour le spectacle « Pasolini », Deutsches Schauspielhaus, Hamburg
Stage setting, costumes and make-up/Bühnenbild, Kostüme und Maske/Scénographie, costumes et maquillage; Director/Regisseur/Metteur en scène Hans Kresnik

Gottfried Helnwein works on the stage setting for "Pasolini"/Gottfried Helnwein bei der Arbeit am
Bühnenbild zu »Pasolini«/Gottfried Helnwein travaillant aux décors de « Pasolini », in the studios
of the Deutsches Schauspielhaus Hamburg, 1996
Mixed media on vinyl, 30 × 45 feet, 10 × 15 cm

Untitled/Ohne Titel/Sans titre, 1996
Mixed media on canvas, 82⅗ × 55 inches, 210 × 140 cm
Tenor Neil Shicoff in a scene from the Opera "Peter Grimes"/Tenor Neil Shicoff in einer
Szene der Oper »Peter Grimes«/Le ténor Neil Shicoff dans une scène de « Peter Grimes »,
by Benjamin Britten, Wiener Staatsoper, 1996

Scratches and scrapes a series of self-portraits and child-photos with luminous stigma.

Child of Light, 1972, photograph, grattage

Self-Portrait, 1972, photograph, grattage

1973 First edition of an etching *Meine Buben haben einen Türken in die Schlucht gestossen* (My Little Rascals Have Shoved a Turk into the Ravine).

More pen-and-ink drawings and happenings with children; ORF (Austrian national TV) film: "Engagierte Kunst?" (Committed Art?), directed by E. Kroiss; Aktion *Sandra* in the Gallery over the Stubenbastei, Vienna.

First cover for the political and cultural magazine *Profil* ("Selbstmord in Österreich" [Suicide in Austria]) showing a little girl slashing her wrists. Strong public reactions; many readers cancel their subscriptions.

1974 Theodor Körner Prize.

Aktion *Weisse Kinder* (White Children) with 15 bandaged children in Kärntnerstrasse, in the center of Vienna.

ZDF (German national TV) film portrait "Helnweins Sehtest" (Helnwein's Eye Test), directed by Heinz Dieckmann.

Aktion White Children, Vienna, 1974

1975 Works on a series of pen-and-ink drawings on the subject of corrective devices (*Metallippe zum Lächeln* [Metal Lip for Smiling]; *Korrekturspange* [Corrective Brace]; *Das Wannenwunder von Watras* [The Bathtub Wonder of Watras]; *Assistent Assmann* [Assistant Assmann]; *Hilfe für Mann ohne Kinn* [Help for Man with no Chin] etc.).

1976 Aktion *Allzeit bereit* (Always Prepared) at the Naschmarkt, Vienna.

Helnwein, watercolor (detail), 1972   Goya, oil on canvas (detail), 1802–1812

1977 Seven-month stay abroad, studying in the USA. Intensive involvement with the work of Kandinsky and Walt Disney.

1979 One-man show with pen-and-ink drawings in the Albertina Museum, Vienna.

Aktion in the International Year of the Child.

R. Höpfinger and E. Regnier hand out sweets and toys bearing texts and Helnwein pictures of wounded and tortured children to passers-by in Zurich.

With an open letter and the picture of a dead child lying with its head in a plate of poisoned food (*Lebensunwertes Leben*)

Lebensunwertes Leben, 1979, watercolor

he protests against Austria's number one forensic psychiatrist, the former euthanasia doctor, Dr. Gross, who admitted in an interview that in the Nazi era he had poisoned hundreds of children and called this method of killing humane.

Helnwein became intensively involved with the phenomenon of the split between High Art and Trivial Art. He saw this as an apartheid situation in 20th century culture.

1981 Begins a series of works about trivial heroes and myths with a painting of the Austrian soccer star Hans Krankl, *Der Bomber der Nation* (The Bomber of the Nation).

Gottfried Helnwein, his son Cyril and Andy Warhol
Museum of Modern Art, Vienna, 1981

There followed the pictures of *Peter der Grosse* (Peter the Great) – the Austrian singer Peter Alexander – and *Niki Lauda,* the Austrian Formula 1 champion; the NDR film "Helnwein malt Lauda" (Helnwein paints Lauda) directed by Viktoria von Fleming.

The art establishment and the critics are shocked by these works and reject them. The Austrian playwright Wolfgang Bauer, on the other hand, is enthusiastic about these works and calls them "painting for eternity". The critic of the *Neue Zeit* retorts: "Let us hope that eternity will resist such impertinence."

Inspired by Helnwein's James Dean apotheosis, Wolfgang Bauer writes the ballad "Song for Helnwein – Boulevard of Broken Dreams".

First encounter and start of the friendship with H. C. Artmann; first monography, texts: H. C. Artmann, Botho Strauss, Wolfgang Bauer and Barbara Frischmuth.

1982 Meets the Rolling Stones in London. Mick Jagger, Keith Richards, Ron Wood, Charlie Watts and Bill Wyman pose for Helnwein.

Helnwein's portrait of Kennedy makes the cover of *Time* for the 20th anniversary of the President's death.

The Higher College of Visual Art in Hamburg offers Helnwein a Chair. Helnwein declines the offer.

Mick Jagger and Gottfried Helnwein, London, 1982

Aktion *Mit Kind und Kegel*, Frankfurt, 1982

For *Zeit Magazin*, Peter Sager writes a cover story about Helnwein.

The self-portrait as a screaming blinded man is used for this cover story and later for the cover of the Scorpions album *Blackout*.

Bavarian Television produces a film portrait of Helnwein, directed by Hans-Dieter Hartl.

Helnwein self-portrait
on the cover of the Scorpions album *Blackout*

Boulevard of Broken Dreams, 1981, watercolor

ZEIT*magazin*

L'Espres

GUERRA
ALLA DROGA

Germany, 1982

Italy, 1984

Japan, 1983

Muhammad Ali, Gottfried Helnwein and his son Ali, Los Angeles, 1983

Scene from the film "Helnwein", Vienna, 1984

1983 One-man show in the Stadtmuseum Munich. The exhibition is seen by more than a hundred thousand people. Andy Warhol poses for Helnwein in New York for a series of photos.

First encounter with theater director Peter Zadek.

"Rettet die Donau" (Save the Danube) – the Austrian art-collector and patron Hans Dichand finances a campaign with large billboards of Helnwein's artwork throughout Austria against the destruction of the last great riverside meadowland woods in Europe by the Austrian power-station company Donaukraftwerke AG.

ZDF and ORF produce the film "Helnwein", directed by Peter Hajek.

In the radio program "Teestunde" (Tea-time), Helnwein uses obscenities to insult the inventor of the neutron bomb, Sam T. Cohen, criticizes the education and training system at schools and art schools, draws attention to the high number of student suicides, and calls upon young people simply to stay away from school. The directors of Austrian Radio cancel this program.

In Los Angeles Helnwein meets Muhammad Ali, who appears in his film. His self-portrait is shown in the exhibition "Köpfe und Gesichter" (Heads and Faces) in the Darmstadt Kunsthalle.

1984 "Helnwein", the film by Peter Hajek, opens the Austrian Week in the Berlin film festival, "Berlinale". The film is awarded the Adolf Grimme Prize and in the same year wins the Eduard Rhein Prize and the Golden Kader of the city of Vienna for outstanding camera work.

A self-portrait collage as a contribution to the "1984 – Orwell and the Present Day" exhibition in the Museum of Modern Art in Vienna.

The office of Soviet foreign minister Gromyko tries to acquire Helnwein's portrait of Gromyko, which appeared as a *Time* cover. But the painting is already part of a collection in the Smithsonian Museum in Washington D.C.

Helnwein's self-portrait is on the cover of *L'Espresso*, in Italy. Helnwein meets Walt Disney artist Carl Barks, creator of the Donald Duck legend. Helnwein maintains that he learned more about art and life from Donald Duck than from all the schools he ever attended.

Mick Jagger
by Gottfried Helnwein, 1982

John Lennon
by Andy Warhol, 1980

J. F. Kennedy
by Gottfried Helnwein, 1983

Robert Kennedy
by Roy Lichtenstein, 1968

Participation in the portfolio of graphic art for the Olympic Games in Sarajevo '84 with Henry Moore, James Rosenquist, Mimmo Paladino, Cy Twombly, Andy Warhol and others. Photo session with Clint Eastwood in the Stadtmuseum, Munich.

1985 One-man show at the Albertina museum, Vienna. Catalogue with texts by Walter Koschatzky and Peter Gorsen. Moves to Germany and lives and works in a castle near Cologne. He radically changes his way of working and now begins a series of large-format pictures consisting of several

Helnwein in his studio, Germany, 1985

parts (diptychs, triptychs, poliptychs). In doing so he combines photomurals with abstract gestural and monochrome painting in oil and acrylic, also using reproductions of Caspar David Friedrich paintings and war documentary photographs which he assembles to form what the critic Peter Gorsen calls "Bilderstrassen" (picture lanes). In doing this, Helnwein closely examines taboo areas and tackles terms such as "Untermensch" (sub-human), "entartete Kunst" (degenerate art), "lebensunwertes Leben" (life unworthy of life).

Rudolf Hausner proposes Helnwein as his successor as head of the masterclass for painters at the Academy of Visual Art in Vienna.

William S. Burroughs and Gottfried Helnwein, in Lawrence, Kansas, 1989

Time magazine commissions Robert Rauschenberg and Gottfried Helnwein to design covers with Deng Xiaoping. *Time* magazine commissions Gottfried Helnwein to do a portrait of Mikhail Gorbachev. At this time, Brezhnev is still alive. Gorbachev is at this point the candidate with the least chance of succeeding to the office of president.

Dance of the Ape, 1987, photograph

Aktion *Untermensch*, camp of the Austrian Army, Spratzern, 1978

1986 He works on a series of large-format self-portrait metamorphoses, which have their origin in the self-portrait as screaming man blinded by forks.

Start of a series of photographic self-dramatizations using the themes of dying hero, SS man, martyr, sufferer, friend of children, and mummified corpse (*Gott der Untermenschen* [God of Sub-Humans]; *Das stille Leuchten der Avantgarde* [The Silent Glow of the Avant-Garde]; *Bete Herr, denn wir sind nah!* [Pray, Lord, for We Are Near!]. *Eine Träne auf Reisen* [A Tear on a Journey]; *Der Tod des Expertentums* [The Death of Expertise]; *Partisanenliebe* [Partisan Love]; *Blitzkrieg der Liebe* [Blitz of Love]; *Geheime Elite* [Secret Elite]; *Gefäss der Leidenschaft* [Vessel of Passion]).

One-man show in the Mittelrhein Museum, Koblenz, and in the Freie Volksbühne theater in Berlin. Podium discussion "Violence, Sexuality, Antiquity" with Heiner Müller, Hans Neuenfels, Ernest Bornemann, and Gottfried Helnwein.

1987 Parallel to the large-format, multi-part pictures and the photographic work, he now also turns to crayon drawings (*Knabe und Neger* [Boy and Negro]; *Triumph der Wissenschaft* [Triumph of Science]; *Nachgeburt der Venus* [The Afterbirth of Venus]; *Das Lügengebet* [The Prayer of Lies]).

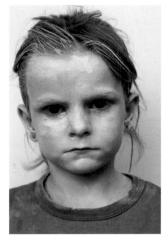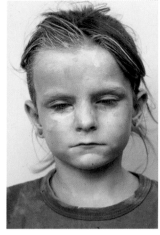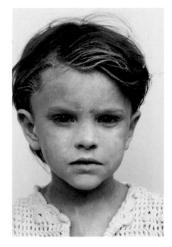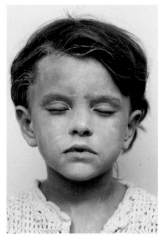

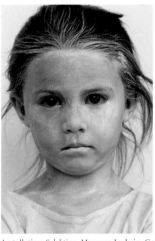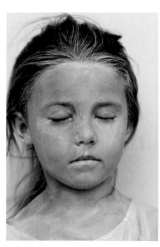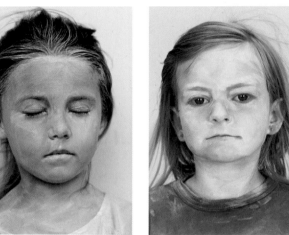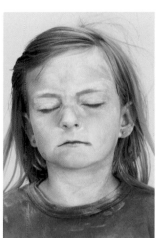

Installation *Selektion*, Museum Ludwig, Cologne, 1988

One-man exhibition in the Leopold Hoesch Museum, Düren; in the Villa Stuck, Munich; and in the Musée d'Art Moderne in Strasbourg.

Installation and Exhibition Opera *Der Untermensch* in the Kunsthalle, Bremen.

The monography "Der Untermensch", self-portraits from 1979–1987 is published by Verlag Edition Braus. Texts by Heiner Müller and Peter Gorsen.

1988 Large installation in front of the Ludwig Museum in Cologne: *Selektion (Ninth November Night)* is a four-meter-high, hundred-meter-long picture lane in which Gottfried Helnwein recalls the "Reichskristallnacht", the start of the Holocaust, on 9 November 1938. He confronts the passers-by with larger-than-life children's faces lined up in a seemingly endless row, as if for concentration camp selection.

Installation *Selektion*, Museum Ludwig, Cologne, 1988

Helnwein now works simultaneously on large-format monochrome-blue realistic oil and acrylic pictures and on monochrome abstract pictures.

The poster for Peter Zadek's production of "Lulu" by Frank Wedekind in the Schauspielhaus theater in Hamburg unleashes a storm of outrage.

The Deputy Mayor of Hamburg protests against the picture.

One-man show, Musée d'Art Moderne, Strasbourg, 1987

Gesäßformen I, 1988, oil on canvas

A "German-Language Citizens' Initiative for the Protection of Human Dignity" lays charges against Helnwein and Zadek for pornography. The discussion about this picture spreads beyond the borders of the country. The Mayor of the City of Vienna, Helmut Zilk, is enthusiastic about the poster and gives Helnwein his hearty congratulations.

Night V, 1990, mixed media on canvas

critics and is later awarded the Theater Prize of Berlin.

One-man exhibition "Arbeiten auf Papier" (Works on Paper) in the Kunstverein in Ludwigsburg.

Helnwein meets William S. Burroughs in Lawrence, Kansas.

Helnwein meets Norman Mailer in Provincetown, USA.

Works on a series of drawings and pastels: *Modern Sleep; Gott in Panik* (God in Panic); *Das Wunderkind* (Child Prodigy); *Verbrannter Engel* (Burnt Angel).

"Torino Fotografia '89 Biennale Internazionale", exhibition with Clegg and Guttmann and David Hockney.

1990 One-man show in the Musée de l'Elysée, Lausanne.

Helnwein's photographic work from 1970 to 1989 is published by Dai Nippon in Japan. Text by Toshiharu Ito.

Set and costumes for "Die Verfolgung und Ermordung Jean Paul Marats, dargestellt durch die Schauspielgruppe des Hospizes zu Charenton unter Anleitung des Herrn de Sade" (The Persecution and Murder of Jean Paul Marat, Performed by the Drama Group of the Hospice at Charenton under the Direction of Monsieur de Sade) by Peter Weiss, directed by Hans Kresnik at the Staatstheater in Stuttgart.

Set for Sophocles' "Oedipus" at Hans Kresnik's choreographic theater in Heidelberg.

Work on a fragment of the Berlin Wall for the exhibition project "30 Artists in Berlin" together with Robert Longo, Sol LeWitt, Mimmo Paladino and others.

Photo session with Keith Richards at the Berlin Wall.

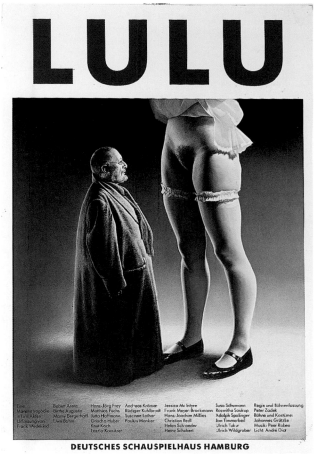

Poster for "Lulu", Deutsches Schauspielhaus Hamburg, 1988

Photo session with Michael Jackson in Germany.

Participates in the exhibition "Selection 4" Polaroid Art of the last 10 years in the Victoria & Albert Museum in London; and in the "Photokina" in Cologne.

1989 One-man show "Zeichnungen und Arbeiten auf Papier" (Drawings and Works on Paper) in the Folkwang Museum in Essen.

Co-operation with East German writer Heiner Müller and choreographer Hans Kresnik and dancer Ismael Ivo on a play about Antonin Artaud.

Work on the set and costumes for "Carmina Burana" by Carl Orff at the Bayerische Staatsoper opera house (opening of the 1990 Munich Festival).

When Wolfgang Sawallisch, the head of the Staatsoper, sees the radical costume design, he is so shocked that he immediately cancels the contracts with Helnwein and director Hans Kresnik.

Set, costumes, and make-up for "Macbeth", a production of Hans Kresnik's choreographic theater in the Stadttheater in Heidelberg.

The play is given an enthusiastic reception by audience and

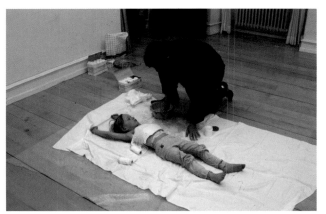

Helnwein and his son Amadeus
work on the installation *White Christmas* in his studio, Germany, 1988

1991 Meets Charles Bukowski and David Bowie in Los Angeles.

"Some facts about myself". Book project with Marlene Dietrich on Berlin after the Wall comes down: Helnwein takes photographs of the new Berlin and Marlene Dietrich writes an accompanying text. Published by Kathleen Madden.

Installation *Kindskopf* (Head of a Child) in the Minoriten Church in Krems, Niederösterreichisches Landesmuseum (Museum of Lower Austria). Helnwein paints a 6×4 meter (18×12 feet) child's head for the apse of the early Gothic

Heiner Müller and Gottfried Helnwein in Basel, 1989

GERMANIA
TOD IN BERLIN
HEINER MÜLLER

Nationaltheater Mannheim 87/88

Poster for "Germania, Tod in Berlin"

basilica. Ten days before the opening he has his children Amadeus, Ali Elvis and Mercedes paint large-format canvases which he then arranges in the basilica.

Works on the *48 Portraits,* a series of 48 monochrome red pictures of women (oil on canvas) as a counterpart to Gerhard Richter's *48 Portraits* of 1971, which depict only men in monochrome gray.

The cycle of paintings is first shown in the Gallery Koppelmann in Cologne.

Helnwein applies more and more layers of oil varnish to his realistic blue monochrome pictures till the subjects are almost indiscernible.

1992 Photo session with Roy Lichtenstein in New York, at the Leo Costelli Gallery.

Group exhibition in the Los Angeles County Museum of Art.

White Christmas installation in the Leopold Hoesch Museum in Düren for the 4th International Biennale of Paper Art.

First one-man show at the Modernism Gallery in San Francisco.

One-man show at the Pfalzgalerie Museum in Kaiserslautern and at the Kunstmuseum in Thun.

"Aktion-Reaktion", exhibition of Rainer, Nitsch, Brus, and Helnwein at the Foundation Fiecht Austria, Schömer collection.

"Faces", one-man show in the Munich Stadtmuseum.

"Faces", one man show, Centre International Contemporain d'Art, Montreal, 1994

1993 One-man show "Faces" in the Rheinisches Landesmuseum, Bonn.

In the Ludwig Forum in Aachen the *48 Portraits* are shown in the "Künstlerportraits" exhibition.

Deutsche Fototage, Frankfurt: Group Exhibition "Ansichten von Alexandra S." (Views of Alexandra S.).

1994 "Das Jahrzehnt der Malerei" (The Decade of Painting), Schömer Collection in the Kunstverein, Augsburg.

"Faces" one-man show in the Centre International d'Art Contemporain in Montreal.

One-man show in the Städtisches Museum, Schleswig.

Helnwein works on the *Fire* cycle in oil and acrylic, dark monochrome plates with the faces cf rebels such as Arthur Rimbaud, Jim Morrison, Malcolm X, Mishima, Mayakovski, Rosa Luxemburg, Ulrike Meinhof, Marcel Duchamp, Pier Paolo Pasolini and others.

He works intensively on the development of new artistic

Gottfried Helnwein and Keith Richards, Berlin Wall, 1990

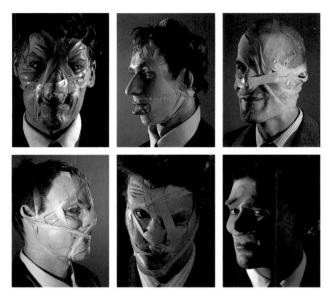

Rammstein, 1997, photographs

techniques. On the computer he processes and modifies photographs and paintings, then transfers them to the canvas and develops them further by painting over them.

Installation of a picture of a monochromic blue face of 25×16 meters (75×50 feet) in Vienna on a building in the city center.

1995 Group exhibition in the Städtische Galerie, Ludwig Institut Oberhausen: "Versuche zu trauern" (Attempts to Mourn), masterpieces from the Ludwig Collection from antiquity to the present day. Group exhibition in the Phoenix Museum of Art, Arizona; Contemporary Arts Center,

"Die Hamletmaschine", 47th Berliner Festwochen, Arena, Berlin, 1997

Cincinnati, Ohio; Lakeview Museum of Arts and Sciences, Peoria, Illinois; Nexus Contemporary Arts Center, Atlanta, Georgia; Rock and Roll Hall of Fame and Museum in Cleveland.

"Faces" one-man show, Houston Center for Photography.

The collector Peter Ludwig commissions Helnwein to paint portraits of himself and his wife, Irene, for the new Ludwig Museum in the Russian Museum in St. Petersburg.

Peter and Irene Ludwig purchase *Head of a Child* for the museum in St. Petersburg and *Dresden* for the Ludwig Museum in Beijing.

1996 Helnwein works on portraits of Peter and Irene Ludwig for the Ludwig Museum in Beijing.

Work on a series of photographic pictures of people who have died a violent death; using computer techniques, he modifies them again and again, ultimately to the point of dissolution.

Set and costumes for "Pasolini" in the Schauspielhaus theater in Hamburg; directed by Hans Kresnik.

San Francisco Museum of Modern Art, photography exhibition selected from the museum collection.

One-man show in the Fine Arts Museum, Otaru, Japan.

Opening group show of the Ludwig Museum, Beijing.

Peter and Irene Ludwig with Gottfried Helnwein in his studio, Germany, 1995

1997 Moves to Ireland and lives and works in a castle near Dublin.

One-man show in the State Russian Museum, St. Petersburg, Ludwig Museum in the Russian Museum.

One-man show in the Wäinö Aaltonen Museum of Art, Turku, Finland.

Photosession with the German musicians Rammstein.

Set for "Die Hamletmaschine" by Heiner Müller, Director Gert Hof. 47th Berliner Festwochen, Arena, Berlin and Muffathalle, Munich.

Mayakovski and Muller, 1996, mixed media on canvas

The works presented in this book were included in a large retrospective in the State Russian
Museum, St. Petersburg in 1997.
Thanks to everybody who supported this project,
especially to all the collectors who have lent their work for this exhibition.
Special thanks to Renate Helnwein, Peter Feierabend, Frank Bülow, Bruno Franzen,
Martin Muller and Katya Kashkooli

Director, Russian Museum: Vladimir Gusev

Vice-Director, Russian Museum: Evgenia Petrova

Curator for Contemporary Art at the Russian Museum: Alexander Borovsky

Exhibition Manager: Joseph Kiblitsky

Text, page 17: Peter Selz, Professor Emeritus, Department of Art History, University of California, Berkeley, Former Curator at the Museum of Modern
Art in New York and Founding Director of the Berkeley Art Museum

Text, page 175: Klaus Honnef, Curator for Contemporary Art at the Rheinisches Landesmuseum, Bonn

The text on pages 29 and 130 are extracts from the text by Peter Gorsen:

Helnwein, der Künstler als Aggressor und vermaledeiter Moralist, Katalog Helnwein, Graphische Sammlung Albertina, Wien, 1985

Layout: Peter Wassermann, Andrea Hostettler, Switzerland

Layout Assistants: Erhard Mika, Renate Helnwein, Cologne

Transparencies: Ralf Krieger, Cologne

Translation German/English: Edward Martin, Bell, and Gertraud Trivedi, London

Translation English/German (Selz): Jeannette Hark, Editing: Daniela Kumor

Contributing Editor: Heike Straßburger

Color Separation: Graficart s.n.c., Formia, Italy

Coordination for the Exhibition and Catalogue: Renate Helnwein

Mixed media on canvas = oil, acrylic and ink-jet on canvas

Photographic Credits:

cover and pages 8+9: Bernhard Schaub, Cologne; pages 38+39: Farbfoto Harz, Düsseldorf

pages 42+43: Joker Verlag, Bonn; pages 88–93: Gabriela Brandenstein, Vienna

pages 188–191: Wolfgang Hauptmann, Vienna

page 241, pages 243–256 and 258: Fotoassistenz: Martina Kudlacek

pages 310+311 and pages 325–331: Bernhard Schaub, Cologne

page 385: Andor Gasser, Paris; pages 388+389: Bernd Uhlig, Berlin

pages 396+397: Bernhard Widman, Stuttgart; pages 400+401: Martina Kudlacek, Prague, Cologne;

page 407: the painting "Boulevard of Broken Dreams" was inspired by a photograph by Dennis Stock.

Biography: US Press, Vienna; Martina Kudlacek, Cologne; Ralf Krieger, Cologne

Martina Dettlof, Berlin

www.helnwein.com

© 1998 Könemann Verlagsgesellschaft mbH

Bonner Str. 126, D–50968 Köln

Project Manager: Sally Bald

Project Editor: Susanne Kassung

Production Director: Detlev Schaper

Production Assistant: Nicola Leurs

Typesetting: Oliver Hessmann, Thomas Lindner, divis GmbH, Cologne

Printing and Binding: Sing Cheong Co. Ltd., Hong Kong

Printed in China

ISBN 3-8290-1448-1

10 9 8 7 6 5 4 3 2 1